THE ART OF WILLIAM FAULKNER

THE ART OF
WILLIAM FAULKNER

John Pikoulis

BARNES & NOBLE BOOKS
TOTOWA, NEW JERSEY

First Published in the U.S.A. 1982 by
BARNES & NOBLE BOOKS
81, Adams Drive, Totowa,
New Jersey, 07512
ISBN 0–389–20076–X

Printed in Great Britain

Library of Congress Cataloging in Publication Data

Pikoulis, John, 1941–
   The art of William Faulkner.

   Bibliography: p.
   Includes index.
   1. Faulkner, William, 1897–1962—Criticism
and interpretation. I. Title.
PS3511.A86Z9462   1982   813'.52   81–22893
ISBN 0–389–20076–X   AACR2

To John Armstrong

Contents

Acknowledgements

The author and publishers wish to thank the following who have kindly given permission for the use of copyright material: Chatto & Windus Ltd, Random House Inc. and Curtis Brown Ltd, on behalf of the Estate of William Faulkner, for the extracts from the author's works; Horace Liveright, Inc. for the extracts from *Mosquitoes*, copyright 1927, renewed 1955; Faber and Faber Ltd and Harcourt Brace Jovanovich Inc., for the extracts from *Collected Poems 1909–1962* by T. S. Eliot; Faber and Faber Ltd and Random House Inc., for the extract from 'The Novelist' from *Collected Poems* by W. H. Auden; Faber and Faber Ltd and Harcourt Brace Jovanovich Inc., for 'Looking into History III' from *Poems 1943–56* and *Things of this World* © 1956 (US edition) by Richard Wilbur; and Laurence Pollinger Ltd on behalf of Edmund Volpe, and Farrar, Straus & Giroux Inc., for details from a genealogical table in *A Reader's Guide to William Faulkner*.

Preface

Two very great American writers of the twentieth century stayed at home while most of their contemporaries ventured into Europe. Perhaps as a consequence, these writers, although admittedly difficult to appreciate, have received less than their due in this country. I refer to Wallace Stevens and William Faulkner. Stevens has lately received some attention, but no comparable quickening of interest has occurred with Faulkner. He remains the stereotype of the 'Southern' writer dealing with morbid excesses of behaviour in an impenetrably convoluted style. He is recognised as a writer of power but one who is nonetheless too alien, lacking the English novelist's decorum, his willingness to invite the reader into his fiction. It is in the hope that these essays will promote a more generous assessment of his work that they are presented to the reader.

At the same time, they contribute to the voluminous debate which his work has excited in the United States, a debate which may very roughly be said to have been conducted along two lines, the 'sensationalist' and the 'moralist', most conveniently divided in the middle 1940s by the publication of *The Portable Faulkner*, a compendium put together by Malcolm Cowley.[1] This book, coming at a time when Faulkner's fortunes were low and most of his novels out of print, is generally credited with renewing interest in his work and heralded extensive critical appreciation of it. Before then, the 'sensationalist' view had prevailed, responding (with approval or otherwise) to the power of early works like *The Sound and the Fury, Sanctuary* and *Light in August* with their depiction of the modern waste land. The moralists, helped by Cowley and by the fact that Faulkner himself had by now moved on to a period of more conceptual narratives, saw below the surface of shock and excess, below the restless experimentation of style, to discover (again, with approval or otherwise) a traditional engagement in the problems of human behaviour. Mr Cowley pointed the way.

> ... Faulkner, at least in those early days, was not so much
> composing stories for the public as telling them to himself—
> like a lonely child in his imaginary world, but also like a writer
> of genius. (*The Portable Faulkner*, p. xi)

Again,

> ... Faulkner writes, not what he wants, but what he just has to
> write whether he wants to or not. (*ibid*, p. xxiv)

By intervening to select and order such compulsive material, the
editor provides what the author, in his daemonic genius, cannot
do. That which is dictated into the imagination achieves
coherence only rarely, and then by chance: Faulknerian fragments, Cowlerian synopsis. The end result is the many commen-
taries that have sought to establish Faulkner as a great humanist
metaphysician working in the novel.

There is still, however, much to be said for essays like Alfred
Kazin's 'The Rhetoric and the Agony', with its puzzled reaction
to the gap between Faulkner's power, all deliberate and intense,
and its source in 'debasement or perplexity or a calculating
terror', his style,

> perhaps the most elaborate, intermittently incoherent and
> ungrammatical, thunderous polyphonic rhetoric in all Ameri-
> can writing [which] explains why he always plays as great a
> role in his novels as any of his characters to the point of acting
> out their characters in himself....[2]

and his agony, which Professor Kazin says is

> the agony of a culture, his culture; but it has been even more
> the agony of his relation to that culture.... It has been the
> agony inherent in every effort to transcend some basic
> confusion by force of will alone. [His characters] are the tonal
> expression of Faulkner's own torment, the waking phantas-
> magoria, sensation beating against sensation, of his perpetual
> tension. (*On Native Grounds*, p. 465)

More recently, Walter J. Slatoff has offered an account of Faulkner's tension in his stylistic study, *The Quest for Failure*,[3] drawing attention to his use of the oxymoron which, he believes, argues a

> desperately divided and tormented perspective, a condition of mind which tries to move simultaneously and intensely toward both order and chaos and which understandably seizes upon the figure which most nearly moves in both directions, the oxymoron. (*The Quest for Failure*, p. 251)

Professor Slatoff declares tension, as of a gathering of breath, panting, suffocation or similarly explosive respiratory strain, to be

> the dominant, even the normal, condition in [Faulkner's] world. Primarily these states of tension are achieved by various forms of antithesis, simultaneous suggestion, and irresolution, by Faulkner's overwhelming tendency to place entities of all kinds in opposition. (*ibid.*, p. 52)

This emphasis on Faulkner's 'polar imagination' is accompanied by not a little irritation on Professor Slatoff's part. We sense that he is disappointed in Faulkner's indecisions; any great novelist ought to be able to master them. Hence the suggestion that Faulkner 'may be more ambiguous and more resistant to rational analysis than has often been supposed (*ibid.*, p. 137).

> ... both the form and meanings of his works are governed much less by a controlling idea, or themes, or dramatic or aesthetic considerations than by a succession of temperamental impulses and responses. The finished work becomes, in a sense, the record of a process, the record of the artist's struggles with his materials, rather than the record of his victory over his materials.... (*ibid.*, p. 253)

It is another, more refined way of saying what Professor Kazin said and it admirably records the sound of Faulkner's pencil scratching across the page. But it is not the whole truth, and in the following pages I offer my view from my own very different perspective.

Faulkner is, I think, the only American novelist apart from Henry James to have produced a sizeable number of books for each of which the highest claims can plausibly be advanced. These, in my opinion, are (in order of publication) *Sartoris, The Sound and the Fury, Absalom, Absalom!, The Unvanquished, The Hamlet, Go Down, Moses* and *The Reivers.* Accordingly, it is to these that I have directed my attention, to the first quite briefly, to the last not at all since I take it to be one of those works best appreciated by readers familiar with Faulkner's work and therefore not altogether in place here. Instead, I have dealt with *Sanctuary,* a lesser work but one which is intensely revealing and much underestimated. Two omissions may cause some surprise: *As I Lay Dying* and *Light in August.* These are usually regarded as major works but I cannot share that opinion and so have had no choice but to leave them out.

My acknowledgements are twofold: first, to the Faulkner critics, from whom I have learnt much. I make only a relatively few references to them in the pages that follow (by no means all I could have wished to make) and I am glad to be able to record my appreciation of them here in this necessarily general way. I should also like to thank the staff of the Inter-Library loans desk in the Humanities Library, University College, Cardiff, for their help, without which I could scarcely have hoped to embark on this project.

Dinas Powis, June 1980

... I'd like to know whether epochs that possessed culture knew the word at all, or used it. Naïvete, unconsciousness, taken-for-grantedness, seems to me to be the first criterion of the constitution to which we give this name. What we are losing is just this naïvete, and this lack, if one may so speak of it, protects us from many a colourful barbarism which altogether perfectly agreed with culture, even with very high culture. I mean: our state is that of civilization—a very praiseworthy state no doubt, but also neither was there any doubt that we should have to become very much more barbaric to be capable of culture again. Technique and comfort—in that state one talks about culture but one has not got it.

Thomas Mann, *Doctor Faustus*

The tale is the form most natural to a people with a passionate historical sense of life. For in the tale, events march on, passing sometimes over and sometimes around human lives. Individual character is interwoven with the events but is subordinate. That is why the Southern novel is, at first glance, so very deficient in the portrayal of human character. As Lacy Buchan, the narrator of [Allen Tate's] *The Fathers*, says, 'I have a story to tell but I cannot explain the story ...'.

Herbert Marshall McLuhan,
'The Southern Quality'

'You can't repeat the past.'
'Can't repeat the past?' he cried incredulously. 'Why of course you can!'

F. Scott Fitzgerald, *The Great Gatsby*

PART ONE

Benjy's Hell

1 Writer in the Faraway Country

Questioner: Do you think there's a particular order in which your works should
    be read?...
Faulkner: ... begin with a book called *Sartois*.[1] That has the germ of my
    apocrypha in it.[2]

I

Sartoris (1929) is rightly considered by many to be a seminal
work but fewer would agree that it is a remarkable achievement
in its own right, one that brings Faulkner suddenly into
command of his art. As his earlier work shows, a way of giving
convincing expression to youthful emotion had eluded his grasp
until, with this book, the myth of the South came to activate his
imagination, grounding his feelings in a context and suggesting a
method that could do justice to them by being indulgent and
indirectly critical at one and the same time. While, therefore,
Sartoris is subordinated to Bayard Sartoris and works for him in
the arrangement of light and dark, the movement of the seasons,
the disposition of the characters and the atmosphere of 'glamorous fatality', it also allows us to see him more dispassionately as
a man at war with himself, one who is a child both of the old
South and the new and an embodiment of the conflicts between
them.

It was of immense advantage to Faulkner that he should be
able to release himself in this way through a protagonist who was
equivalent to the stress he felt. Despite the memorable characters who emerge in the novels, he was not a chronicler of
personality by nature. He could not command the kind of
attention necessary to the disinterested representation of people.
He could work only by immersion, immersion first of all in
himself. Many of his characters are facets of their author's mind
brooding on itself and extended on to the page with all the
complexity of art, fictions masking an inner identity. This is not

to suggest that they are narrowly autobiographical nor that he had no eye for the minutiae of life but to emphasise the degree to which they had to be absorbed into himself before they could be animated, in contradistinction to the process whereby the novelist deepens his awareness of other lives by becoming absorbed in them ('he must /Become the whole of boredom, subject to /Vulgar complaints like love, among the Just/ Be Just, among the Filthy filthy too', as Auden has it). That is why Faulkner treats people less as parts of an observed world than as players in a private drama whose origins may have lain outside himself but who have become, like figures in a family history, part of his expanded consciousness of self, as intimate as memory.

Yoknapatawpha is just such a mental landscape as would give habitation to characters like these, a discrete arena of existence which, to a significant degree, emerges in answer to Bayard's suffering and deliberately intensifies it. It is a world in which actuality is distorted, suspended in the hiatus between past and present, the former glamorous, bold and rewarding, the latter overshadowed by it and by the First World War (one of whose casualties is Bayard's brother, John; his wife, Caroline, also died during the war). To catch the many implications of this situation, Faulkner decided to eschew realism for a mode that would of necessity forgo the amenities of the detached observer and with them the normative morality of the novel in favour of Henry James's romance, 'experience liberated', as he put it in his Preface to *The American*, 'experience disengaged, disembroiled, disencumbered, exempt from the conditions that we usually know to attach to it...'. It is 'the disconnected and uncontrolled experience—uncontrolled by our general sense of the "way things happen"—which romance alone more or less successfully palms off on us', so that the ultimate justification of the mode is its account of 'the things that, with all the faculties in the world, all the wealth and all the courage and all the wit and all the adventure, we can never directly know; the things that can reach us only through the beautiful circuit and subterfuge of our thought and our desire.'[3] Or as Faulkner put it when describing his short story, 'Carcassone':

I was still writing about a young man in conflict with his environment ... it seemed to me that fantasy was the best way to tell that story. To have told it in terms of simple realism would have lost something, in my opinion. To use fantasy was the best, and that's a piece that I've always liked because there was the poet again. I wanted to be a poet, and I think of myself now as a failed poet, not as a novelist at all but a failed poet who had to take up what he could do.[4]

To talk of 'failed poetry', however, runs up against two problems when it is cited in defence of *Sartoris*. The first is that the appeal of the romance lies outside the terms to which modern criticism of the novel is committed. The second is that the culture of which it is here a part often appears to be no more than slick or unhealthy. Nevertheless, Faulkner wished to acknowledge the old South for what it was, in part, to those who created it—but only in part, since he writes as one who can do justice to it but at the same time (and by virtue of that very talent) suggest how much of a monster it could also be. The reader should not, therefore, mistake the complexity of attitude in his portrait. There is the world evoked by the statue of Bayard's great-grandfather, Colonel John Sartoris (the Civil War hero modelled on Faulkner's own great-grandfather), the world of master-servant relations, the chivalric warrior-gentleman and virtuous lady, the extended interlocking families with their custom and ceremony, but it is no longer the ideal it used to be now that Bayard's experience is redirecting him to a more passive conception of heroism.

We first see the Sartoris museum, image of the civilisation of the old South, at twilight. It is something grand and affecting yet largely silent, empty, a thing of echoes and memories. The descriptions of the house, its contents, its grounds, its nostalgic charm, are all accomplished as friezes or tableaux, as if the house had become another statue to obsolescent—if not obsolete—greatness.

The stairway with its white spindles and red carpet mounted in a tall slender curve into upper gloom. From the center of the ceiling hung a chandelier of crystal prisms and shades.... To the right of the entrance, beside folding doors rolled back upon a dim room emanating an atmosphere of solemn and seldom violated stateliness and known as the parlor, stood a tall mirror filled with grave obscurity like a still pool of evening water. At the opposite end of the hall checkered sunlight fell in a long slant across the door, and from somewhere beyond the bar of sunlight a voice rose and fell in a steady pre-occupied minor, like a chant. (p.7)

We are reading about a quality wonderfully rich but enervated. Bayard responds by trying to fight free from it, but whether he acts for or against his family, he is always characteristically one of them. Even then, his revolt is not without sanction from the keepers of the covenant. Old man Falls, who reveres the Colonel, can distinguish between his heroism and his killing of the Burdens after the Civil War.

When a feller has to start killin' folks, he 'most always has to keep on killin' 'em. And when he does, he's already dead hisself. (p.23)

When, therefore, the Colonel's death, like the first Bayard's, is repeated as a fine tale, it is instinct with a corruption which, though unmentioned in the telling of it, Bayard has acted upon.

Part of the complexity of *Sartoris* can in this way be traced to the interaction of Bayard's rebellious subjectivity and the converging yet distinctive orthodoxy of people like his grandfather Bayard, Miss Jenny, Will Falls, Dr Peabody and the MacCallums, in which fact and fantasy are variously compounded. Bayard's point of view, that is, is comprehensible only in terms of a whole tradition, 'Bayard' the man being the characterisation of 'Bayard' the sensibility of a community through several generations. And behind both parties lies the pervasive autobiographical element that, over and above its effect on individual characters, lends the portrait of Jefferson its swell of feeling. This might be termed the ground bass of *Sartoris* were it not part of so interacting a complex, for if the Southern agony is Faulkner's concerted theme, the Southern way of life is his granted one. On almost every page there is a quiet rendition of what it felt like to be alive in a particular spot at a particular point of time. Part of the effect of such detail comes from the realisation that, for the first time, Faulkner is discovering himself to himself by uncovering the lineaments of his great theme. After the Georgia of *Soldiers' Pay*, the Gulf setting of *Mosquitoes* and the unfocused or merely fanciful terrain of the poetry, Yok-

napatawpha is born. The result is to maintain a balance between
Bayard and his context, between his consciousness of failure
(which touches his war record but also a fearfully suppressed
sexuality) and a sense of continuity. It is not a perfect balance
and is not meant to be, but it rescues the romance from the
overpersonal while still allowing the personal full expression.

For the most part, it is in dialogue that all the humour and
bustle of life are found. When the narrative resumes, it very often
steadies into a lament; the depressed rhythms and spellbound
sense impressions combine to create *Sartoris'* melancholy in one
slow, long, grand, cumulative swell. Every page is soaked in it.

> One of the dogs was quite old and nearly blind .... toward the
> middle of the afternoon it went around to the front and waited
> there quietly and gravely until the carriage came up the drive;
> and when Bayard had descended and entered the house it
> returned up to the back and waited again until Isom led the
> mare up and Bayard came out and mounted. Then together
> they spent the afternoon going quietly and unhurriedly about
> the meadows and fields and woods in their seasonal mu-
> tations—the man on his horse and the ticked setter gravely
> beside him, while the descending evening of their lives drew
> toward its peaceful close upon the kind land that had bred
> them both. (p.35)

Such is the 'ritual of the everyday' in a 'world of ennui' that
Sartre described so well:

> this boredom ... is only an appearance.... The real drama is
> *behind*, behind the lethargy, behind the gestures, behind the
> consciousness.[5]

It is with this in mind that Sartre identified Bayard as a man
whom

> One cannot grasp ... through his gestures ... nor through his
> stories ... nor through his acts ... a nature pre-eminently
> poetical and magical, whose contradictions are numerous but
> veiled.[6]

That is because Bayard is a triumph of indirect portraiture, one we feel to be, in Henry James's phrase, 'deeply indigenous' to the South. And central to this indirection is the fact that he properly enters the book only a quarter or so of the way through (once, that is, 'Sartoris' has been dramatised) and that thereafter his distress is located in the world rather than in himself, in descriptions of Yoknapatawpha and not in any 'psychological' revelations. Bayard is the atmosphere that surrounds him.

Faulkner often remained true to his genius in these early years by concentrating on 'poetical and magical' characters like Bayard (Quentin Compson, Darl Bundren, Horace Benbow—the major exception, and the flaw has not been remarked, is Joe Christmas), all of whom suffer from a malady which, though given some circumstantial justification, remains unspecified, some paralysis of feeling that is, by displacement, to be found in the fabric of their novels. Such manipulation of perspective is no mere trick of technique. It grows from the restricted nature of the Southerner's 'private' life, which ensures that the emphasis falls not on the individual complexion of his behaviour but on the broader drama of his estrangement from the South. And since that culture is divorced—and divorces him—from contemporary reality, his alienation is complete.

The form this alienation takes emerges more explicitly from the death of John Sartoris in 'All the Dead Pilots'.

And that's all. That's it. The courage, the recklessness, call it what you will, is the flash, the instant of sublimation; then flick! the old darkness again. That's why. It's too strong for a steady diet. And if it were a steady diet, it would not be a flash, a glare. And so, being momentary, it can be preserved and prolonged only on paper: a picture, a few written words that any match, a minute and harmless flame that any child can engender, can obliterate in an instant. A one-inch sliver of sulphur-tipped wood is longer than memory or grief; a flame no larger than sixpence is fiercer than courage or despair.[7]

(The 'instant of sublimation', indeed; an inspired slip whereby 'sublime illumination' becomes 'sublimation'.) With which compare 'Carcassone''s

I want to perform something bold and tragical and austere... me on a buckskin pony with eyes like blue electricity and a mane like tangled fire, galloping up the hill and right off into the high heaven of the world.[8]

There speaks the Bayardesque hero, in love with deathly achievement. Owing to some failure in his emotional life, he has sought 'the courage, the recklessness, call it what you will' in 'the manly arts of Mars'. When this, too, fails (as it must, being satisfactory only when freed into bouts of daring that scrape near to death), he reaches breaking point and feeds off himself in every way, turning in the end to literature, his buckskin Pegasus, as a substitute for the active life. But then comes the realisation that books can never recapture the feelings that give birth to them. Like the words they are made up of, they are inferior to, because an abstraction from, the life of gallantry.

We gain further insight into these attitudes in the aftermath of Bayard's being thrown by a stallion. As he is carried away by his companion, Suratt, and while in considerable pain, he sees in a reverie the image of Narcissa Benbow amidst a chaos of fighting. Her manner is serene, in sharp contrast to her surroundings and to his own mysterious feeling of guilt about his brother's plane crash. Consequently, the image he entertains here suggests that he is torn between life and death (indeed, after the juxtaposition of Narcissa and the war, he goes on to weary of the prospect of having to live three score and ten years). It also suggests some frustration of manliness, be it military or amatory, and a hidden connection between the two. It further suggests that Faulkner's muse, his 'white lady', was born in the war, thus defining his view of the relation between the imagination and a man's humiliations implicit in the book.[9]

Bayard's predicament is therefore radical and it depends on our sense of him as the co-author of *Sartoris*. The book's subjectivity, that is to say, is of its essence, for in as much as we realise that it is Bayard's eye which sees, his the consciousness which interprets and his the sensibility which colours every page, so much are we nearer to understanding the hidden crisis of disaffection he symbolises.

There was a fire of logs on the hearth now and they would sit in the glow of it—Miss Jenny beneath the light with her lurid daily paper; old Bayard with his slippered feet propped against the fireplace, his head wreathed in smoke and the old setter dreaming fitfully beside the chair, reliving proud and ancient stands perhaps, or further back still, the lean, gawky days of his young doghood, when the world was full of scents that maddened the blood in him and pride had not taught him self-restraint; Narcissa and Bayard between them—Narcissa dreaming too in the firelight, grave and tranquil, and young Bayard smoking his cigarettes in his leashed and moody repose. (p.281)

Here, in one of those languorous tableaux with which the book is replete, the commitment to the Sartorises implied by the affectionate atmosphere modulates into an adverse comment on their sapped energies. Similarly, the family's poise belies the fact that what is presented is the remnant of a family: an aged widow and widower, a young man bereft of his brother (not to mention his first wife and son) and, between the two, a whole generation missing. Young Bayard epitomises the ambiguity in the fireside scene where, though he appears before us, the description manages to impress itself on us as part of his 'leashed and moody' reflections. This double focus, now subtly differentiated, now hardly distinct, makes him omnipresent in the scene. *He* is the dog dreaming of juvenescence; *he* is the Sartorises in stasis by the fireside; *he* is the creator of the telling details (the various dreamings, including Jenny's paper; old Bayard's smoke-wreathed head and his grandson's cigarettes). Above all, he is the observer who detects in such multifarious activity a secret message, and it is *this* that gives rise to the vague unease which permeates the book because it tells him that he is a split personality whose ability to function as a writer is a consequence of his failure to distinguish himself as an authentic Southerner. In his essay 'The South and the Faraway Country', Louis D. Rubin, Jr. shows how membership of the old South signified belongingness, a communal definition of self. The very fact of the emergence of Bayard–Faulkner argues the disintegration of such homogeneity since 'the very sensibilities that made him a novelist are precisely those that isolated him from the community'.[10] The imagination is exiled and its fundamental theme becomes the story of its exile; it interrogates itself to explain to those who have left the South, physically or not, why they cannot go home again. As Faulkner remarked,

... it is himself that the Southerner is writing about, not about his environment; who has, figuratively speaking, taken the artist in him in one hand and his milieu in the other and thrust the one into the other ... and he writes.[11]

In a fragment of a poem called 'The Ace', he wrote:

The silent earth looms liquid in the dawning
Black as poured ink beneath the grey
Mist's spectral clutching fingers

The sun light
Paints him as he stalks, huge through the morning
In his fleece and leather, gilds his bright
Hair and his cigarette.

Makes góold his fleéce and leather, ańd his bright
Hair.
        Then, like a shooting stár,[12]

That sort of attractive riskiness which damned and glorified the early flying man, apparently so defiant and yet courting death every minute, that physical liberation from earth and feeling of having one's mettle tested—both are raised into a fitting emblem of 'the modern'. Much to his regret, Bayard lacks the flair for such derring-do; he is not a pilot stalking the skies but, as the revealing metaphor in the first verse of 'The Ace' implies, a gaunt writer in the ghost-ridden world of the Sartorises.

The 1914–18 war, which drew Faulkner from the South for the first time and gave birth to him as a writer, becomes a trope of his exile. Yet the separation is caused not by any change that has occurred in the land while he has been away; it is rather that the attrition it has suffered unknown to itself since the end of its own Civil War has caught up with it unawares, the shock of recognition being confused with the speed of the change. Accordingly, when Bayard returns from Europe, the family house, his 'aunt' and grandfather, the plantation, the negroes and poor whites, a whole tradition he had once taken for granted at last begins to make a less than favourable impression on him. But that in itself does not account for the depth of anxiety he feels, for others than he have concluded that something is amiss with the South, yet none reacts as he does because none suffers like him from the ability to feel first sufficiently conscious of and then sufficiently detached from the South to be able to regard it as a 'home' separately experienced from 'self'. It is not the unfavourable impression the South makes on him that signifies, therefore; it is the fact that it should have made any impression at all.

Even so, the state he used to inhabit has not vanished altogether. It now inhabits him, having assumed the status of 'the country within [his] mind', the South of his childhood, 'when [he] had not recognised within [himself] the intense perceptions that gradually set [him] apart'.[13] And it is in this breach between ideal and actual South that Yoknapatawpha is born, wherein the writer fashions an order of reality that acknowledges even as it tries to transform the chequered order of everyday life—and thus to heal the division within himself that has led to such activity in the first place.

Both as a man and as a lover of Venetian glassware and the poetry of Keats, Horace Benbow echoes the larger historical theme worked out in Bayard. Indeed, he is another Bayard (as the original *Sanctuary* suggests). Horace, the man who feels himself 'ordered by words' and is thus enfeebled in everyday life, is the objective correlative of the writer in the faraway country plagued by his aestheticism and his desire for a married woman who, like the marble faun of the poems, ends up trapped in the self's imaginings. Knowing this, we know something of Faulkner, too.

John Sartoris is another projection of Bayard—and behind both lies an autobiographical reference (as in the loss of Caroline in October 1918).[14] Though he trained as a pilot in Canada, Faulkner did not actually see service and the frustration this occasioned issues in the dual portrait of John, the dashing hero-who-might-have-been who died in the war, and the paralysis of his 'twin' brother. While John is the idealised active self (evidently deriving from his namesake, the Colonel), Horace, the man who goes to war with the YMCA and feels he lacks courage, may be closer to the reality Bayard feels guilty about (hence his risking his life in daring escapades) and all three men complementary facets of a single personality in which Horace is the man who suffers, Bayard the mind which creates and John that which is created.

II

Mosquitoes (1927), Faulkner's second novel, explores the Bayardesque personality further. It describes a party of Southerners becalmed on a yacht in Lake Pontchartrain, idle socialites, for the most part, whom Faulkner has little difficulty in satirising. But when, at the dead of noon, we come across this:

> Talk, talk, talk: the utter and heartbreaking stupidity of words. It seemed endless, as though it might go on forever. Ideas, thoughts, became mere sounds to be bandied about until they were dead. (p.156)

we are reminded of Margaret Powers saying, 'Women know more about words than men ever will. And they know how little they can ever possibly mean.' (*Soldiers' Pay*, p. 252) and discover the origin of Addie Bundren's complaint in *As I Lay Dying* 'that words are no good; that words don't ever fit even what they are trying to say at' because they are 'just a shape to fill a lack' and life a meagre preparation for death (pp.159–60). Consequently, we need to register the fact that the protest *Mosquitoes* makes against Mrs Maurier's party is, in truth, self-directed. A creative impulse is stirring but it has very great doubts about itself, doubts as to whether it can ever be legitimate or whether its value can be asserted only when it is eliciting images of ourselves and not when it is engaged in mimetic narratives of the life about us.

The argument is pursued by the novelist Dawson Fairchild.

> 'Well, it is a kind of sterility—Words,' Fairchild admitted. 'You begin to substitute words for things and deeds, like the withered cuckold husband that took the Decameron to bed with him every night...' (p.175)

Words must not be mistaken for the objects and actions they denote, especially by the novelist, for his vocation is a substitute for the life he no longer possesses, a fiction which consoles him.

> When youth goes out of you, you get out of it. Out of life, I mean. Up to that time you just live; after that, you are aware of living and living becomes a conscious process. Like thinking

does in time, you know. You become conscious of thinking,
and then you start right off to think in words. And first thing
you know, you don't have thoughts in your mind at all: you
just have words in it. But when you are young, you just be.
Then you reach a stage where you do. Then a stage where you
think, and last of all, where you remember. Or try to. (p.192)

Fairchild may elsewhere be an affectionate send-up of Sherwood
Anderson, particularly when the characters discuss his novels,
but he is here a medium for Faulkner in his insistence on youth
as the most valuable moment in man's life. One uses words,
indeed, one thinks thoughts, only when one's childhood has
passed away. The fact that words and thoughts and conscious
actions exist is a measure of the divide in one's life and the only
fruitful purpose in thinking and writing is to throw a bridge
across the chasm.

At least that is true of the male adult, for women, however
young or old, are something else again. They are 'practical
creatures' whereas men are the ones to 'hold on to conventions
for moral reasons' (p.185). Fairchild again makes the salient
points:

Women are never stupid. Their mental equipment is too
sublimely sufficient to do what little directing their bodies
require. And when your mentality is sufficient to your bodily
needs, where there is such a perfect mating of capability and
necessity, there can't be any stupidity. (pp.200–1)

The only time when men approach such wholeness is when they
are young, when, as Fairchild's description of women suggests,
mind and body are in harmony. Once the male grows up, once,
that is, he becomes sexually active, his equilibrium is disturbed.
The rest of his life is spent trying to re-establish it, not by
action—for that is part of the disease, not a cure—but by the
effort to regress into the past. And since the regression is
purposeful, it is not necessarily a debilitating fancy. Nor is it,
strictly speaking, a regression at all, since youth is not a static
quantity nor one which is merely chronological. It is a recoverable state of being, just as children themselves are 'psychic'; they
'can distil the whole gamut of experiences [they have] never
actually known, into a single instant' (p.194). They are unself-

conscious, they exist whole, they are above all innocent—but they are not ignorant. Physically, they are part of a developing process but psychically their state is comprehensive because proleptic. They experience life in profound, unstatable ways which the adult can recapture by becoming, after much effort, childlike himself.

As an illustration of this complex, Fairchild tells his audience of an experience that befell him as a twelve-year-old when visiting his grandfather in Indiana one summer. A girl with blue eyes and golden curls who was part of the family reunion vaguely caught his attention (since childhood is unknowing and unthinking, no description of his response to her is possible in words). Chancing to visit an outhouse—his childhood predates 'water works and sewage systems'—he noticed the girl approaching the women's half of the house, divided from the men's by a partition. He locked himself in the cubicle, hushing himself until she went away. Naturally, there is no apparent reason for this behaviour; the boy acted as he had to, instinctively. Then, since he did not hear anything from the girl's side, 'I put my head down through the seat', presumably to verify for himself her presence and, no doubt, her functions. He discovered that she had pre-empted his move; the boy saw (and the mature man sees as clearly),

> two wide curious blue eyes into which an inverted surprise came clear as water, and long golden curls swinging downward above the ordure; ... (p.195)

There, for the twelve-year-old, the experience ended. To say that boy and girl had been furtively attracted to each other and had seized the opportunity to express their interest by peeping at each other would be to offer a later verbalisation which can only fail to capture the quintessence of the event, something which now resides in Fairchild's memory and which was then an ineffable spontaneity of light, colour, movement, sound, heat, who-knows-what emotions, a tissued thing of atmosphere. All that the older person can do as artist is to recreate as faithfully as he can what he remembers, though his recreation can never be other than unsatisfactory. More than that, it reminds us that Fairchild (the punning name is obviously apt) has lost the ability to behave like the boy he was. A whole dimension of life, much the most important part of it, has gone.[15]

As with people, so with words. When they are used by the *Nausikaa's* party, they are impotent. The artist, however, can use them purposefully.

> ... by the time the child is old enough to add anything to our knowledge of the mind, it has forgotten. The soul sheds every year, like snakes do, I believe. You can't recall the emotions you felt last year: you remember only that an emotion was associated with some physical fact of experience. But all you have of it now is a kind of ghost of happiness and a vague and meaningless regret. (p.194)

Since adults exist within attenuations of feeling in what is a continuous dilution from the period of childhood, they can most profitably set themselves the Proust-like task of recalling the 'physical facts' of past experience, as Fairchild does in his Indiana story.

> I don't claim that words have life in themselves. But words brought into happy conjunction produce something that lives, just as soil and climate and an acorn in proper conjunction will produce a tree. (p.175)

The vital objective hinted at in this passage is not difficult to define since, if art arises when men become sexual, its peculiar task is to recapture the ideal (in love as in life) by creating images of young women who are '*motionless and virginal and passionately eternal*'. This is what the sculptor Gordon does. The young girl, Jenny, repeats the ideal for she suggests the Eula Varner-like torpidity that is preferable to sex, a woman who is both pubertal and innocent.[16]
 Unfortunately, even the words the artist uses suffer from dilution. Fairchild remarks

> That first infatuation ...; that sheer infatuation with and marveling over the beauty and power of words. That has gone out of me. Used up, I guess. So I can't write poetry any more. It takes me too long to say things, now. (p.207)

We are immediately reminded of Faulkner's deprecating reference to himself as a 'failed poet'.

It's a kind of childlike faith in the efficacy of words, you see, a kind of belief that circumstances will invest the veriest platitude with magic ... there comes a time when it will be invested with something not of this life, this world, at all. It's a kind of fire, you know.... (p.208; second ellipsis in text)

Such 'fire', 'Carcassone''s 'tangled fire', produces the following lines (borrowed from the fourth poem of *The Green Bough*, where the line break comes after 'april'):

... above unsapped convolvulae of hills
april a bee sipping perplexed with pleasure ...
                                        (p.208; ellipses in text)

This is a late Romantic poetry of infinite sadness and delicately morbid delights, precisely 'not of this life, this world at all'. Traces of it exist in *Mosquitoes*:

September - a month of languorous days regretful as wood-smoke. (p.14)

... summer lay supine, unchaste with decay. (p.15)[17]

Intermixed with descriptions like these are others which show Faulkner the would-be modern, the reader of Eliot.[18] The result is a weird compound of old and new. The shocking originality of 'Twilight ran in like a quiet violet dog ...' (p.17) rubs uneasily with the descriptions of stars flowering 'like pale and tarnished gardenias' (p.19). The more characteristically Faulknerian touches (the sound of rubber on asphalt 'like a tearing of endless silk' or 'The small boneless hands of water lapping against the hull ...' (p.188)) are usually the more effective because the two styles have been combined to create a new one, though much less admirable effects remain.

One final point of interest attaches to Fairchild/Faulkner's aesthetic. In an important passage, he develops correspondences suggested by his former pronouncements. My comment is bracketed.

It's getting into life, getting into it and wrapping it around you, becoming a part of you. [Self and not-self are seamlessly one to boys.] Women can do it without art—old biology takes care of that. But men, men.... A woman conceives: does she care afterward whose seed it was? Not she. And bears, and all the rest of her life—her young, troubling years, that is—is filled. Of course the father can look at it occasionally. But in art, a man can create without any assistance at all: what he does is his. A perversion, I grant you, but a perversion that builds Chartres and invents Lear is a pretty good thing. (p.265; ellipsis in text)

This, taken in conjunction with Fairchild's earlier opinion that art is created with a particular woman in mind (the forlorn loved one crossed with the Muse), outlines assumptions and beliefs which Faulkner clung to for the rest of his life. The notion of art as a 'perversion', in this case a verbal autogenesis, is not at all fanciful and those interested should consult Anton Ehrenzweig's *The Hidden Order of Art*[19] for a description of the psychology of creation wherein the male artist, partly in emulation of the mother-muse, breaks himself down in order to recreate himself anew in the work of art. He becomes a dying god. (This is the sense in which the title of *As I Lay Dying*, I think, refers to its author.) As André Bleikasten remarks of the line of heroes deriving from Bayard Sartoris:

Through these other selves, the novelist attempted to pass from 'I' to 'he' (which becomes 'I' again, but a fictional 'I' in the monologues of Darl and Quentin); by keeping his invented characters at a distance, by withdrawing from their destinies, by making them where necessary die in his stead, he achieved the immunity of the creator.[20]

He was saved from himself.

III

Soldiers' Pay (1926), Faulkner's first novel, raises a problem that is inextricably associated with the suffering of his heroes: women. The hero of *Soldiers' Pay*, Donald Mahon, is involved with three lovers, Emmy, Cecily and Margaret. Emmy is the poor, faithful servant girl, a figure of adolescent memory, once loved, much missed. The girl who succeeds her, Cecily, is a more urgently desired yet strangely feared person though, as Mahon's love for the two suggests, she is no more than another aspect of Emmy or, rather, what Emmy may be said to have become and as such has been expelled from her portrait, one who is specifically sexual and capricious with it. To pass from Emmy to Cecily is to pass from sensuous reverie to sensual reality and this Mahon manages to do only to suffer rejection for his pains. The resentment he feels thereafter is mitigated only by the attraction she continues to exercise for him. His third mistress, Margaret Powers, is a chastened figure, one who impulsively married the wrong man during the war and is determined to make amends for it. To this extent, she is what Emmy and Cecily may be said to have become, an obviously more adult person though at the same time much less known because less intimately felt. She is the beloved who, having repented her treatment of her lover, returns to him in the guise of helpmate and protector. Alas, she comes at a time when he can least enjoy her. He is now a mute, paralysed thing in the grip of death. Yet, even if he were not, he still could not respond to her because he can no longer be satisfied by any one of her images, however reformed. His experience has taught him to think of her as containing three separate personalities—Emily, Cecily, Margaret—and he is bewildered both by their variety and by the fact that they *can* be contained by any one woman. Indeed, it is this fear of woman that is the secret cause of his paralysis. The Compson brothers in *The Sound and the Fury* are the first but not the last characters to share these feelings and to deduce from them that Emmy-like adolescents are the most desirable because most promising and least threatening of women, though combined with this is a Horace-like apprehension that even they will in time be transformed into fickle adults, golden curls above the ordure.[21]

2 The Compson Devilment

I

Despite the voluminous commentary it has attracted, *The Sound and the Fury* (1929) remains a puzzle, admitting as it does no straightforward assessment of the characters usually identified with each of its sections in turn. Most critics have sought to establish a hierarchy of values whereby Benjy and Dilsey are granted the esteem denied Quentin and Jason, but this is merely to repeat the error described by R. W. B. Lewis in another connection:

> We still tend ... to read a poem the way we watch a tennis-match; turning our heads and minds back and forth between what we presume to be unchanging opponents, as though a poem moved between fixed choices of attitude before plumping conclusively for one of them as the unequivocal winner. The best kind of poem is a process of generation—in which one attitude or metaphor, subjected to intense pressure, gives symbolic birth to the next, which reveals the color of its origin even as it gives way in turn by 'dying into' its successor. Such a poem does not deal in dichotomies but in live sequences.[1]

This conclusion is just as true of *The Sound and the Fury* and it accounts for the fact that the sympathy aroused in us by any one of the book's characters, far from being exclusive, is compounded by our equally sympathetic reaction to the others. At the end, therefore, we are left with at least four complementary claims on us which, in a story of so many defeats, are subsumed under our awareness of the all-embracing failure of the South.

The opening section of the book is reflected through the consciousness of the retarded youngest son of the Compson family, Benjy Compson, though his portrait, while apparently giving us a convincing representation of an idiot's mind, is, in fact, entirely arbitrary, not the mental life of an idiot but a novelist's simulation of it for his own purposes. Even then, the idiocy evoked is not a clinical state.[2] It is a trope for an extreme state of the mind of spoilt youth, as we can tell from *As I Lay Dying*, where Faulkner has the young Vardaman Bundren sound like Benjy after his mother's death because he is grief-stricken. The question of idiocy is irrelevant.

We need to grasp the manner of presentation in Benjy's case because it helps show Faulkner's difficulty with his material and how he solved it. The life of the Compsons engaged his whole attention. He gave it various names to emphasise one or other of its aspects; 'Caddy' is one such name but so fleeting is the quality she represents that he perforce approached her indirectly through her brothers. Similarly, he prepares us for an understanding of the family by having Benjy appear at the start so that his disorientation can free us from the logic and values of orderly narrative and sensitise us to the kind of truth with which *The Sound and the Fury* has to do. Only in Benjy's amoral world can we become intimate with people who are, like him, sealed up in themselves and who labour to give an account of themselves, the fiction they compose emerging through successive consciousnesses whose Benjy-like fragmentation constitutes a definition of their suffering which is vividly enacted rather than described by the novelist at one remove, as it were.

Benjy is thus not to be set aside from the Compsons as their victim; nor is he a stick to be taken to them. He *is* the Compsons at their most abject and therefore their most fitting—because most vulnerable and appealing—representative. As Faulkner himself said:

> The only emotion I can have for Benjy is grief and pity for all mankind. You can't feel anything for Benjy because he doesn't feel anything. The only thing I can feel about him personally is concern as to whether he is believable as I created him. He was a prologue like the gravedigger in Elizabethan dramas. He serves his purpose and is gone....[3]

In this way, the Benjy of the first section establishes the book's tonality. But he does not exactly vanish once he has spoken his mind. He *becomes* Quentin and Jason, all of them the slaves of time, Benjy to a dimension in which the distinctions between tenses are collapsed, Quentin to the past, Jason to the succession of present moments that are forever robbing him of success. Whether it be through action, withdrawal or endurance, an identity of interest is insisted upon, one that issues in that demented force called 'Benjy' which each brother carries within, the sound and the fury, the nihilism or derangement of meaning they all have to brave as a mark of the degree to which their outer lives have failed and their inner lives become possessed by that failure.

For this reason, it will not do to accord Benjy the status of an independent character. Quentin, Jason and the others we grant that solidity of specification; we feel Faulkner knew them in the flesh. Benjy, however, is an imaginative quantity prior to individual existence, a personification of human suffering, as the Christ-like coincidence of his age and the Easter festival suggests.

> Without thought or comprehension: shapeless, neuter, like something eyeless and voiceless which might have lived, existed merely because of its ability to suffer. . . .[4]

His most typical and repeated utterance confesses as much while vainly complaining against all he represents:

> Then Ben wailed again, hopeless and prolonged. It was nothing. Just sound. It might have been all time and injustice and sorrow become vocal for an instant by a conjunction of planets. (p.288)

Benjy may be Luster's 'loony' but he is more decisively Jason's 'crazy' world, the 'mad house' he and his niece complain about in which sickness and strife predominate; he is also, as the imagery insists, the projection of a local into a universal calamity. That being so, the idiot we meet in the last three sections is not always the Benjy of the first. He is the product of sleight-of-hand as Faulkner develops from the frame of mind of the first section a being called Benjy who is certifiably less than sane.[5]

Benjy's section covers some thirty years of the Compson's history, from the death of his grandmother (Damuddy) to his thirty-third birthday. Faulkner's bravura here is immense. Through scraps and pieces—at first genuinely perplexing—he constructs a significant history. Four deaths, those of Damuddy, Quentin, Mr Compson and the negro servant Roskus, punctuate the design; there are two Maurys (Benjy himself, until he has his name changed, and his uncle), two Jasons (father and son) and two Quentins (the first boy and his niece, Caddy's daughter). At first, Benjy's aimless movements with Luster (his negro companion), Uncle Maury's comic entanglement with Mrs Patterson and the drive to Mr Compson's cemetery appear to exist in a random relation, though Benjy's sensuous memory of his sister's purity remains to suggest a lost world which the juxtaposition of news of Damuddy's death immediately takes up. Here, within the context of an adult order impinging on a children's one, there occurs the first intimation of a sequence of loss and grief that is to lend structure to the various passages as it is developed. All the while, discriminations are quietly registered: the dominance of Quentin and Caddy over Jason and the as-yet-unrenamed Maury; between the first pair, the ascendancy of Caddy—vital, capricious, independent—and between the second the contrast between Jason and the uncomplaining Maury. (We note as prophetic Jason's refusal to submit to Caddy's authority on the day in question.)

While any verbal stimulus might carry the reader from one event to another without seeming logic or preparation, Benjy's cries and the accumulation of deaths soon suggest connections, as in Roskus's:

> ... They ain't no luck going be on no place where one of they own chillens' name ain't never spoke.... [Benjy] know lot more than folks thinks.... He knowed they time was coming, like that pointer done. He could tell you when hisn coming, if he could talk. Or yours. Or mine. (pp.29–30)

Faulkner augments this superstitious attitude by the frequent collocation of Damuddy's death and Caddy's wedding as momentous events for the South and for Benjy personally (the loss of his name, the loss of his love).[6] In particular, because it commemorates the passing of the ante-bellum generation and the children's loss of innocence, Damuddy's death assumes a governing importance as symbol of the fall of the South and, with it, the fall of the Compsons. The death of the old lady and the growth to consciousness of the children are pictured in the muddied drawers (Damuddy equals muddy) sported by Caddy as she balances in a pear tree looking into her grandmother's room. Her later history, accompanied by snatches of parental dispute and Benjy's complaints, underscores the image and is promptly contrasted with Quentin's response to Benjy's howls of protest. Daughter, mother and great-grandmother are allied as figures in different stages of decay and we see how much further it has harmed the daughter (that early sketch of Temple Drake). The account of events leading up to Benjy's castration follows at once and the pattern implied by the juxtaposition driven home: Caddy's sexual lapse prompts Benjy's intemperance (his attack on the schoolgirls) as it drives Quentin to suicide. It is typical that Faulkner should have chosen a venerable old woman and a young girl to carry his burden, even more so that he should have framed them by the consciousness of an eternal child.

Because of his exclusive devotion to her, Quentin comes to the meaning of Damuddy's death only later through Caddy. That is not true of his brothers. Jason, who as a child liked to sleep with his grandmother, bears the impact of her passing in an estrangement which the context reveals to be more than simply personal while Benjy perceives immediately what is happening. Roskus was right to regard the name-change as premonitory because he sees that Benjy not only typifies the breach between past and present but has the sixth sense to understand as much. Dilsey supports him movingly by appealing to the divinity that shapes our ends.[7]

> *His name's Benjy now, Caddy said.*
>
> *How come it is, Dilsey said. He ain't wore out the name he was born with yet, is he. . . . Folks don't have no luck, changing names. My name been Dilsey since fore I could remember and it be Dilsey when they's long forgot me.*
>
> *How will they know it's Dilsey, when it's long forgot, Dilsey, Caddy said.*
>
> *It'll be in the Book, honey, Dilsey said. Writ out.*
>
> *Can you read it, Caddy said.*
>
> *Won't have to, Dilsey said. They'll read it for me. All I got to do is say Ise here.* (p.56)

Benjy's name-change and Damuddy's death are thus seen to involve a breach of identity consequent upon a lapse in steadfastness on the part of the Compsons. They now begin to suffer the humiliation long known to Dilsey and her family, one that has schooled them to the virtue of fortitude, which is a result of belief as of integrity—*All I got to do is say Ise here.*

It is interesting to note how, in the last-quoted scene, Benjy the idiot no longer matters. Far from determining the description, he is simply a convenient outlet for Faulkner and as such is indistinguishable from a traditional narrator. In varying degrees, this is true of the several descriptions we have of life in the Compson home. As Irene Kaluża has pointed out, it is the material concerning other people, quoted without distortion by Benjy, which dominates his section; that relating to himself is much less frequent.[8] It is as if the character Benjy, who is mentally defective, is a figure who appears in the scenes the narrator Benjy, who is mentally precocious, describes. The 'abnormality' of the idiot and the different 'abnormality' of the novelist find common purpose in him, so that to the fragmented operations of the boy-man's mind is added Faulkner's selective portrait of a failing family. The very detachment he brings to his task and the cunning whereby transitions from one event to another are effected signal the presence of an omniscient author operating hand-in-hand with the ostensible one. It is Faulkner, not Benjy, who exemplifies Dilsey's fears by framing her indignant speech with scenes of contemporary Compson life, just as it is Faulkner who brings together Jason cutting up Benjy's paper dolls with Jason the family overlord in the following section. He is spontaneously locating meaning less in individual episodes than in their juxtaposition. The episodes themselves are straightforward, related in the sparest vocabulary and syntax. What we lack are background, introductions and explanations and we are deprived of them so that we may concentrate on huge shifts of feeling from one period to another, for it is they which more than anything else are responsible for the impression of Benjy's idiocy and all that flows therefrom. At the same time, the very brevity and artlessness of the man keep the melodrama at bay. In lesser hands, we might have had a portentous family saga of decaying fortunes. Here, dissension is lightly touched on and the key stages of the Compsons' decline uninsistently manifested.

As a one-man chorus, Benjy watches, suffers and cries while the blows fall. As chorus-prologue, he presents in embryo all the major characters and events which succeeding sections are to amplify. As a man mentally (and later physically) imprisoned in childhood, he is a fit memorialist of a story whose major theme is the loss of innocence. He laments; he is the lament; he is—with Caddy—the subject of the lament. In other words, he is at one and the same time a narrator, a consciousness and an active representation of a way of life. In this way, he is the most complex figure I know to have been used as a first-person spokesman.

There is a pathos in having suffered with Benjy a birthday so reminiscent of past joy and, in the gloom of night at the end, so empty of hope. The lack of emotion with which he remembers the anniversaries that mark the change suggests that this is how it is with him day after day. His pain has been habituated. Jason's final act—that of righting the progress of the surrey round the statue of the Confederate soldier in the town square—develops the point memorably. It reminds us that he treats Benjy compassionately as well as cruelly, admiring his brother's capacity for punishment because it touches so sharply on his own, though, granted the circumstances, it is only to be expected that the cruelty should predominate and that the compassion should so resemble a gesture of defeat. Benjy's 'hoarse agony' is assuaged; normal expectations are restored and a kind of security achieved under the Confederate monument, 'each in its ordered place'. (This striking phrase belongs, as *The Unvan-quished* suggests—see page 115—to the ante-bellum South, now used to confirm its failure.) Yet the journey is one to death, both for the Compsons and the South. Literally, of course, Benjy is on his way to his father's grave. He holds in his hand a broken narcissus which Luster has mended with a splint, a reminder of the Sartorises' static, self-absorbed life, now even more intensely done. The Confederate soldier, gazing 'with empty eyes beneath his marble hand into wind and weather', is compared to Benjy, whose eyes, 'empty and blue and serene again', long for the ordered view the soldier is perpetually to enjoy (as did the marble faun of the poems not long before). It is a brilliant conjunction of images, wherein the catastrophe of the Civil War, thoroughly as it impacted on the South at the time, is seen to have been held in suspension until the turn of the century, when it was finally released.

The Sound and the Fury's concept of historical destiny, together with the Compsons' profound sense of consanguinity, extends this sense of failure to everybody. It is not only Benjy who sees his world as 'mad', nor is the negro the only one who tries to alleviate it with faithful service, since Faulkner insists on refracting these qualities through disparate temperaments, thereby enriching any of their specific manifestations. That is why *The Sound and the Fury* is always pushing in the direction of sustained metaphors of behaviour located in individuals, Benjy's 'madness' being the first we meet. That, too, is why our capacity for tolerance is so fully stretched by the book. It extends to Mr Compson, a man already saddened by his family's plight but increasingly driven to drink and an early grave by the grief he feels for his two favourite children, Caddy and Quentin.[9] It also extends to Mrs Compson with her perennial complaints, a comic portrait of a weak person become monstrous by feeding off her own weakness. Earl, Jason's business partner and a straightforward man, speaks of her kindly enough and we have no reason to disbelieve her protest that Caddy and Quentin always treated her as an outsider—though more in temperament than in anything else, even if the years of self-pity have convinced her otherwise and encouraged her to take refuge in illusions of superior worth, a caricature of the Southern 'aristocracy'.

Mrs Compson's view of herself as one who is at the mercy of circumstance (that, too, is how Dilsey thinks of the niece, interestingly enough) may be extended to her family, in which the exclusions and conspiracies she complains of are rife, not so much as a result of selfish rivalries but more as a sign that, whatever their motives (these are, in fact, rarely worse than mixed or thoughtless), people no longer come together, things no longer hang together, save in a crazy way. When we learn in *The Mansion* that Jason, having prevailed on his mother to commit Benjy to an asylum, relents in the face of her whining only to see him burn down their house a few years later, we understand how tangled their affairs have become. And when Jason buys back the pasture his father sold to send Quentin to Harvard and in outreaching himself loses it to Flem Snopes, who devotes it to modern housing in the name of the woman who most intensely embodies Faulkner's vision, we see clearly the implicit tendency of *The Sound and the Fury*. It is the 'Compson devilment' at work, the surrender of the South to its own antipathetic spawn.

II

It is to the historical trauma that the Compsons are experiencing that we first turn for the clue to Quentin's behaviour, for if Benjy protests the loss of innocence, he protests that of the 'aristocratic' tradition, in which he sees himself as a chevalier of purity. Such a realm, of family love and relations free from the interrogation of self-awareness, is for him the source of all the values that matter and the atmosphere it breathes is one of flow, of continuity. Like the paradisal garden, he sees it as existing in time but free from chronology (precisely Benjy's way with events, we notice) and resistant to direct expression since the necessity for talking about it occurs at the moment when it no longer exists, when one has passed from grace into history.

Unluckily for Quentin, the worm has been at the bud. He himself comes of age, Caddy deserts him and the Compson's disarray becomes manifest. Sooner than resign himself to these blows, he sets out to recover life from them by attempting to protect his sister from other men. That way, he can prolong his childhood and find some shelter for himself from his mother's non-existent love and his father's broken will. (The relation between Quentin and his father recalls that between Axel Heyst and his father, the nihilist who wrote a book called *Storm and Dust*.) Jason, too, suffers from an all-too-present mother and an absent father; Caddy apart, it is Quentin's situation in reverse. His solution is self-dependency and he carries it off because he has enough worldly energy to be a breadwinner and enough psychic energy to justify himself to himself. Quentin has no such reserves of strength. His solitude is both more oppressive and bewildering because it has been more recently imposed and because it exacts its penalties on one whose wounds are more sensitive, his feelings finer. When Caddy falls, there is no consolation to be found for him, only a mounting desperation as he burrows deeper and deeper into himself. As a result, he comes increasingly to be haunted by shadows: the shadow of his own body (reminding him of his mortality and his dejected exist-ence), the shadow of the past and the shadow that is his consciousness of time itself. We recall the Shadow that falls with such paralysing effect in T. S. Eliot's 'The Hollow Men' or the shadows that haunt the protagonist of 'The Waste Land' (another victim of 'memory and desire'):

> ... your shadow at morning striding behind you
> Or your shadow at evening rising to meet you;

On his last day, Quentin reflects on his life in the form of a deadpan register of events shot through with unpunctuated reminiscence and argument. The way in which his memories surface is instructive. On the one hand, there are Benjy-style shifts, neatly dovetailed verbal or sensory links between past and present, together with episodes from the past that are conventionally embedded in the text, memories of sad affection, meditative or nostalgic (many of them involving negroes or episodes from his childhood), unlike the former, which represent the cross-currents of his disturbed emotions. On the other hand, there are switches in tense and subject which, in the speed and suddenness of their occurrence, are new. Benjy's literal reports, as of the observing eye which knows and feels more than it sees, give way to the ruder involvement of his brother, though there are several transitional passages before we get the measure of his more allusive descriptions. These are not only juxtaposed, however sharply. They punctuate his mind in flashes as memory piles on memory or hides lurking within another, so much so that they appear to be the eruption of material he is helpless any longer to combat or control. The contrast between them and the enjambed passages concerning Harvard in the summer of 1910 is absolute: internal and external worlds are set at loggerheads— which is as much as to say that the techniques we were persuaded to accept in the first section have been adapted for use in this one and, because Quentin is not mentally deficient, have become dramatic in quite another way. They tell how his life has become forfeit to his memories.

The young boys fishing and the Italian girl he meets are final, distant reminders of all that he loses thereby. At the same time, they suggest the more personal complexion of his dilemma, as is apparent when we contrast them with Dalton Ames, Gerald Bland, Caddy and Natalie, all of them proof of how clock-time ruins the young by forcing them to grow up and become sexually active. But it is not sexuality alone that rankles, nor even female sexuality, despite Mr Compson's references to 'periodical filth' and 'liquid putrefaction'. It is the belief that women do not suffer man's outrage at the loss of innocence nor share his interest in trying to recover it. For Mr Compson (who, despite his disillusionment, is as much an idealist in some matters as Quentin, which is why his cynicism should be both self-protective and intended to shake his son as well as believed in), Caddy's activities are only the latest reminder of the ability of women to adapt themselves to sex with a facility that leads him to conclude that they are secretly allied to evil and thus never have any innocence to lose. That is why, though they remain objects of veneration when immature or ingenuously regarded, women are so often execrated by the Faulknerian boy-man. That, too, is why, with attitudes like these (attitudes quite independent of the argument about the decline of the Compsons) Quentin should reluctantly try to preserve his chastity by admiring women from a distance. This then becomes the hidden spring of his behaviour:

> ... and I thought about how I'd thought about I could not be a virgin, with so many of them walking in the shadows and whispering with their soft girl voices lingering in the shadowy places ...[10] but if it was that simple to do it wouldn't be anything and if it wasn't anything, what was I.... (p.146)

For Quentin, women must be pure to be loved, physically tantalising but without putting him to the test, not least because he feels the reality of making love to be incommensurate with the emotions it is intended to express, if not destructive of them. Hence his admiration of negroes for they, like Benjy, are childlike in themselves and treat others as if they were children; such simplicity 'tends and protects them it loves out of all reason' (p.85). Best, Quentin thinks recalling Versh's story of a man who castrated himself, never to have known sex; his father's corrective emphasis on nature as process does not touch him. But since he does know sex, he cannot be content with chastity alone and turns to incest for release. Incest

> represents a desire for self-sufficiency.... What a great temptation, how god-like, to be whole, to be alone, unified, integral, to be the more completely self-sufficient, entirely

independent, ... by union with a part of oneself.[11]

To become whole again like this would free Quentin from self-awareness and with it his obsession with time—and it can come about because incest keeps intact his refusal to mature sexually while offering him a once-for-all surrender to his masculinity which will restore him to a new if beleaguered relation with his sister.

> *If it could just be a hell beyond that: the clean flame the two of us more than dead. Then you will have only me then only me then the two of us amid the pointing and the horror beyond the clean flame.* (p.115)

When it comes to the point, however, Quentin cannot force Caddy into incest. For one thing, he does not actually want to possess her. It is only that, hating the fires of lust he now feels, he wishes to convert them into purifying flames with the one who recalls the happy time when he knew neither. (Benjy's reaction to fire and his emasculation contribute to the complex.) For another, '... I was afraid she might [commit the act] and then it wouldn't have done any good' (p.176). Only the poetry of sex matters to him because it alone can reconcile him, as much as anything can, to his loss of wholeness. When, on the morning of his suicide, he tries to destroy his watch, he tries to halt the process that is separating him from the past. He is trying to achieve something Mr Compson knows to be impossible (hence his intelligent resignation):

> Because Father said clocks slay time. He said time is dead as long as it is being clicked off by little wheels; only when the clock stops does time come to life. (p.82)

If only the clock of history were stopped, time would come to life again and men could once more inhabit an innocent world. Being of a more singular intensity than any other Faulknerian, Quentin takes the thought to its literal conclusion by submitting his body to the flow of water, the ultimate feminine haven, the death of the mind.

Like the more spiritually-minded protagonist of 'The Waste Land', he has come to this pass because the sex that is life repeatedly collides with the sex that is death (of the body or spirit) and drives with conflicting emotions that can never be satisfactorily resolved. Through both men stalks the shadow of a divided self. Through both appear memories of radiance and shame. Quentin is haunted by one such memory in particular: Caddy's muddying her drawers on the day Damuddy died. For him, this assumes the force of prophecy since it betokens her besmirchment, the dirty drawers signifying her lapse into sexuality via menstruation. (Faulkner originally began the second section with Quentin recalling Benjy pawing at Caddy's dress 'signifying his recognition of her fall from virtue'.[12] There then followed his suicide pact with Caddy and his attempt to prevent her meeting Ames. The inner logic of this sequence is less transparent in the richer texture of the version we have, as is the anticipatory nature of Benjy's distress.)

Even so, Caddy's emblematic status derives from apprehensions that are more truthfully self-directed, since it is Quentin's slapping her after she has defiantly removed her wet dress at the creek that causes her to fall and muddy her drawers; it is after he has been aroused by another girl, Natalie, that he smears mud from his body on to hers; and finally, in the highlight of this section, it is he who reminds her of the drawers as she lies soaking in the creek water up to her hips, and points a knife at her throat to end it all. What is being hinted at by these events is not women's sexuality so much as the inability of men like Quentin to bear it. Hence the alternatively protective and disgusted reactions of the brothers to Caddy: upon her is lavished the love but also projected the anxiety of inadequate men. More than that, the preoccupation each brother has with her is the expression of the Southerner's attitude to the land—cumulatively, as a set of images relating to nature, goodness, affection and security (Benjy), as the guarantor of his code of honour (Quentin) and finally as a focus of resentment for the fact that the past has come to blight the present, the land itself merely a source of exploitation (Jason).

Quentin's adventure with the Italian girl harks back to his love for Caddy, though the girl herself does more than remind him of his sister. She is also an image of Little Sister Death, whom Quentin is now courting in the hope that she will help him recover his first love.[13] A similar contrast exists between his fight with Dalton Ames, Caddy's old boyfriend, and his fellow undergraduate, Gerald Bland, another sexual male he is driven by guilty fear to assault. On this his last day, both episodes make him realise afresh how much he and his brothers are lost in the dungeon of the South, which he remembers being illustrated for him by

> a picture in one of our books, a dark place into which a single weak ray of light came slanting upon two faces lifted out of the shadow.

He can only identify himself with the objects of his despair:

> I'd have to turn back to it until the dungeon was Mother herself she and Father upward into weak light holding hands and us lost somewhere below even them without even a ray of light.

Caddy, however, is free from such cramping effects. With a mixture of admiration and resentment that she should possess the strength he lacks, Quentin recalls her saying:

> *You know what I'd do if I were King?* she never was a queen or a fairy she was always a king or a giant or a general *I'd break that place open and drag them out and I'd whip them good....* (p.172)

It is the same instinct for life that leads her to foil his double-suicide pact by calling his bluff. However much she loves Benjy and Quentin, they are for her still prisoners who would restrain her in the dungeon, Benjy to keep her sweet-smelling, Quentin to prevent her from growing up. She must range more widely and it is only right that she should do so for she is a spirit of earth. Unfortunately, she is also the unwitting cause of much injury, injury that in the present analysis signifies the incompatibility of nature and civilisation, innocence and the motion of life.[14]

III

Quentin's section, giving rise as it does to some of Faulkner's finest sustained passages, is, I think, the *locus classicus* of the stream-of-consciousness novel in as much as it ascribes the technique not simply to the passive mind articulating its experiences but to one so enervated by the conflicts it harbours that it is incapable of action and is reduced instead to feeding off itself. Quentin thus bears out Robert Penn Warren's observation that the events of the book are related through the consciousness of the doomed characters 'or rather, through the special consciousness which, in each case, is in itself ... the doom'.[15] This is nowhere more brilliantly demonstrated than in the third section, spoken by the middle brother, Jason Compson. That Jason is in many ways reprehensible needs no further emphasis here though there are two important points to be made about him: first, that he is a comic creation and, second, that his reaction to modern life accords with many of Faulkner's own views, he being not only an example of modern man cut adrift from the old morality but also a condemnation of such a man, himself a critic of what he has become. Jason is the thing Faulkner hates and gives vent to the hatred he feels; he is at once ally and enemy. That is why he is a comic villain. That, too, is why he is the most vulnerable Compson, one in whom the established order of Grenier and Habersham gives way to the brave new world of Stevens and Snopes.

Behind Jason lies a great deal of historical feeling against the forces tearing apart family and community. He expresses the frustrations of those who oppose the decline of the agrarian South and champions the rights of the small man against big business generally. He is a protestor in a distinctive tradition, one realised in all his shabby prejudices, his self-pity, his distorted and undeclared ideals. But for all that his ideals are real and we should not be blinded to the fact by the inspiration which led Faulkner to make him victim and proponent of the very system he rails against.

Jason's relations with his niece, Quentin, are like a running argument with himself about those ideals. Like his brothers, he is obsessed by the need to protect the ghost of a Southern lady's virtue and in so doing commits himself to the bolder task of defending Jeffersonian life in the throes of dissolution. Like his brothers, too, he is an innocent; only the show of brutishness conceals the likeness. The world is now damned. On that point, all the Compsons agree. Accordingly, it is to the internal soliloquy that they turn for the expression of their chaotic feelings, each character sundered from the other as they are all shut off from any intelligent participation in life, great solitaries leading their lives on two levels—the public one, full of fixed attitudes and responses, and the private one, furious with perception, crammed with argument, memory, emotion, the split self talking to itself.

Jason is especially distinguished by the Dickensian vigour of his reflections because he reflects the discrepancy between appearance and reality more sharply than anyone else. He is a frightened man who would be a bully, a prisoner of his family who must play its warden and boast his lack of 'the sort of conscience I've got to nurse like a sick puppy all the time' (p.228). It is in such moments that his brusqueness may be measured. After the confusions and passions of the preceding sections, his bluntness is invigorating and, together with his whiplash humour, achieves a sense of detachment as liberating in its way as Dilsey's. It is related to the 'sanity' Faulkner later attributed to him, what Richard Chase described as 'the flow of native language [which] makes him what he is, allowing us to see him... in all his unforgettable cruelty, vulgarity, and human appeal...'.[16] Here at last is a familiar man, transparently of ourselves, giving a performance that is less literary than dramatic, in marked contrast to those of his brothers, which are, in varying degrees, collaborations between character and author. We hear not Benjy's strange simplicity of address nor the currents of a submerged mind like Quentin's but a fresh, mimetic voice engaged in an outburst of appalling candour. This coup is vital to the book. For one thing, it prevents the reader's nascent impatience (and worse) with the Compsons ever erupting. At the same time, some of the sting is taken out of Jason himself when we realise how feeble the Compsons are and the burden he has to bear in consequence, a point equivocally reinforced by his whining declarations on the subject and by the fact that many of the things he prides himself on—business acumen or chicanery, a no-nonsense approach to life, aggressive discipline over his family—all fail.

Jason is caustic, condemnatory; he is also apprehensive lest he becomes the subject of his tirades.

And there I was, without any hat, looking like I was crazy too. Like a man would naturally think, one of them is crazy and another one drowned himself and the other one was turned out into the street by her husband, what's the reason the rest of them are not crazy too. (pp.232–3)

Jason's awareness of such craziness, whether congenital or environmental, has created his harshness partly as a shield of protection, partly as a safety-valve. He fears the consequences to himself of sheltering people who in the past have had no scruple in betraying him to unhappiness and is undecided between using his position to help them and turning it into an instrument of his revenge. The result is less ironical than another contributing factor to his pathetic villainy.

When he looks at the town birds outside his office window, Jason observes:

> I counted over a hundred half-hatched pigeons on the ground. You'd think they'd have sense enough to leave town. It's a good thing I don't have any more ties than a pigeon, I'll say that. (p.247)

The tone characteristically mixes cynicism and sentiment in equal parts, for if the pigeons remind him of his own frustration, they also allow him to drain all pity to himself. He is thus left to enjoy their plight with laconic relish, only to discover his affinity for them in a new way when he tries to shed the burden of his troublesome humanity. A similar rhythm occurs when he looks at the sparrows in the courthouse yard. At first, he thinks of ways of exterminating them. Then, subtly, unconsciously, he moves on to praise 'country businesses' and 'a country town' in passages that are haunted by a sense that 'country life' is nonetheless vanishing. This, in turn, carries with it a submerged connection to the birds who, ironically, know no other home than Jefferson and who, like him, are severed from it.

> Sometimes the sparrows never got still until full dark. The night they turned on the lights around the courthouse it waked them up and they were flying around and blundering into the lights all night long. They kept it up two or three nights, then one morning they were all gone. Then after two months they all came back again. (p.252)

All the strands that help make Jason are caught here: persecution, bewilderment, futility, routine, a life fouled up.

Jason sees himself as one who sticks by the South but is ill-repaid for it. Hence the contradictions in his behaviour. He puts down the townsfolk by reminding them that the Compsons were aristocrats when they were scratching dirt while at other times scoffing at the family's pretensions. He attacks Quentin for hypocrisy yet also fears he will meet her copulating in the street. He condemns negroes for their indolence but wishes he were one in order to escape from worrying about Quentin (a wish Luster returns by refusing to get involved in 'white folks' business'). In guarding Quentin, we see just how mixed his motives are: he quietens his mother; he punishes the girl for the injury to his chances she represents; he appeals, however mutely, to a sense of family honour; he ensures that the profit accruing from Quentin's dependency will continue; he expresses his revulsion at her behaviour.

Jason often gives a misleading impression because he is not sure what, if anything, can be done to counter the prevailing malaise but is determined to do it bluntly—and the greater the insecurity, the greater the bravado. When Quentin bursts out, 'If I'm bad, it's because I had to be. You made me. I wish I was dead. I wish we were all dead', he comments tartly, 'That's the first sensible thing she ever said' (p.260). The remark is revelatory of his despair, in spite of its being intended as a deflating sally. It is the sort of kindly cruel reply we should expect of a man who goes through the motions but who no longer believes he can save his family.

Aware that, as a result, life is a treadmill of shame for him, Jason brings to it an equally ceaseless commentary, a secret reordering of experience in which he may vindicate himself to himself in compensation for the satisfactions he is being denied. When he reports Earl threatening to tell Mrs Compson how he bought his automobile, he says he is 'Listening to what he would say before I shut him up' (p.228) and then remarks:

> I never said anything more. It doesn't do any good. I've found that when a man gets into a rut the best thing you can do is let him stay there. (p.228)

But these are merely verbal victories, such as people win for themselves when replaying embarrassing experiences. Jason did not 'shut him up' nor is Earl 'in a rut'; those are Jason's ways of despatching him. Again, he imagines himself grabbing the sheriff (who has just before refused him help) and knocking down the owner of a team he requires for the chase after Quentin (just before he is injured by a man who resents his would-be strong-arm tactics) or using soldiers and sheriff to overthrow 'Omnipotence' (shortly before it defeats him once more). Real and imaginary worlds are thus divided and thus collide, though even reverie must at some point acknowledge the facts it seeks to avoid. So it is here, for after performing his brave deeds, Jason imagines himself in bed with his whore, Lorraine, 'pleading' for help like the hopeless being he is.

It is all in the inside of his head, as when he reports the town's gossip about Quentin to his mother:

> You don't know what goes on I says, you don't hear the talk that I hear and you can just bet I shut them up too. (p.239)

Once more, we can be sure he did no such thing. The point is important since too many readers take Jason's Jason at face value. He is always *justifying* himself to himself; he is a character aware of behaving before an audience and his style responds accordingly (note, for example, how the past tense often gives way to the historic present when he reports exchanges). A detached portrait would produce someone very different from this, someone much less sharp, bitter, quick. It is precisely what happens in the last section, when the self-styled master crumbles in a narrative that is not his to manipulate. *This* Jason is more than likely the one his fellow Jeffersonians know. (Frenchman's Bend knows him as Jody Varner.) He is the man Jason himself is guilty about, the one for whom he wins rewards by cheating his mother, stealing Quentin's money—and reordering events in his commentary.

Jason's comic talent is another part of his attempt to argue with his unlucky fate. Quentin may have been an intelligence, but look what happened to him:

> ... I never had university advantages because at Harvard they teach you how to go for a swim at night without knowing how to swim and at Sewanee they don't even teach you what water is. (p.195)

So he has elected to stay at home. After all, someone has to provide for the family. Perhaps Benjy, that 'hog for punishment', can help.

> Rent him out to a side show; there must be folks somewhere
> that would pay a dime to see him.... (p.195)

Or, now that his father is dead, perhaps Uncle Maury, who
attends the funeral masking his alcoholic breath with clove
stems:

> I reckon he thought that the least he could do at Father's
> funeral or maybe the sideboard thought it was still Father and
> tripped him up when he passed. (p.197)

Certainly the niece herself won't help. So here is a man beset by
'invalids and idiots and niggers'. But aren't the last-mentioned,
particularly Dilsey, helpful? She, at least, thinks so.

> 'And whar else do she belong?' Dilsey says. 'Who else gwine
> raise her cep me? Ain't I raised ev'y one of y'all?'
> 'And a damn fine job you made of it,' I says. (p.197)

Touché, though Jason unwittingly includes himself amongst the
damned. (Or does he know? It is hard to tell.) Truthful Jason
exposes everyone save, as he likes to think, himself.
   Even if he had doubts, these would be stilled by the person he
fears most but can never escape from because he can never hate
her enough to want to: his mother. He is her slave, one who has
'to chase up and down back alleys because of [her] good name'
(p.232). (This reminds us of Mr Compson telling Quentin that
'no Compson has ever disappointed a lady' (p.177).) But Jason
is more than simply mother's slave. He is also, improbable as it
may sound, mother's boy. What with his blinding headaches
and his nervous allergy to petrol fumes, can we doubt that the
symptoms are classic? Not that he has accepted the part without
reluctance, as we can tell from the masquerade of virility in his
monologue or from his response to a remark of his mother's that
he may marry once she is dead, even though no woman is good
enough for him. He, however, believes that no marriage could
occur without her rising from the grave.
   Jason's relations with his mother reduce to a simple mechan-
ism whereby he does what he can to please her while simul-

taneously defrauding her. He is smuggling into his duties a cry
for his rights as urgent when it is addressed to her as when it is
addressed to the Easterners in the cotton market:

> 'But sometimes I become afraid that in [refusing Caddy's
> cheques] I am depriving you all of what is rightfully yours....
> If you want me to, I will smother my pride and accept them.'
> 'What would be the good in beginning now, when you've
> been destroying them for fifteen years?' (p.219)

The Jason who says that is a weaker man than is usually
described. Because Mrs Compson is so formidable, he can afford
to speak to her like this, just as he can upbraid her for neglecting
Quentin, because he knows that he will not make any impression
on her.

It is in the nature of things that he can protest but sparingly
and then in a dismissive voice which may well be compared as
an expression of distress with Benjy's broken, bare narration and
the weave and flow of Quentin's exacerbated sensibility. (Faulkner himself suggested the comparison. Benjy, he wrote, 'must
never grow up to where the grief of bereavement could be
leavened with understanding and hence the alleviation of rage as
in the case of Jason and oblivion, as in the case of Quentin'.[17]
Benjy, we notice, expresses grief without knowing why he does
so; his brothers' superior comprehension may be measured in
Jason's 'rage' and Quentin's death-wish, precisely the features
that make them obnoxious to some.) When Jason says he wants
to teach Luster to drive so that Luster can chase Quentin, he
does so, he says, because he wants to stay at home and play with
Benjy. There is no reason why remarks like this should be read
merely as bad jokes. That would be to confuse the stratagems of
expression with the core of meaning. The same is true of his
retort to Mrs Compson's remark that she would take Caddy
back if it were left to herself. '"Let her come back," I says, "far
as I'm concerned."' Calling her bluff? Partly so, but also a real
sentiment deriving from feelings so obscured that they are
hidden even from himself.

When he chases Quentin at the end, Jason's adolescent
suffering erupts in passages of astonishing power. Stealing
money from Caddy has been his way of claiming what was due
to him when she jettisoned his job with Herbert Head. The niece

merely repeats the original offence, 'the fresh battle toward which he was carrying ancient wounds' (p.306). He cannot but believe that buildings, the law, the weather, people, the universal Deity Himself have finally joined in the conspiracy against him. In this state, the stifling, stultifying oppression he feels insensibly gives way to reveries in which pain is conjured up the better to be enjoyed—as his mother enjoys hers. With that depressing irony, his bid for liberation is over.

IV

Jason's section introduces us to the idea of servitude or bondage, thus complementing Benjy's 'madness' and Quentin's metaphor of death. It is a quality powerfully developed in the last section by Dilsey, the family servant. For many, Dilsey remains the only character to escape the Compsons' lot, thanks to her great strength and fortitude. Is she, then, a countervailing instance of affirmation or is she, by her very nature, a confirmation of the South's fate? Dilsey's sterling qualities cannot blind us to the fact that her ministering to her masters is of little avail, either to herself or to them. Perhaps this does not count for much since it reflects more on the Compsons than herself. Nor is moral effort to be judged by the successes it achieves. However, in so nihilistic a work as *The Sound and the Fury*, it is likely to be confirmation of the essentially secondary role she plays—as a servant, a woman, a negro and Christian. Quentin defines her role and that of her people thus:

> They come into white people's lives like that in sudden sharp black trickles that isolate white facts for an instant in unarguable truth like under a microscope; the rest of the time just voices that laugh when you see nothing to laugh at, tears when no reason for tears. (p.169)

Negroes, it seems, are little more than isolating agents for the white man's experience. They help define him by providing an atmospheric background to his drama. As at the end of *Soldiers' Pay*, they are held in awe for their emotional religion and paid a good deal of tender-hearted regard for their ability to bear so many misfortunes. Such attitudes, together with the relative clarity of the narrative at this point, could not but have encouraged readers to seize on Dilsey with relief:

> ... in the fourth section we break into sunlight of a solid world—an objective world. It is Dilsey's world; but it is not merely her world, for it is a public, not a private world. Here the solipsism of the private worlds is expanded into something communal.[18]

Not so solid or objective, though: the negro's world is what the white man creates to prevent his giving way altogether. It is less a criterion than an indulgent lament combined with an obscure feeling that even he will somehow survive. This sense of endurance is not, as it was later to become, positive, rather the faith which can console when all else fails, a thing to fill one's eyes with tears.

The point is reinforced by Dilsey's appearance at the start, where she is described as being both 'regal and moribund', a noble person and a skeleton, her bones and skin disjointed. Compare this with the description of Benjy's body, lacking unity, deathly-looking, moving like that of a trained bear, and we realise that the parallel between the two is one of Faulkner's surest intuitions. As he was later to remark:

> There was Dilsey to be the future, to stand above the fallen ruins of the family like a ruined chimney, gaunt patient and indomitable; and Benjy to be the past. He had to be an idiot so that, like Dilsey, he could be impervious to the future, though unlike her by refusing to accept it at all.[19]

Here, then, are two companions in defeat—and, because of that fact, two of its likeliest survivors. But just as it was not people like Dilsey who brought ruin to the South, so it is the more vulnerable characters who have a prior claim on us. Her attitude to time may be more profoundly achieved than Quentin's but it draws much of its strength from being placed in the context of his more searching (if also more flawed) inquiry into the meaning of time. It is Quentin who carries on the central debate of the age and his doing so is contingent on the fact that he is not Dilsey and is denied her knowledge.

How could it be otherwise? Dilsey's virtues are granted her

through her experience as a member of a subjugated race. They are as yet beyond the reach of the white man because he is still struggling to accept the fact that he *has* been defeated—indeed, would much rather persist with his traditional ideals, and these emphatically contradict anything the negro might have to teach him. More—

> What growth there was consisted of rank weeds and ... trees that partook also of the foul desiccation which surrounded the houses; trees whose very burgeoning seemed to be the sad and stubborn remnant of September, as if even spring had passed them by, leaving them to feed upon the rich and unmistakable smell of the negroes in which they grew. (p.291)

Nature, too, we notice, depends on the negro for what little fertility there is; nevertheless, the trees 'partook also of the foul desiccation' and they are no more to be blamed than the Compsons for failing to draw more from him. Nor only they.

> The clock tick-tocked, solemn and profound. It might have been the dry pulse of the decaying house itself.... (p.285)

Chronology itself is implicated in the general movement, as the book emphasises by subverting the spring and midsummer months to the Compson agony. It is not Dilsey's time, in which the eternal and temporal intersect, but even she is forced to relate the Easter message more narrowly to it—'I seed de beginnin, en now I sees de endin.'

There is now an all but universal conspiracy of fate and this, together with Faulkner's sentimental rather than substantial understanding of the negro, prevents us from regarding the fourth section as Dilsey's, however dominant her presence. Moreover, as has been observed before, of all the leading figures, she alone fails to reveal herself through monologue. Set against Benjy, Quentin and Jason, she comes to us as different in kind from them, deeply rewarding but without their ability to move us with their terrible intimacy.

At this point, with the support of a narrative which directs attention away from her to Jason and finally to Benjy, technique reveals theme, for it is an implication of the monologues that language is something that only disappointed men come to rely on. Reality is anterior and superior to expression, a Faulknerian conviction bred in the bones. If, therefore, the monologists are divorced from satisfying action, they are also divorced from wholly meaningful language. When we meet them, all that is positive in their lives is over; language is their sole means of comfort and explanation, the words themselves a mark of the misfortune that has overtaken them. The peculiar nature of the book grows from this attitude to language, as if it were the last thing left a people in their attempt not just to rediscover but to return to their lost reality.

In being thus doomed to be continually on the alert to themselves, the Compson brothers dramatise the predicament of their author. With two undistinguished novels and a number of inferior poems to his credit, one novel (*Elmer*) abandoned, another (*Sartoris*) still awaiting acceptance and a projected novel about the Snopeses not going beyond the first chapter, Faulkner, barely turned 30 at the time, was in a difficult situation, aggravated by the personal complications he himself hinted at to his French translator (which we may guess concerned his affairs with his wife-to-be, a divorcee whom he married shortly after completing *The Sound and the Fury*. She was the childhood sweetheart whose first marriage took place while Faulkner was visiting his friend Phil Stone at Yale, a situation echoed by Quentin receiving his invitation to Caddy's wedding at Harvard). Though he knew that he had achieved something authentic with *Sartoris*, Faulkner could not regard his activities as a writer as anything but ominous. No aesthetic considerations, still less financial ones, drove him to this conclusion. It was just that he understood that, like the Compsons, he had become a novelist only because he had failed to fulfil himself as a man. 'Art', he declared, 'is no part of [real] Southern life.'[20] Yet the unhappy times insisted that men like him should have emerged, for whom art was their 'breath, blood, flesh, all', representative figures at a turning point in their country's history. Faulkner was the most important of these and he understood all too well how tied he was to a medium—literature—which appeared to him to confirm his own subjection to the Benjy disease and to a means of expression—language—he distrusted all his life. 'I do not believe,' he once declared, 'there lives the Southern writer who can say without lying that writing is any fun to him.'[21] *The Sound and the Fury*, therefore, discloses to us an extreme example of the reluctant novelist, one impelled to write books against his deepest instincts but doing so with an extraordinarily passionate commitment because he knows there is nothing else for him to do.

Faulkner's quandary is enacted in the fourth section, when he himself takes over the work. In various interviews, he returned repeatedly to the point: 'I had to write another section from the outside with an outsider, which was the writer', or 'Then I tried to tell the story', or 'I tried to gather the pieces together and fill in the gaps by making myself a spokesman'.[22] Accordingly, while the last section appears to be objective, it is in fact most personal, an unconscious manifesto of Faulkner's difficulties during which he vanishes into his tale. For the length of the section, he exists nowhere other than in its pages. The point is implied, I think, by the prefatory note he drafted several years later, in which he describes the book as being the only one that had given him 'that ecstasy, that eager and joyous faith and anticipation of surprise which the yet unmarried sheet beneath my hand held inviolate and unfailing, waiting for release'. He then declared, 'When I began it I had no plan at all. I wasn't even writing a book....'[23] We can believe him. The times are out of joint; one either luxuriates in misery (as Quentin tends to do) or lashes out in anger (as Jason does); one has only one's creations to turn to, as one does obsessively, hardly aware of their nature or direction. And when the moment comes to give them shape, they incline to disorder. Where the writer seeks some conclusion, no conclusion is available, for he is most unusually implicated in his material and rises above it only with difficulty and then imperfectly.

This conflict between Faulkner and his characters is central to the book. In *The Hidden Order of Art*,[24] Anton Ehrenzweig bids us regard creativity as a process that begins with the disintegration of the artist's inner self under the pressure of psychological tensions; the resulting fragments are then scattered before being eventually reaccepted in the newly-ordered whole which is the work of art. Such activity takes place on different levels and in devious ways, though in the greatest works it resolves itself into the figure of the dying god, what he calls a 'poemagogic' image of the creative act. It is difficult not to relate 'the hidden order of art' to *The Sound and the Fury* and to see in it the result of Faulkner's response to the most pressing of internal conflicts. We are aided in our task by Carvel Collins with his observation that Benjy, Quentin and Jason represent the Freudian id, ego and superego respectively.[25] The error here is to imagine that these are the equations of a determined technique whereas they do no more than reflect the various stages of the decomposition of the writer in the act of creation, Quentin being the nearest approximation to the dying god.

In his *The Psychological Novel 1900–1950*, Leon Edel reflects on the fact that the minds of the three narrators spring from Faulkner's and asks, 'Is the creation of off-shoots of consciousness—however rich the off-shoots—in essence a form of autobiography, the emptying of the artist's mind to artistic ends?'[26] He thinks probably not, but the question remains—if, that is, it has not been answered by Faulkner himself. In his introduction to *The Sound and the Fury*, he noted that, because of the special circumstances attending his emergence, the Southern novelist writes with a 'violent partizanship', projecting

> ... into every line and phrase his violent despairs and rages and frustrations or his violent prophesies of still more violent hopes. That cold intellect which can write with calm and complete detachment and gusto of its contemporary scene is not among us....[27]

This remarkable passage is tantamount to a confession that the book it was meant to preface deals not with several characters but with a single consciousness fractured into pieces. It is the consciousness of Compson, in turn the consciousness of the South, as mirrored in the consciousness of Faulkner.

Such fracturing is well suggested by his oft-repeated descriptions of the way in which he wrote *The Sound and the Fury*:

> ... the first thing I thought of was the picture of the muddy seat of that little girl's drawers climbing the pear tree ... and I decided that the most effective way to tell that would be through the eyes of the idiot child who didn't even know, couldn't understand what was going on. And that went on for a while, and I thought it was going to be a ten-page story. The first thing I knew I had about a hundred pages. I finished, and I still hadn't told that story. So I chose another one of the children, let him try. That went on for a hundred pages, and I

still hadn't told that story. So I picked out the other one, the one that was nearest to what we call sane, to see if maybe he could unravel the thing. He talked for a hundred pages, he hadn't told it, then I let Faulkner try it for a hundred pages. And when I got done, it still wasn't finished, and so twenty years later I wrote an appendix to it, tried to tell that story.[28]

The author begins in a state of unknowingness—indeed, 'I wasn't even writing a book'. He is the artist as idiot, as much possessed by as in possession of his material. Gradually, his perceptions grow clearer and he becomes the artist as reasoner. Benjy gives way to Jason. Alas, he is no more able to 'unravel the thing' than the idiot was, so there follows a last shot at it by 'Faulkner'. This, however, is not his first appearance in the book, for his presence was announced in the second section by Quentin, who surveys the South from his vantage point in the East just as Faulkner did in 1918 at the moment he began to emerge as a writer. Quentin's section, then, is Faulkner's earlier, premature contribution to the work. It nearly succeeds in giving shape to it but the swell of feeling that accompanies it tells us that mastery over himself—whether as man or writer—is denied him. The section ends not with Quentin secure in his intention to commit suicide but with his rehearsal of the debate with his father, as if it still floated in his mind awaiting deeper resolution. Like incest, death by water abides the issue. More, it fails to tell the whole truth of the issue because it is inadequate to explain Jason's South, Dilsey's South, Benjy's South.

So it is that Faulkner finally abjures surrogates and enters his fiction directly. Now more than ever he is determined to bring it to definition, but the very attempt declares his inability to do so. All he can manage is confirmation that his 'sound and fury' signifies 'nothing', emptiness, collapse. His confession of failure is thus built into the book and with it he joins a work heaped with similar confessions. It is as if Faulkner had finally despaired of fitting form and content while remaining as true as possible to his vision. The Christian overtones can now be understood in terms of the dying artist-Christ, image of that which triumphs over the world's suffering by containing it in a metaphysic—and image of the order of art which has eluded Faulkner.

Hence, to the established metaphors of madness, death and servitude is added the metaphor of order: the order Dilsey enunciates in her celebration of Christ, the order Jason tries to reassert as he goes after his niece, the order Benjy howls for and Jason enforces at the end and, encompassing all, the order which the writer tries to establish as he tells his story. And it is in the conflict between the metaphor of order and the other metaphors that the book comes to a halt. It is carnival time again. Benjy reacts as usual to the golfers' cry of 'caddie', Jason, like Quentin, wrestles with time and fantasies of death, the daughter repeats her mother's escape, Jason again loses what he believes is rightfully owed him. Even the Reverend Shegog's 'recollection' of the life and death of the Saviour is reduced to the ominous circularity that is bringing the story full round. Once more we hear Benjy's 'grave hopeless sound of all voiceless misery under the sun' (p.316). It is the sound of the Compsons' enforced capitulation to their fate. As Mr Compson and Dilsey, from their different perspectives, now both advise, the South has no other choice but to stay awake and see evil done a while. An immense reluctance accompanies the verdict and it culminates in the freezing of conflict presided over by the statue of the Confederate soldier. The artist-idiot and the artist-sane man fight to a deadlock before the statue of a failed, Christ-like martial dying god. Like Jason, Faulkner has managed to provide only a kind of order: abrupt, imposed, negative, fragile.

Save for our familiarity with *The Sound and the Fury*, we should not believe that its experience has been mastered or that its ending—particularly the exceptionally unsettling final phrase—constitutes a satisfying conclusion. The failure is relative, of course; had it been too great, the book would have fallen apart. As it is, the last section narrows the gap, turns the book in on itself, as it were, and shows how its imperfections derive from the Compsons' genesis in an image which was resistant to explication but from which grew the matter we now have, a set of brilliant fragments shored against its ruin.

> At best, the novel aims to make the chaos familiar not to render it any less chaotic ... like Benjy we have been restored only from an unfamiliar to a customary chaos.[29]

If we take the opposite view and hold that the ending is a suitable conclusion to a work which, despite appearances, is traditional in its social and moral concerns, we shall have to agree with Richard Chase that *The Sound and the Fury*, like its author, is

> biased, bardic, parochial, and, in the societal or cultural sense, unmannered. Davy Crockett still screams in the Southern wilderness ... Faulkner is capable of very fine and very extensive and complex fictional constructions, [but] he can fail us exactly at the level of existence where the subtle complications of human behavior have to be established. Faulkner works inward from the extremities, from the mechanics and ecstasies of life.[30]

One does not get 'the subtle complications of human behavior' from Faulkner because he is a radical romancer of 'extremities' who, in *The Sound and the Fury*, was overwhelmed by a visceral reaction against the eclipse of the South. It was, we may surmise, a private emotion which triggered the feeling off and which thereafter grew to accommodate the larger one, the two together generating the book's intensity of feeling. The reasons for the crisis were not gone into, just as a core of values to set against it were but glimpsed at. Such were to come in the work that followed. For the present, it is the shock of discovery, unflinching in its honesty, that dominates.

Throughout, there appears a tension between the image and its embodiment in people, between essentially poetic resources and novelistic resourcefulness. The first two sections in particular try—with what accomplishment we know—to mediate between them. The nature of the reconciliation I have indicated by referring to 'metaphor', midway between the poetic exploration of states of being and the novelistic tendency to statement and resolution. It is, as we shall see, the basis of Faulkner's greatness.

3 That Time and That Wilderness

The consequences of the Compsons' failure in *The Sound and the Fury* are to be traced in *Sanctuary* (1931), which describes the final moment of collapse for the old South and the shocked reaction to it of a young man as he contemplates its replacement by a strange new mechanistic society. For him, this is no matter of simple opposition—women like Temple Drake court their own destruction because they no longer possess the will or the right to demand anything other while their opponents, the gangster Popeye chief among them, are but victims, men who have been subjected to the kind of life which makes their degeneracy inevitable. Such circuitousness of guilt dominates the book and encourages us to regard Temple and Popeye not as adversaries so much as answering extremes of the South's behaviour, the one not only invoking but positively deserving the other. What happens between them is in large part what happens to the American Dream in the twentieth century.

Faulkner's devotion to the Dream may be most easily grasped in his essay 'On Privacy (The American Dream: What Happened to It)', a subtitle which succinctly defines his work as a novelist. Indeed, the title of the present book is glossed by the essay when it describes the Dream as

> a sanctuary on the earth for individual man.... Not just an idea, but a condition: a living human condition designed to be coeval with the birth of America itself...

> ...that dream was man's aspiration in the true meaning of the word aspiration. It was not merely the blind and voiceless hope of his heart; it was the actual inbreathe of his lungs, his lights, his living and unsleeping metabolism, so that we

actually lived the Dream. We did not live *in* the dream, we lived the Dream itself, just as we do not merely live *in* air and climate, but we live Air and Climate; we ourselves individually representative of the Dream....[1]

This rare embodiment of perfection (we read of it again in 'The Bear' and 'The Old People') is matched by the equally physical response to its loss in *Sanctuary*, which is a fiction born of fright, that phenomenon when one steels oneself to contemplate the worst that is likely to occur with the result that one is seized by a numbing chill. The writing bears the signs of such painful apprehension in its spareness of diction, its greater than usual deliberation of phrasing, its general air of conscious fashioning. (Adjectives and verbs have been specially worked with an eye to effect, as in the 'glittering collapse' of the face of the woman who takes Ruby Lamar in after Lee Goodwin's arrest.) This vivid, chastened manner sharpens Faulkner's foreboding, makes his fear of the future felt on the pulse, as appears when we compare it to the original version of *Sanctuary*, which has more the still, sad music of *Sartoris*. Episodes turn on items of tense, concentrated action unsupported by much authorial commentary and resolved with finality, as if a curtain were being run down. This impression of the stage is apt for *Sanctuary* is a theatrical work that needs to be performed on the page; its material has, as it were, demanded and received a dramatic rather than a narrative authority. Accordingly, each chapter or group of chapters is orchestrated to a pitch and paced with a speed and emphasis that heighten its impact. That is why the potential ironies go for nothing; they are trampled underfoot by the book's headlong movement.

A good example is the visit of the young Virgil and Fonzo Snopes to Memphis in Chapter 21. This is sometimes adduced as an instance of comic relief, though that is only its minor function, if it is a function at all, since whatever amusement we may feel at the expense of two youngsters living unawares in the company of prostitutes is soon dispelled when, cured of their ignorance and more than ever keen to enjoy themselves, they are led into another whorehouse only to find themselves repelled by the colour of the women they meet there. '"Course they're niggers," Clarence said. "But see this?" He waved a banknote in his cousin's face. "This stuff is colour-blind"' (p.159). A

comparable moment in *The Reivers* is one of Faulkner's happiest
inspirations. Here, the smile is wiped off the reader's face as the
scene goes about its business with a simplemindedness that
amounts to relish. The same souring of the comic recurs with
young Bud after the gangster Red's funeral and the point
insisted on: innocence succumbs to what Miss Reba calls 'this
world's meanness' because it hungers after corruption. Temple,
Little Belle and Popeye enlarge on the theme. It is of the essence
of *Sanctuary*.

If such laconic disenchantment answers to one aspect of the
theme, there is in the time scheme of gradually delayed
revelation a countervailing quality of postponement and, when
that is no longer possible, of appalled recognition on the part of a
gentle being who is being drawn into infinite areas of suffering,
taking up now this thread, now that, and sinking with slow
confusion into the mire. As a result, what may appear somewhat
lurid in the telling is made inward by virtue of its relation to the
suffering of the teller. This undertone of feeling is intensified by
imagery which plays repeatedly on shadows, eyes, effects of light
and dark intermingling (usually stippled, in pencils or patches,
through windows, trees, bars)—all elements of the nightmare
that embraces the players. These shadowy images combine into
one when Temple looks at a clock of Miss Reba's at twilight and
there discovers a 'nothingness' that is both historical, like the
futility of *The Sound and the Fury*, and cosmic, a 'chaos' that spins
on to meet 'new disasters'.

The characters match this dreadful environment. They are
less individuals than representative figures in each of whom
inhere aspects of the South's eclipse. Accordingly, no amount of
sketching contrasts is sufficient to capture the significance of
what is happening to them. We are obliged instead to concentrate on complementary qualities (Temple's sick excitement at
the prospect of rape and Popeye's fear of natural surroundings,
Horace's sad lust and Popeye's lubricious impotence, Ruby's
fidelity and the treachery of others, Narcissa's callousness and
Miss Reba's blousy humanity) in a theatre of violence regulated—indeed, made tolerable—by Faulkner's concern for his
people. And once we notice these features, we find our attention
being fixed on common ground, the ground on which Horace
Benbow and Popeye meet at the start of the book. On that
occasion, Jeffersonian respectability and Memphis immorality

are seen to return to the place where they once co-existed in markedly altered form as robust, spontaneous, amoral beings. Alas, such co-existence is no longer possible. The tensions that negotiated disparities like theirs have vanished. Likewise, the horse-trading which, as *The Hamlet* makes clear, allowed each his expression has dwindled into a variety of activities, legal or illegal, that have split town from country and converted pioneer life into a hypocritical code that allows Jefferson to go through some of the motions of civilisation but with none of its spirit.

The wilderness, however, still knocks within at the Old Frenchman place, which is the true sanctuary of the title. (This is more sentimentally explicit in the original *Sanctuary*, where the Old Frenchman place, the Sartoris way of life 'in the throes of . . . rigor-mortis' and present-day Jefferson represent three historical stages against which is played Horace's search for the 'region of truth divorced from all reality', as ever promised by the figure of the young girl.)[2] No wonder Temple, its symbolic travesty, fears it when she stumbles on it after her car accident: Popeye is not the sole cause of her dread.

> The house came into sight, above the cedar grove beyond whose black interstices an apple orchard flaunted in the sunny afternoon. It was set in a ruined lawn, surrounded by abandoned grounds and fallen outbuildings. But nowhere was any sign of husbandry—plow or tool; in no direction was a planted field in sight—only a gaunt weather-stained ruin in a sombre grove through which the breeze drew with a sad, murmurous sound. (p.34)

The house itself is little more than a shell, its formal gardens are overgrown with saplings, it houses a seedy collection of people, criminals and down-and-outs. Yet there is enough humanity, enough energy and roughness in them for someone like Horace to feel nearer reality with them than with anyone else. The blind old man in the company suggests the important link, as Horace proposes:

> I never knew who he was. . . . Maybe that old Frenchman that built the house a hundred years ago didn't want him either and just left him there. . . . (p.87)

Here, then, is someone who keeps the Dream alive, an aged prophet who, like Tiresias in 'The Waste Land', foresees all and suffers all.

A more explicit reference to Eliot's poem occurs in the scene where Temple is raped by Popeye with a corncob. As Popeye advances towards her, it is 'to the old man with yellow clots for eyes' that she cries out, 'something is happening to me!' (p.82). It is not clear whether Temple is appealing to the old man for help, confessing herself to him or confiding in him as tutelary genius of the place. Whatever the case, the moment before her rape, she herself becomes 'an old man with a long white beard', the one a carbuncular clerk made love to in London a decade before and whom Popeye now violates with his cob.[3]

That Temple should be humiliated in this way reflects on the fact that, like Caddy Compson (whom she resembles in an unlovely way) and like all Faulkner's leading women, she personifies the state of the South at any given moment. She is thus paradoxically identified both with the land and with contemporary Jefferson; in their contest she is snatched from a college-girl's round with a ferocity that suggests an inherent rottenness being exposed. And so it proves for, despite her protests, she is soon shown to be ignorant of the virtues she espouses, being as much fascinated as repelled by men like Popeye. With supreme irony, he returns her interest in him by making her the object of his gesture of love (albeit a brutal one) towards a dimension of existence he has not enjoyed but which he obscurely recognises once flourished at Frenchman's Bend.

Thereafter, he takes her to Miss Reba's place, where she languishes 'like a thin ghost, a pale shadow moving in the uttermost profundity of shadow' (p.118), the shadow, perhaps, of Eliot's hollow men or Jung's private unconscious, storehouse of the repressed emotions in which the shadow of one's past self is now contained. (Indeed, Temple as a creation belongs here.) Beyond that, the shadow portends the threatened disintegration of life, of the universe itself. Hence the one-handed china clock Temple observes at dusk, seeing in it 'the ordered chaos of the intricate and shadowy world....' (p.120). The timelessness of this broken-down clock contrasts with the timelessness of the land we have met earlier in the book. The reminders offered here are pertinent ones: of the futility of imposing mechanical routines on nature, as Jefferson has done, and of the necessity for constructing a sensitive order against chaos, as the pre-Pettigrew pioneers failed to do.

In both positive and negative senses, the ruin of the Old Frenchman place stands as a memorial to these errors. More than that, it calls to mind all that survives them, the spirit of the plainfolk of the South, here, as in *The Hamlet*, trapped between contradictory tendencies. At one moment, as when Horace sees them on a Saturday in Jefferson, they are reassuringly familiar, the golden codgers of Yoknapatawpha:

Slow as sheep they moved, tranquil, impassable, filling the passages, contemplating the fretful hurrying of those in urban shirts and collars with the large, mild inscrutability of cattle or of gods, functioning outside of time, having left time lying upon the slow and imponderable land green with corn and cotton in the yellow afternoon. (p.88)

Against this is set a version of its successor:

The sunny air was filled with competitive radios and phonographs in the doors of drug- and music-stores. Before these doors a throng stood all day, listening. The pieces which moved them were ballads simple in melody and theme, of bereavement and retribution and repentance metallically sung, blurred, emphasized by static or needle—disembodied voices blaring from imitation wood cabinets or pebble-grain horn-mouths above the rapt faces, the gnarled slow hands long shaped to the imperious earth, lugubrious, harsh, and sad. (pp.88–9)

It is an uneasy record of man's submission to the machine, as eloquent in its way as Popeye's use of a corncob or Narcissa's 'life of serene vegetation like perpetual corn or wheat in a sheltered garden instead of a field' (p.84).

Horace's memory of childhood returns us to the ideal state, where human beings are lost, through the 'actual inbreathe' of their lungs, in life at its most vital. Only later, when they are separated from it, do they grow aware of it as 'merely [their] blind and voiceless hope'; until then, it remains part of their metabolism, a magical innocence which Faulkner captures in a passage concerning the young Horace and Narcissa at play. It might be Quentin and Caddy we were reading of.

> The street was narrow, quiet. It was paved now, though he
> could remember when, after a rain, it had been a canal of
> blackish substance half earth, half water, with murmuring
> gutters in which he and Narcissa paddled and plashed with
> tucked-up garments and muddy bottoms ... or made loblol-
> lies by treading and treading in one spot with the intense
> oblivion of alchemists. He could remember when, innocent of
> concrete, the street was bordered on either side by paths of red
> brick tediously and unevenly laid and worn in rich, random
> maroon mosaic into the black earth which the noon sun never
> reached; at that moment, pressed into the concrete, near the
> entrance of the drive, were the prints of his and his sister's
> naked feet in the artificial stone. (pp.96–7)

Everything now, alas, threatens to turn to 'artificial stone'.

It is against such an eventuality that Horace commits himself
to fight when he becomes involved in Temple's affair. Meeting
Ruby, he tells her:

> 'But that girl.... She was all right. When you were coming
> back to the house the next morning after the baby's bottle, you
> saw her and knew she was all right.' The room gave on to the
> square. Through the window he could see the young men
> pitching dollars in the courthouse yard, and the wagons
> passing or tethered about the hitching chains, and he could
> hear the footsteps and voices of people on the slow and
> unhurried pavement below the window; the people buying
> comfortable things to take home and eat at quiet tables. 'You
> know she was all right.' (p.131)

Horace's not wanting to believe the worst about Temple and the
relaxed hum of life that comes to him through the window are
directly related to each other, for in trying to establish the truth
about the weekend's events, he has the window scene as a clue to
guide him to the ideal they have brought into jeopardy.

When he enters the fray, he can scarcely believe the evil he
encounters: justice is gagged and bound by the likes of Temple's
father, a judge; the legislature is in the hands of venal politicians
like Clarence Snopes; the epitome of Virginian chivalry is

Gowan Stevens. Above all, Southern woman is now Temple
Drake, defiled on a Sunday morning in spring, the Dream
ultimately desecrated. Sensing the threat to herself at the Old
Frenchman place, Temple tells Ruby:

> 'I'm not afraid. Things like that dont happen. Do they?
> They're just like other people. You're just like other people.
> With a little baby. And besides, my father's a ju-judge. The
> gu-governor comes to our house to e-eat—What a cute little
> bu-ba-a-by,' she wailed, lifting the child to her face; 'if bad
> man hurts Temple, us'll tell the governor's soldiers, won't us?'
> (pp.45–6)

So much for fake childishness—and for the law, which can no
longer be equated with justice. But then, as *Requiem for a Nun*
makes clear, all legal systems are inherently inadequate, whatever their condition, because they give codified expression to the
pioneer's vision and in so doing betray it. Perhaps man gets
round to formulating laws as inevitably as he grows up but once
he comes to rely on them, he is in peril. In the present
circumstances, adherence to law may distinguish a man as one
who clings to the good, as is evidently the case with Horace. All
the same, we cannot be blind to the imperfections of his
profession. These are everywhere insisted on, not only by Judge
Drake or Eustace Graham or those responsible for the deaths of
Lee Goodwin and Popeye but also by Horace himself and the
conventional morality that has claimed his sister and Temple.
   It is interesting to note that when he first visits the Old
Frenchman place, Horace is running away from his wife, Belle,
who originally (as *Sartoris* shows) attracted him by her overpow-
ering sensuality. That is one good reason why he should follow
Temple's career with a guilty interest. Another emerges from his
ready response to the 'delicate and urgent mammalian whisper
of [his step-daughter's] curious small flesh' (p.133). Gazing
across the spring at Popeye, the grey-flannelled, tweed-suited
heir to the Dream meets a frustrated man like himself, with his
'bloodless' face and 'vicious depthless quality of stamped tin'
(p.5). (Narcissa, always in white, completes the figure: white
and black flank grey on either side.) The grove in which they
meet 'in which broken sunlight lay sourceless' (p.5)—another
Eliot echo, perhaps?—is part of the complex to which Horace

contributes further when he draws the equations 'nature is "she" and Progress is "he"; nature made the grape arbor, but Progress invented the mirror' (p.14). Yet, if he tries to escape masculine self-consciousness in Kinston for the timeless feminine principle in Frenchman's Bend, he nevertheless finds there the collapse of his hopes. His shock is figured in Temple, the very flower of girlhood now so perverted as to be scarcely distinguishable from Popeye's world.

That he fails in the end to redeem her is not surprising. Yoknapatawpha's is a communal crisis and only a communal response can hope to solve it. But where institutions connive at evil, men like Lee Goodwin are possible, who believes in the 'common sense' of his peers (if not in Horace's 'law, justice, civilisation') and in the certainty of being acquitted of the charge of Temple's rape while at the same time not daring to disclose Popeye's presence at the Old Frenchman house. For him, truth is divisible so that, while he falls victim to a split society, he is that society, too. Accordingly, we react to his death as Popeye greets his own arrest—protestingly but without surprise.

The South's collective culpability is memorably emphasised towards the end of the book when Horace returns to Kinston. His train is met by an old man (reminiscent of Temple's old man).

> He was thin, with gray eyes and a gray moustache with waxed ends. In the old days, before the town boomed suddenly into a lumber town, he was a planter, a landholder, son of one of the first settlers. He lost his property through greed and gulli- bility, and he began to drive a hack back and forth between town and the trains, with his waxed moustache, in a top hat and a worn Prince Albert coat, telling the drummers how he used to lead Kinston society; now he drove it. (p.238)

This failed 'aristocrat' is as much an anachronism in the 'free Democratico-Protestant atmosphere of Yoknapatawpha county' today as Horace. Equally, he has been his own worst enemy. The cancer spreads from within.

While, therefore, our sympathies are engaged with Horace, they extend to all who cause or share in his suffering—Popeye included. Conceived out of wedlock, born on Christmas Day, his mother and he deserted by his father, nearly burnt to death in a fire, an undersized weakling, his fate is pronounced for him early by a doctor:

> And he will never be a man, properly speaking. With care, he will live some time longer. But he will never be any older than he is now. (p.246)

There is a name for the illness diagnosed here: the Benjy disease. Popeye suffers from it because he is the issue of the old Frenchman line as Benjy was of the Compsons', separate versions of the same process. But even though he is severed from its values, he still obscurely hankers after them and the impasse forces him to punish what he would otherwise have worshipped—Temple. In the final chapter (not part of his original conception), Faulkner is at pains to make the point explicit by insisting that Popeye is as much a victim as an agent of evil, superseded by the sensuality he arouses in girls and ending his days tending cigarette butts in his cell with a passion for orderly arrangement. At this stage, we are reminded of the similar fates of Harry Wilbourne and the convict in *The Wild Palms*—with good reason for, like them, Popeye is an extreme version of the modern Southerner, a mock protagonist characterised by the same anxiety felt by all who pursue the Dream. Soon after finishing *Sanctuary*, Faulkner explored the point further in that most alienated of men, Joe Christmas.[4]

After his defeat in court, Horace is driven home by Narcissa. While in tears for the travesty of justice he has witnessed, he refuses to despair and tries to turn the suffering of the last few months to advantage. '"It does last," Horace said. "Spring does. You'd almost think there was some purpose to it...."' (p.234). 'Spring', once associated with nubile girls and the frontier past, has survived their decay and re-emerges once again in the cotton along the road and the locust blossoms on the drive as the car sweeps by. Yet, 'It had been a gray day, a gray summer, a gray year' (p.253) and Horace cannot forget the impression made on him by the girls he saw in Oxford while pursuing Temple. Despite their physical appeal, he felt no joy with them because he realises that the time for youth, in both personal and national terms, is over. Only the emptiness of failure remains, and it embraces everything—the affective life, manly endeavour, the very substantiality of his universe.

He stood there while on both sides of him they passed in a
steady stream of little colored dresses, bare-armed, with close
bright heads, with that identical cool, innocent, unabashed
expression which he knew well in their eyes, above the savage
identical paint upon their mouths; like music moving, like
honey poured in sunlight, pagan and evanescent and serene,
thinly evocative of all lost and outpaced delights, in the sun.
Bright, trembling with heat, it lay in open glades of mirage-
like glimpses of stone or brick: columns without tops, towers
apparently floating above a green cloud in slow ruin against
the southwest wind, sinister, imponderable, bland; and he
standing there listening to the sweet cloistral bell, thinking
Now what? What now? and answering himself: Why, nothing.
Nothing. It's finished. (pp.137–8)

This vision of drift into the nadir, developed from the analysis
begun in *Sartoris* and *The Sound and the Fury*, is *Sanctuary*'s most
critical insight. Ruby and Reba, like Dilsey, offer some relief, but
they are without amplification, overwhelmed by 'the horror'
Horace senses one night when he listens to the noise of the
insects outside his window and perceives 'the chemical agony of
a world left stark and undying above the tide-edge of the fluid
in which it lived and breathed' (p. 177). The 'fluid' here recalls Faulkner's description of the Dream cited earlier in the
chapter; having betrayed their ideal, Southerners are now like
fish that have lost their 'condition of being'. They have been
beached.[5]

Up to this point, I have treated *Sanctuary* as a parable, or, as
Malcolm Cowley has it, 'an example of the Freudian method
turned backward, being full of sexual nightmares that are in
reality social symbols'.[6] However, this does not adequately
account for the book's charge of emotion. The last-quoted
passage is a good illustration of the point for, while it contributes
to the debate about the South's condition, it has a bearing on
matters altogether more private since it can be read as a lament
not just for one's life but for having been born at all, for having
been expelled from the womb as much as from the paradisal
enclave. (Popeye's rape evinces the same infantile resentment.)
In trying to understand why this should be so, we are led, as
frequently in Faulkner, to place his work in the context of his
own life. In his preface to the Modern Library edition of

Sanctuary in 1932 (a preface parodying the Hemingway of *The Torrents of Spring*[7]), he declared that, after the exhaustion of *The Sound and the Fury* and the rejection of *Sartoris*, he had resigned himself not to think of publishing again, though once *Sartoris* was finally accepted, he turned to *Sanctuary* and what he termed a 'cheap idea' which could be made lucrative for him as his previous novels had not been. What he wrote in the early summer of 1929—relevantly, at about the time of his marriage— was then substantially revised towards the end of the following year and published early in 1931. (The original version made clearer the close ties that exist between *Sanctuary* and *Sartoris*, ties which the revision made paradigmatic rather than discursive by placing greater emphasis on Temple; the substance of the work was unaffected.) In the period between the two versions, *As I Lay Dying* was written, according to Faulkner, in a period of six weeks, which suggests that *Sanctuary*, by deliberately exploiting part of his talent, acted as a release. Something broke within and drove him to this.

> And I'd lie there with the shucks laughing at me and me jerking away in front of his hand.... I could feel the jerking going on inside my knickers ahead of his hand and me lying there trying not to laugh about how surprised and mad he was going to be in about a minute. Then all of a sudden I went to sleep.
> ... I couldn't even feel myself jerking in front of his hand, but I could hear the shucks. (pp.175–6)

Like the concept of a corncob rape, the language Temple uses here belongs to fantasy, the sort of compulsive mental eroticism which may be analogous to Faulkner's relating how he took whisky with him into the crib of a barn and 'tore off' 5000 words, though the date of the incident and the nature of the material he wrote remain unspecified.[8]

When Horace listens to Temple's recital of her rape and its aftermath, he is filled with shock and despair. He sees a man and a woman untouching in an 'alley mouth', the man propositioning the woman obscenely, she in 'voluptuous ecstasy'. He then imagines the eyes of the dead and, over all, the fact of evil and suffering 'during wind and rain'. Sex has gone to his head and there seethes with the discovery that it is in secret alliance with violence and sinfulness. Listening to Temple has been

> a dream filled with all the nightmare shapes it had taken him
> forty-three years to invent, concentrated in a hot, hard lump
> in his stomach. (p.177)

The sequence is an acute description both of *Sanctuary* and of the creative process which produced it.

In this context, Horace is best regarded as a development of Bayard Sartoris a few years on. He is now married to a divorced woman and feels inadequate as a husband. He has come late to sex and then passionately; as the barriers of frustration fall, his conscience is awakened in reproach for deeds and desires real or imagined. In time, this leads to a jaundiced view of women, whom he grows to regard as responsible for his unhappiness. It also contributes to the nausea with sex that permeates the book and gives it its central idea—the reaching after permanent value in a phantasmagoria of lust—a haunted flavour.

Temple and Popeye compound Horace's suffering. The latter appears to be Horace's opposite in nearly every particular, yet their first meeting suggests that they may not be strangers to each other after all, for when Horace decides to seek a divorce from Belle, he is described as 'feeling quiet and empty for the first time since he had found Popeye watching him across the spring four weeks ago' (p.209), which suggests that their meeting is related to his desire to leave his wife. Domestic and sexual man come face to face with each other during a depressive crisis brought about by the realisation of what the married state actually entails. The delicate conscience of the one projects itself into the bizarre figure of the other, a Horatian correlative who enacts his most shameful fancy—the rape of a young woman—before being expunged altogether. Thus, behind the drama of Goodwin and the mob, that of justice in a community, remains this private passage, the justice a man seeks for himself by trying to come to terms with the brute beast within.[9]

This notion of Horace and Popeye's submerged connection is supported by several passages from the early drafts. For example, while explaining his desertion of Belle to his Old Frenchman audience, Horace watches the 'thug' 'as though he were the one he must establish himself with....'[10] Shortly afterwards, fearing he will kill him, he tells himself, 'You'd think there'd have to be a kinship between two people who looked on death at the same time, even though it was from opposite sides'.[11] Again, it is Popeye whom Horace curses as he contemplates a photograph of Little Belle—for the very good reason that he has made him realise the Popeye within himself.

In this perspective, all the leading characters in *Sanctuary* may be said to isolate different aspects of the one man and woman whose story it is, a notion made plainer in the original version, where Belle and Narcissa are associated as equivalent women whom Horace turns to for succour after his mother's death. (Ruby is another, more frankly maternal substitute he is attracted to.) In the same way, Temple's rape becomes not a fortuitous event but a manifestation of his attitude to Little Belle, while mother and daughter together trace the degeneration of his love for his wife into the weekly carriage of shrimps from station to home.

The failure of Horace's marriage has everything to do with the fact that he likes to think of women as nature's very 'she'. Unfortunately, Little Belle, the model of his illusion, grows up and his fondness for her, as for a childhood sweetheart, becomes tainted with lust. In a portentous passage, Quentin's honeysuckle love for Caddy repeats itself as Horace's honeysuckle love for Little Belle and then yields to the discovery, so nauseating as to induce vomiting, that it belongs to Temple's experience on a shuck mattress. As he vomits, he relives the attack on Temple.

> Lying with her head lifted slightly, her chin depressed like a figure lifted down from a crucifix, she watched something black and furious go roaring out of her pale body. (p.178)

Ruel E. Foster interprets the last-quoted sentence as representing both Temple's blood-letting and, by inversion, the attack on her. By the same token, Temple's imagined climax becomes Popeye's—but since his impotence is well established, it becomes Horace's more directly than Professor Foster allows with his comment that Horace is 'feminine enough to invest himself with the feminine emotions and to put himself in their place'.[12] The description appears to be more masculine than feminine, though with elements of both; the feminine is described as the masculine imagines it:

The car shot bodily from the tunnel in a long upward slant,
the darkness overhead now shredded with parallel attenuations of living fire, towards a crescendo like a held breath, an
interval in which she would swing faintly and lazily in
nothingness filled with pale, myriad points of light. (p.179)

Image and reality meet in a moment of recognition as Horace
throws up.

Gowan Stevens, the enfeebled scion of the South, is a younger
version of Horace in as much as he courts two kinds of women,
the goddess (Narcissa) and the bitch (Temple), precisely the
same duality Horace notices in Little Belle as he stares at her
photograph. At first, she is associated with fruition and subtle,
wholesome physical invitations. Then,

He moved suddenly. As of its own accord the photograph
had shifted, slipping a little from its precarious balancing
against the book. The image blurred into the highlight, like
something familiar seen beneath disturbed though clear
water; he looked at the familiar image with a kind of quiet
horror and despair, at a face suddenly older in sin than he
would ever be, a face more blurred than sweet, at eyes more
secret than soft. In reaching for it, he knocked it flat;
whereupon once more the face mused tenderly behind the
rigid travesty of the painted mouth, contemplating something
beyond his shoulder. (p.133)

The disparity thus discovered is, he realises, to be found in all
women, it being but a short step from Little Belle's 'secret eyes'
to Temple herself, 'cool, predatory and discreet' (p.25). When
an understanding of this hits him in the stomach, the crisis
ensues because it shatters his faith in the purity of women and
everything that depends thereon. Significantly, his revulsion on
hearing Temple's account of the rape is not directed at Popeye's
viciousness; instead, he re-enacts Temple's orgasm. Horace
becomes Temple; he vomits, she goes through her climax—and
the actions are simultaneous.[13]

The original *Sanctuary* contains a strange dream that elabor-
ates on the cause of his revulsion. In it, Horace imagines that his
mother appears as a compound of Ruby's dress and Belle's
mouth. He tries frantically to prevent her from speaking but

fails: 'a thick, black liquid welled in a bursting bubble that splayed out upon her fading chin ... and he was thinking He smells black. He smells like that black stuff that ran out of Bovary's mouth when they raised her head'.[14] The smelly 'He' here is Popeye, the man born in recoil from the fact that, like Emma Bovary, mothers and wives are sexual and may have lovers or remarry. The imagery of 'black stuff' is our clue to such an interpretation for, like Mr Compson's view of women 'like pale rubber flabbily filled' (*The Sound and the Fury*, p. 127) and Joe Christmas's 'urns' issuing 'something liquid, deathcoloured, and foul' (*Light in August*, p.178), it refers to menstruation, Belle's mouth being the vagina.

It is not difficult to see how all these attitudes have clashed and merged to produce in Temple a symbol of that element in young girls that betrays their virtue, something that explains how (as their names suggest) Little Belle can become—in a sense has already become—Belle Benbow. Temple is the displaced expression of the relation between these two women and Popeye a secret self who discovers that what has been long desired in them turns out to be that which robs them of their attraction for him. Indeed, his dread of sensual women *is* his impotence. For having helped reveal the truth about the Southern belle, he is himself included in the general disenchantment. Having come this far, Horace decides that it is better to avoid the hypocrisy of women who pretend to virtue for someone like Ruby, the melodramatically faithful whore and common-law wife, faithful (like Reba to Mr Binsford) simply because she is sexually frank, unlike the Belles and Temples and without Narcissa's withdrawal from life. It is no accident that the severest criticism Temple suffers comes repeatedly from her.

When Horace remonstrates with his stepdaughter about her boyfriends, she wounds him with a reminder of his domesticity. By way of apology, she embraces him.

> There was a mirror behind her and another behind me, and she was watching herself in the one behind me, forgetting about the other one in which I could see her face, see her watching the back of my head with pure dissimulation. (p.14)

On the same day, he deserts his family. Such duplicity would be enough to drive him away, but that is not the only reason for his going.

> When you marry your own wife, you start off from scratch. . . .
> When you marry somebody else's wife, you start off maybe ten
> years behind, from somebody else's scratch and scratching. I
> just wanted a hill to lie on for a while. (p.15)

His aim is not just to get back to nature or to free himself from
Kinston's stifling routine but to escape from *this* kind of
marriage. His avowed reason for leaving, as he tells his audience
at the Old Frenchman place, is his finding, as he expected he
would, 'a rag with rouge on it', 'a handkerchief where [Belle]
had wiped off the surplus paint when she dressed. . . .' (p.15).
This apparently eccentric trigger to his rebellion leads on, in the
same speech, to his voicing resentment against his wife for
having been married before. Like Harry Wilbourne, he seems to
find it impossible to understand how a married woman can leave
her husband and settle down again with another man to whom
she can sincerely transfer her affections and how, with such
apparent calm, she can resume the conventional life without the
agonies of readjustment he has to suffer. It is not, as Horace
declares in a letter cancelled from the published version, evil
itself that repels. It is women's affinity for it, as evidenced by
their ability to ride the most violent change in their lives with
such utter self-possession. 'It's that they can be so impervious to
the mire which they reveal and teach us to abhor; can swallow
without tarnishment in the very stuff in the comparison with
which their bright, tragic, fleeting magic lies.'[15] Or, as Faulkner
himself put it to a correspondent while writing the first *Sanctuary*:
'Women are completely impervious to evil'. Hence his own
interest in 'how all this evil flowed off of [Temple] like water off a
duck's back'[16] and his hero's chagrin on seeing her turn from
college flirt to kept woman to injured innocent all within the
space of a few months. Belle's rouged rag, symbol of feminine
dissimulation, acts as a goad because it tells the same story.

Horace's recoil from women, then, is prompted not so much
by the discovery of a sexual appetite in them but by the
realisation that the two—innocence and sexuality—can *coexist*, in
Temple's case, in one figure, elsewhere in the life-denying
saintliness of Narcissa and the life-affirming squalor of Ruby. It
is very much to the point that when he deserts his Belles, he

makes for Narcissa as if to his original love, who has grown up but remained chaste to him, her marriage to Bayard Sartoris (which he did his best to prevent) notwithstanding. Unfortunately, she turns out to be as wicked as the rest of them and promptly helps return him to the arms of his wife, where he is left to ponder on his elusive ideal: an eternal, almost pubertal girl comprising earth, springtime, childhood, simple groups of people. The one who best embodies it is that paradoxical creature, the mature girl—someone like Eula Varner. That is why the portrait of a woman who can combine the ideal and real and be not only tolerated but celebrated for so being is reserved (once Charlotte Rittenmeyer has resurrected the old ghost and slain it) for Eula. It is one of the main reasons for the joyous force of her creation. Certainly, she stands at the end of a long line of Faulkner's attempts to come to terms with women who are not innocents or bitches or grand old ladies.

By the end, the fever has abated somewhat. A quality of absorbed shock, of tremendous fright which has been confronted but which lies only just below the surface, pervades the coda, in which those fugitives from truth, Temple and her father, are discovered in the Luxembourg Gardens (another Eliot echo?). The passage is remarkable for the assurance with which it suggests, through the controlled and evocative interplay of sound, action and image, an atmosphere which is both edgy and nerveless, as of the refined dread of those who have, albeit ignominiously, weathered the storm. We sense that the ghosts have not been placated, that the scene offers an implicit comment on the harrowing past. While Horace is trapped with Belle in Kinston, Temple is free to roam the world and is protected from the pain she has caused him—and through Belle (the silent key to *Sanctuary*) still causes him.[17]

4 Innocence and History

I

Absalom, Absalom! (1936), like *The Sound and the Fury*, moves in an analogical, allusive manner, circling and expanding on its material as it proceeds. There are many reasons why this should be, but none more cogent than that it was written in the grip of a barely mastered complex of feeling. The book is shot through with a most passionate sense of foreboding, and if any commentary is to give an adequate account of it, it will need to remain faithful to its most characteristic qualities, which do not include among them the finality of deeply pondered conclusions (even conclusions about the impossibility of reaching conclusions) or, indeed, of things seen clearly, steadily and whole.

The note is struck at once in the opening chapter, when we learn how intermixed the past and present are to people like Rosa Coldfield and Quentin Compson.

> he would seem to listen to two separate Quentins now—the Quentin Compson preparing for Harvard in the South, the deep South dead since 1865 and peopled with garrulous outraged baffled ghosts, listening, having to listen, to one of the ghosts which had refused to lie still even longer than most had, telling him about old ghost-times; and the Quentin Compson who was still too young to deserve yet to be a ghost, but nevertheless having to be one for all that...—the two separate Quentins now talking to one another in the long silence of notpeople, in notlanguage .... (p.9)

One Southerner has been frozen in the past (she is the Civil War's elegist); her young visitor may sense that the same fate awaits him as awaits all those who are obsessed by time. He lives neither wholly in the present nor wholly in the past but in some

66

combination of the two, some ghostly limbo which so affects him that he can no longer claim to be an individual person but a spectral consciousness that contains the past, a creature of imaginative introspection.

> His childhood was full of [the Sutpen story]; his very body was an empty hall echoing with sonorous defeated names; he was not a being, an entity, he was a commonwealth. (p.12)

Everything we learn of Quentin and Rosa in the opening chapter suggests how unlikely it is that their storytelling venture into the past can yield satisfactory interpretations. They cannot be dispassionate, let alone disinterested, their motives are confused and their powers, both critical and creative, impaired,

> looking with stubborn recalcitrance backward beyond the fever [the ending of the Civil War] and into the disease [the war itself] with actual regret, weak from the fever yet free of the disease and not even aware that the freedom was that of impotence. (p.12)

Nearly fifty years separate the two yet, for all that, they are both Southerners alike in their impotence and in their refusal to recognise their condition. Indeed, so close is the resemblance that it would be difficult to tell them apart. Such interchangeability of character is made possible by a common view of time (today is yesterday is forever) and the existence of a destiny in whose presence what is shared by individuals bulks larger than their differences.

> What is it to me that the land of the earth or whatever it was got tired of [Sutpen] at last and turned and destroyed him? What if it did destroy [Rosa's] family too? It's going to turn and destroy us all some day, whether our name happens to be Sutpen or Coldfield or not. (p.12)

Impotence and fatalism within a continuum of time are thus established as central concerns from the start.

The opening pages also affirm how personal is the Southerner's sense of the past—and how puzzling.

It's just incredible. It just does not explain. Or perhaps that's it: they dont explain and we are not supposed to know. We have a few old mouth-to-mouth tales; we exhume from old trunks and boxes and drawers letters without salutation or signature, in which men and women who once lived and breathed are now merely initials or nicknames out of some now incomprehensible affection which sounds to us like Sanskrit or Chocktaw; we see dimly people, the people in whose living blood and seed we ourselves lay dormant and waiting, in this shadowy attenuation of time possessing now heroic proportions, performing their acts of simple passion and simple violence, impervious to time and inexplicable... you bring them together in the proportions called for, but nothing happens; you re-read, tedious and intent, poring, making sure that you have forgotten nothing, made no miscalculation; you bring them together again and again nothing happens: just the words, the symbols, the shapes themselves, shadowy inscrutable and serene, against that turgid background of a horrible and bloody mischancing of human affairs. (pp.100–1)

It might be *Absalom, Absalom!* itself we were reading of here, as if the voice were not Mr Compson's but Faulkner's own as he confesses to the difficulties he experienced in writing his work. And behind Mr Compson sounds his father's voice telling those many years ago that language is a 'meagre and fragile thread' joining the 'surface corners and edges of men's secret' lives for an instant before sinking back into the darkness again. It is a familar message: man is an isolate, language a limited, temporary expression of himself (by inference when the pressure of experience demands it); relations with others are as evanescent as the language used to describe them and the words we use furtive declarations of that condition.

Yet, even if life is inexplicable, it does not deter attempts at its interpretation; it only makes them more compulsive. Literature, condemned though it be to failure, brings us nearest the truth and we measure its attempts, as Faulkner said he judged himself and his fellow-novelists, not by their success but by the magnitude of their ambition and the degree of their failure. In the present case, the ambition is unquestionably of a very high order indeed for when men like Quentin go hunting in the past, they hunt for the seeds of themselves in men who represent some earlier self, historically and psychologically. 'The past', Quentin might say, 'is me.' It is a field of 'perception, consciousness, apprehension of self. ... When the American confronts history, he has the illusion that he is confronting himself....'[1] Illusion, maybe, yet if each man is 'a commonwealth', then each man is, in his own time, the fated hero.

The search is always through other people for oneself and it claims for itself the vividness of experience, on the analogy of an adult looking back to childhood. Age rediscovers innocence and, finding itself baffled by all that it learns, asks, 'Was that really me? What went wrong? Who am I? What was I? What, then, happened? Why?'. The 'I' is a multiple one (the several temporal selves which constitute the living self, the several chronological selves in which our historical self is embodied) and it is trying to discover the reasons for its fragmentation.

Back the answer comes in the shape of Thomas Sutpen, the boy who ventured into Tidewater from West Virginia only to discover that men there claim possession to the land as they do to everything else, discriminating amongst themselves according to their possessions. He tried to avenge himself on them by building up a dynasty of his own, first through marriage to Eulalia 'Bon', then through marriage to Ellen Coldfield, then through her sister, Rosa, and finally through the granddaughter of his friend, Wash Jones—all to no avail. In such single-minded activity, we may see a man caught up in the contest between innocence and history, the moment when innocence *becomes* history and the mind falls into consciousness. Yet, weakening as his obsession with time then becomes, it remains a prerequisite to his conception of a purposeful life since it helps him avoid the finality of the tenses and with it the existence of the past as an entity immune from all but verbal revision.

Quentin is particularly intimate with the past, having grown up so immersed in stories about it that it has become a part of himself, another of his senses. Memory for him is thus no simple exercise in recall; it is what his father so finely characterises as 'the recognizable *I*' (p.196) and what he, with equal fineness, describes in this way:

Because you were not listening, because you knew it all already, had learned, absorbed it already without the medium of speech somehow from having been born and living beside it, with it, as children will and do: so that what your father was saying did not tell you anything so much as it struck, word by word, the resonant strings of remembering. You had been here before.... (pp.212–3)

Memory believes before knowing remembers.

The past is active, then. It exists in men's mouths, partly as a true impression, partly for more personal reasons. Whatever the case, the personality of the speaker is of not much less consequence than what he has to say. That being so, chronology may be convincingly disrupted in favour of a thematic grouping of subjects and a more suspenseful way of handling them, on the analogy of impromptu speakers trying—the task is often felt to be too difficult for them—to give shape to recalcitrant material, now making connections between events, now passing judgement on the characters involved and repeatedly mingling description with commentary.

It is also clear that, while no voice can speak the truth, the past is nevertheless a matter of voices, none of which can be discounted. Whether it speaks relative falsehoods or relative truths, it will have to be listened to. As Miss Rosa puts it, '*your illusions are part of you like your bones and flesh and memory*' (p.348). Her opening contribution demonstrates the point, offering what is undoubtedly an exaggerated fable of the past, concentrating attention on Sutpen's ogre-like nature, the foolishness of the Coldfields—herself included—the fatality of the South and the outrage and puzzlement she feels. Yet it remains true that we do not disbelieve her estimate of Sutpen, even when it is qualified by others. It is simply added to. We learn that there was something demonic about him and then that there were other things about him, some less important, some more so. We also learn that his motives were different from those she attributes to him and that she has special reasons for not realising the fact. But that Sutpen *was* demonic is a truth—and not only Miss Rosa's kind of truth—which we shall have to attend to. Sutpen is thus less a complex character than a compound one: 'this quality *and* that quality *and* yet others...' rather than 'this quality which leads to that one which qualifies the next'. And what is true of Sutpen is as true of events generally, whose only plausible structure is that of sequence, not causality. Mystery necessitates the simplest syntax.

Interestingly enough, when the third-person narrator comes to describe Sutpen at the beginning of the second chapter, he uses almost exactly the same tone as Miss Rosa's, thereby undermining her status as an independent voice and confirming the burden of her testimony. This is not because he is an especially authoritative person; we do not gain the impression that he is particularly well-informed (or even, apparently, very noticeable, for he has been frequently ignored in criticism of the book). It is rather that he, too, views Sutpen across the years, interweaving his contributions with those of others and accepting or qualifying them as occasion demands.

It could scarcely be otherwise, for *Absalom, Absalom!* is a work that takes its bearing from a man who is an isolate, a creature of second-hand rumour and report. The speculation that surrounds Sutpen, that is, is not just so much historical guesswork; it reflects with considerable accuracy—as, in time, it created—the Sutpen of legend. Faulkner himself acknowledged as much when he turned to the experiment of using a first-person narrator and, with astonishing ambition, at least quadruplicated it. The increase in the flow and variety of interpretation is prodigious and, as we should expect, it diminishes the omniscient narrator's authority. Where before, a Conradian narrator might share something of the author's status while being located in the novel as a character who is (at least theoretically) subject to the same limitations of perception as his fellows, Faulkner takes up the distinction and constructs a whole book from and about it, granting his narrators precedence over the characters in their tale and allowing the latter to enter it (when they are not already creatures in another person's story) *only as narrators themselves.* The cardinal example is Sutpen himself; Rosa is another. If you are not a narrator, then you do not figure significantly in the book.

In the numerous analyses of the work that have appeared, each narrator has had his particular characteristics amply documented. It is not to gainsay these to insist that the differences between them are not, in fact, very great; as the authorial narrator himself puts it, the 'ratiocination' of Quentin and Shreve is 'a good deal like Sutpen's morality and Miss Coldfield's demonizing...' (p.280). That is because outlook, attitude and interests, not to mention syntax, cadence, vocabulary, tone and idiom, all constitute a common possession. Miss

Rosa varies most remarkably, but, as we shall see, the contrast between her individual narratives is as great internally as externally. Similarly, while Shreve's manner is sometimes idiosyncratic, large stretches of his speeches might be compared to Quentin's with advantage, for they would show little, if any difference (not surprisingly, considering that passages from the one were switched to the other during composition without alteration).[2] Throughout, the narrators proceed on the understanding that they are engaged in an enterprise greater than any one of them alone could hope to undertake. Such individuality as they possess is conditional on it.

The characters themselves are often called upon to perform in ways which blur their outlines as realistic individuals. In the third chapter, for instance, Mr Compson is a representative voice who relates events based on his mother's reports or picked up randomly from news generally available in Jefferson or with the implied sanction of an omniscient narrator, who alone could know of such items as the dinner scene at Sutpen's Hundred that appears here. But this is not his role in the fourth chapter, when he moves from describing the Sutpen–Coldfield relation to the Sutpen–Henry–Bon one in accents which are more obviously personal to him. Indeed, at one moment he tells Quentin what Ellen Sutpen said, at another, what his mother said while talking to Miss Rosa. Each report is evidently of a different provenance—one is hearsay, the other witness—but they coexist without difficulty in a work that does not always recognise distinctions between sources of information as valid. Confronted by a remark like, 'She did not know what happened in the library that night. I don't think she ever suspected ...' (p.91), the reader cannot adjudicate between apparent statement and transparent conjecture. In fact, they constitute different degrees of surmise. No wonder that when the verbal universe is so confused, the people who are its creation should be so too.

By the time we reach Chapter 4, the frankly conjectural begins to dominate proceedings, and this for one particular reason: we move from decisions, acts and events to motives, from that which is publicly assimilable to the recalcitrantly private. The signals proliferate: 'he must have known', 'he must have said to himself', 'he must have said', 'he must have repeated', 'I can imagine ...', 'he must have known', 'he may even have known', 'he must have known' occur within a single paragraph, Mr

Compson's first as he launches into his narrative. The daring activity signified by these phrases is very different from the occasional guesswork indulged in by him earlier. They tell us that, under the pressure of circumstance, he has become less of a storyteller and more of a novelist, filling in the gaps as he goes.

Strangely enough, the change comes about not when he is describing Sutpen but when he is describing his children, as if the further we travelled from the past, the *less* reliable the evidence grows. Talking of Sutpen and his kind, Mr Compson declares:

> ... people too as we are, and victims too as we are, but victims of a different circumstance, simpler and therefore ... more heroic too, not dwarfed and involved but distinct, uncomplex who had the gift of loving once or dying once instead of being diffused and scattered creatures drawn blindly limb from limb from a grab bag and assembled.... (p.89)

A few pages on, we find the identity of the children being blurred into

> that single personality with two bodies both of which had been seduced almost instantaneously by a man whom at the time Judith had never even seen— (pp.91–2)

These are evidently not 'distinct, uncomplex' people but 'scattered creatures' assembled on the page by the imagination.

Not that we are to suppose that this represents any very admirable activity, since it remains true that doing is superior to saying, granted that some deeds are regrettable and some words glorious. Mr Compson thus only repeats a lesson we have learnt before: that the necessity for literature arises once we cease to be heroic single personalities and become 'scattered creatures' subject to the thousand accidents of life. The creative or psychological crisis of the Southerner coincides with the historical one and is inseparable from it. True, literature has the power to integrate this scattering of self—that is its principal structural definition—but it would be better not to have suffered such fragmentation and so not need the salve of the imagination. Better to be a Colonel Sartoris than his descendants, better Thomas Sutpen than Quentin Compson, the latter so 'complicated' and 'diffused' that he has become little more than a vessel for the thoughts of others. He is the individual talent who cannot act without the whole burden of tradition reacting and who feels both actions as if they were equivalent.

> *Maybe we are both Father. Maybe nothing ever happens once and is finished. Maybe happen is never once but like ripples maybe on water after the pebble sinks, the ripples moving on, spreading, the pool attached by a narrow umbilical water-cord to the next pool which the first pool feeds, has fed, did feed, ... Yes, we are both Father. Or maybe Father and I are both Shreve, maybe it took Father and me both to make Shreve or Shreve and me both to make Father or maybe Thomas Sutpen to make all of us.* (pp.261–2)

There comes a time when the telling and retelling of tales becomes a maze in which the teller loses himself, a never-ending round of repetition which so wearies him that he lapses into passivity, a terrible enervation. Mr Compson and Shreve may exempt themselves from such effects (the latter behind the 'protective coloring of levity behind which the youthful shame of being moved hid itself...' (p.280) but Quentin cannot—and before him stands the warning example of Miss Rosa. Nor only she, for when his plans go awry, Sutpen, too, turns to 'literature'. As Mr Compson would have it, his 'distinct' self has become 'complex'.

> He was telling a story. He was not bragging about something he had done; he was just telling a story about something a man named Thomas Sutpen had experienced, which would still have been the same story if the man had had no name at all, if it had been told about any man or no man over whiskey at night. (p.247)

Even his manner is authentic to campfire yarns, 'pleasant faintly forensic anecdotal' (p.250—how well Faulkner describes it!), a very model of detachment and sympathy.

Sutpen's behaviour at this point is critical, as important as anything he has ever done in his life, for his way of trying to rescue himself from the tangle of history is a cue which everyone else in the book has picked up with increasing desperation. It is a distinguishing sign of Southerners in every age that they should do so. That is why Faulkner did. And that is why the narrators nowhere declare themselves Sutpen's heirs so forcefully (and, for the reader, so ironically) than in their various creative habits; forceful, persistent, desperate, self-defeating.

As object and subject, therefore, Sutpen belongs to a literary form of which *Absalom, Absalom!* is only the latest, if a spectacularly developed, manifestation, the spoken tale, here promoting, with beguiling difficulty, a meditation on the meaning of experience. No finality is possible—and not only because the narrators are caught up in different shades of reality for, regardless of whether or not they succeed, they will bequeathe the same task to the following generation and they to the next one, *ad infinitum*. As T. S. Eliot postulated, no event is complete, no profundity finally enunciated; each age must discover them for itself. Only further exploration is possible within the organism—he called it 'tradition'—which sponsors such fresh raids and is, in turn, altered by them.[3]

The intricate narrative pattern is thus a spontaneous habit in Faulkner and the incremental, weaving-in-and-out effect *Absalom, Absalom!*'s single outstanding characteristic—not, as we might suppose, evidence of an omniscient author mediating a coherent purpose in a fractured way but a circumscribed one doing what he can to give shape to his story through the assembly of fragments sufficiently cogent to prevent anarchy but sufficiently diverse to prevent the achievement of any satisfactory order. If we wished to grant the story unity, we should have to read it as history (the South) or tragedy (Sutpen) but, as Patricia Tobin says, this is impossible because *Absalom, Absalom!*'s 'fragmentation of narrative and the reader's immersion in the language itself obscure the powerful accumulation of consequence that is a major effect in both the realistic novel and classical tragedy. When the diachronic structure of the narrative is sacrificed, so also is a great deal of the mimetic identification with reality and the inevitability of tragic doom.'[4]

Mr Compson makes the point in his own way when he observes the indeterminacy of character in Judith, Henry and Bon, his emphasis falling on their youthfulness. Now, this quality is common to nearly every character in the book save Mr Compson himself (though he depends a good deal on his parents' reports for his narrative and takes some of his colouring from them): Sutpen's story is one first of adolescence and then of

early manhood, Miss Rosa, physically like a child, is still frozen
in the attitudes of a girl in her twenties, General Compson 'was a
young man too then' while Quentin and Shreve are barely out of
their teens. Judith and her brothers thus only reinforce what is a
predominantly youthful gathering, as if each had been snatched
from innocence and were now searching for 'that state where,
though visible, young girls appear as though seen through glass
and where even the voice cannot reach them'. (See Linda Snopes
in *The Mansion*.) In other words, they are searching for something that will allow them to retain their youth

> in a pearly lambence without shadows and themselves
> partaking of it; in nebulous suspension held, strange and
> unpredictable, even their very shapes fluid and delicate and
> without substance.... (p.67)

It is the Keatsian ideal of spirit and body, 'wholeness' and
'complexity', held in balance in and out of time, the Eula Varner
ideal of an unself-reflecting people poised on the verge of history.

Incest, narcissism and homosexuality metaphorically announce the inwardness of this quest, the 'fluid and delicate' state
of the people who pursue it. Misegenation proposes something
bolder, as we deduce from the characters it most affects in the
Faulknerian canon. After he is turned away from the front door
of a mansion, Sutpen sets out to recover his lost innocence. He
fails because of miscegenation (his first marriage). Ike McCaslin
sets out to save the wilderness. He fails because of his family's
miscegenation. Joe Christmas sets out to discover himself. He
fails because of his 'mixed' blood. In each case, miscegenation
stands less and less as a fact than as a symbol of the failure of the
South. Indeed, it *is* the South's tragedy, the purity of an ideal
sullied by the admixture of experience. Sutpen's descent from
the hills and the McCaslins' expulsion from the wilderness are
both movements from the pure to the impure and, each time, the
passage is commemorated by the symbol of miscegenation. The
fact of miscegenation is almost wholly incidental; the symbol is
the reality.

It is significant that when Mr Compson turns to Charles Bon,
Sutpen's son, he never thinks it worthwhile dwelling on miscegenation as a clue to his character. For him, Bon is no more than a
figment of the imagination, someone who turns up 'without

background or past or childhood' in the Sutpen house, is befriended by Judith and Henry and subsequently murdered by Henry.

> Yes, shadowy: a myth, a phantom: something which they engendered and created whole themselves; some effluvium of Sutpen blood and character, as though as a man he did not exist at all. (p.104)

Bon remains something of a mystery to the end, but Mr Compson nonetheless manages to suggest a most intelligent interpretation of him, namely, that he was a super-sophisticated decadent, New Orleans-style, an 'indolent fatalist' who had been denied love or any soundly-based values and had been forced to create their semblance for himself by indulging his appetites and allowing the better side of his nature to atrophy as he drifted through life, so that, when faced at last with people who offered him love perhaps for the first time but who nevertheless aroused his envy, he contrived to murder that which he most desired. The implication is that he did so by setting brother and sister against each other in a most unobtrusive way, leaving the seeds of discord to grow as he supposed they would in the naively honourable world of Henry Sutpen.

Henry is Bon's opposite in nearly every respect, a 'Coldfield with the Coldfield cluttering of morality and rules of right and wrong' (p.120). As such, he is denied the close relation with his father that his sister enjoys, she being 'the Sutpen with the ruthless Sutpen code of taking what it wanted provided it were strong enough' (p.120). When Bon appears, he turns to him for friendship as he had earlier turned to Judith for affection, and this leads him to try to bring the two together in marriage. The incestuous motive thus signals Henry's attempt to recover his identity within the restored family circle, precisely what Bon seeks to do when he tries to heal his broken childhood and end his own estrangement from Sutpen, risking even death in the attempt to win Judith—or, rather, since he is a fatalist, to sacrifice himself and so bring retribution to the Sutpens.[5]

Mr Compson's interpretation is a brilliant guess. It may even be the truth, though we can never know. All we know is that Henry and Bon rode off to New Orleans together and joined the war shortly afterwards. How or why these facts occurred remains in doubt. Nor are his conjectures stressed, though we should note that it is the point of his blurring of lines between individuals that they may be tentatively stated.

As he weaves his way through the tangle—was it that Bon was the medium for Henry's manoeuvres after Judith or was it that he loved Henry through Judith (and vice versa) or 'perhaps ... even more than Judith or Henry either: perhaps the life, the existence which they represented?' (p.108)—it becomes clear that Mr Compson's is a distinguished interpretative intelligence working largely (where it matters) in a vacuum. This is nowhere more evident than in his account of Bon's introduction of Henry to New Orleans, a passage which, in the fineness of its movements, is worthy of Henry James. Inevitably, the alternatives he canvasses are not always consistent, especially since, though he holds to a serious view, he enjoys exercising his gifts of deduction and indulging his ingenuity, as in Bon's fantasticated defence of whores. Perhaps it is this that has led some to ignore him in favour of Quentin and Shreve with their own very different interpretation of Bon, but it is worth stressing that theirs is not the only theory to be found in the book nor the most compelling.

The greatest influence on Mr Compson's attitudes is his conviction that all life is contained by what he terms 'the fluid cradle of events (time)' (p.66). In that watery element, there can be no certainty about people, particularly when they are young (and so prone to instability) and when, like Bon, they die, leaving behind them such meagre clues to their identity as to leave the present-day observer wondering whether they could ever have existed. Accordingly, his description of the Judith–Bon–Henry relation is one of constantly shifting complexity as they fuse, dissolve, reform, essences in search of definition. The truth about them is irreduceably multivalent and any conception of their drama necessarily provisional,

> like the mask in Greek tragedy, interchangeable not only from scene to scene, but from actor to actor and behind which the events and occasions took place without chronology or sequence. ... (p.62)

As the only genuinely adult narrator in the book, Mr Compson can afford to take this view where someone like Miss

Rosa believes in the masks she creates. He has cultivated his air of detachment deliberately. He knows that he is touched by the Southern tragedy but does what he can to keep it at a distance lest he, too, fall prey to it. It is no accident that he alone should offer a sympathetic estimate of Goodhue Coldfield's decision to nail himself up in an attic during the war, assuring us that Coldfield

> was not a coward, even though his conscience may have objected, as your grandfather said, not so much to the idea of pouring out human blood and life, but at the idea of waste: of wearing out and eating up and shooting away material in any cause whatever. (p.83)

Again, Coldfield

> was not a coward. He was a man of uncompromising moral strength... (p.82)

What he says about Coldfield could as truthfully be said of himself, as though he had sensed the need to offer an explanation of his own behaviour and had smuggled into these passages an anxious defence of his quietism against Quentin.

This becomes even more apparent in his description of Bon.

> He is the curious one to me. ...who caused all the pother and uproar, yet from the moment when he realized Sutpen was going to prevent the marriage if he could, he (Bon) seems to have withdrawn into a mere spectator, passive, a little sardonic, and completely enigmatic. He seems to hover, shadowy, almost substanceless, a little behind and above all the other straightforward and logical, even though (to him) incomprehensible, ultimatums and affirmations and defiances and challenges and repudiations, with an air of sardonic and indolent detachment.... (pp.93–4)

This sounds very like a description of Mr Compson himself, a cardinal illustration of the way in which the narrators of *Absalom, Absalom!* project themselves into their creations and mould them to their own ends. Nor is this necessarily a shortsighted activity for while, in the Faulknerian view, literature may begin in fancy—'could be', 'might have', 'if'—those same phrases can modulate into 'I can see', 'I imagine', responsible fictions by which we expand on images of ourselves.

Mr Compson survives as a relatively disinterested and unusually self-conscious novelist in a world which, because it is dominated by active heroes, deprecates his existence, with both the strengths and limitations this implies. When, for example, he turns to review Sutpen's career, he says he detects in it

> the illogical machinations of a fatality which had chosen that family in preference to any other in the county or the land exactly as a small boy chooses one ant-hill to pour boiling water into in preference to any other.... (p.102)[6]

The tone is superior, amused but understanding. With which compare Miss Rosa's

> as though there were a fatality and curse on our family....
> Yes, fatality and curse on the South and on our family as though because some ancestor of ours had elected to establish his descent in a land primed for fatality and already cursed with it.... (p.21)

The recognition of fate is common, the attitudes to it divergent. Miss Rosa pre-supposes a design which governs the South, one so permanent as to await the pioneers' arrival in America and to a large extent independent of their misdeeds, while Mr Compson sees a destructive but temporary malignancy without motive. More important, he understands it to operate on only one family—the Sutpens—not on the South at large, still less on his own family. It is part of his blindness that he should fail to perceive that a society which threw up a Sutpen was itself radically flawed. And even if his is not the temperament to do anything about it, his passivity has the effect of encouraging others to step in where he will not. He may have protected himself but only at the cost of abandoning the South to men like the Snopeses.

II

The fifth chapter is given over almost entirely to Miss Rosa and

is, without apparent reason, printed in italics. Here, in gro-
tesquely involved accents, speaks a woman starved of reality and
full of recrimination against the world. Here, too, speaks
Faulkner the verbal millionaire, presently in alliance with a
frustrated spinster as she bemoans her fate. (The italics suggest
that, in doing so, she addresses herself as much as Quentin; or
perhaps it is that the 'two separate Quentins' are still talking to
each other.) Yet, try as we may to sympathise with her, Rosa's
words undoubtedly constitute *Absalom, Absalom!*'s major lapse
into bad writing, all the more so since the Rosa of this chapter is
not the Rosa of the opening one, who spoke in a much more
accommodating style, closer to that of Mr Compson and the
narrator than to her namesake here. Presumably the change
comes about because she is now directly recounting her own
experiences (the first time this has happened in the book). Here
is no mere teller of tales with her commemorative odes and
epitaphs but a living relic of the past grateful for a chance to give
vent to her feelings.

Rosa is a woman cruelly out of joint. The deprived child of her
parents' advanced years, she was betrayed early in life (like
Sutpen and Bon), her mother having died in giving birth to her,
and her sister Ellen marrying Sutpen many years before she was
born. She grows up determined to vindicate herself by punishing
those whom she regards as responsible for her unhappiness—
first her father and, through him, all others of his sex. As if this
were not enough, she is filled with envy for her sister's riches and
her children, both of them older and more attractive than
herself. She is the outcast, the hanger-on, now more than ever
convinced of her superior worth and as secretly determined to
prove it. Hence her Puritan righteousness and her predeliction
for fantasy, the one the better to scold reality with, the other the
better to flee from it.

Reading Rosa's account carefully and availing ourselves for
the first time of dramatic irony as an aid to interpreting
character, we can see how she has long since escaped poverty
and lovelessness by withdrawing into a world of her own. No-one
will insult her there. But she does not want to be left to enjoy it
by herself all over again, so, beginning with Charles Bon, she
peoples it with imaginary creatures who are so real to her that
she doubts whether they could ever have had any existence other
than the one she herself has provided them with.

*because I who had learned nothing of love, not even parents' love—that
fond dear constant violation of privacy, that stultification of the
burgeoning and incorrigible I which is the need and due of all
mammalian meat, became not mistress, not beloved, but more than even
love; I became all polymath love's androgynous advocate.* (p.146)

The purport of this statement is extraordinary. Rosa has created
a man of whom she hears a great deal but whom she never
actually sees or meets and enters into an affair with him in which
she is both the lover she desires and the mistress she longs to be,
both the man and the woman *and* the emotion which draws them
together. Even now, she is so convinced of her magical powers
that she can declare living to be

*one constant and perpetual instant when the arras-veil before what-is-to-
be hangs docile and even glad to the lightest naked thrust if we had
dared, were brave enough (not wise enough: no wisdom needed here) to
make the rending gash.* (pp.142–3)

She who has created another present can also anticipate the
future.

Lest we think that Rosa's is an exceptional case, we had better
remark that she does no more than prove in an obviously
overemotional way what life in the South demands of its people.
Since the reality of the place is so hopelessly at odds with the
ideal they hold for it, they have no choice but to live like this if
they are ever to succeed to

*that doom which we call female victory which is: endure and then
endure, without rhyme or reason or hope of reward—and then endure.*
(p.144)

Victory and defeat are but different names for the same thing—a
conclusion typical of Rosa but by no means peculiar to her in the
Faulknerian canon.

When Bon dies, she immediately goes off to Sutpen's
Hundred, saying she waited there for Sutpen to come home
'exactly as Judith and Clytie waited for him' (p.154). We have a
good idea of what sort of woman Rosa is and it is not as a Judith
or Clytie that we had imagined her. In the following passage, we

discern her original intentions which lie buried beneath her later
interpretation of events.

> *It took me just three months. (Do you mind that I dont say he, but I?)*
> *Yes, I, just three months, who for twenty years had looked on him (when*
> *I did—had to too—look) as an ogre, some beast out of a tale.... Oh, I*
> *... could ... give you a thousand specious reasons good enough for*
> *women, ranging from woman's natural inconsistency to the desire (or*
> *even hope) for possible wealth, position, or even the fear of dying*
> *manless which (so they will doubtless tell you) old maids always have,*
> *or for revenge. No. I hold no brief for me. I could have gone home and I*
> *did not.* (pp.158–9)

The Freudian slip has become the Freudian aside.

It is hard to tell whether Rosa had always loved (or loved-and-
hated) Sutpen, in which case Bon was a substitute for her (as he
was, perhaps, for Henry), or whether he was simply the next in
line for a mind as fertile as hers. It is easier to see how, with one
part of her detesting all men, she should seek some satisfaction
for the part which loves them by allying herself to a man who
satisfies both parts better than anyone else could. Sutpen had
indeed long been the subject of her reveries, in which fascination
and loathing had struggled to gain the upper hand. He had
shown all the coarseness and power which for her distinguish
men. He had helped ruin her family. He was an ogre—but also a
silently magnetic personality, '*who for twenty years had looked on him*
(when I did—[7]*had to too—*[8]*look ...* ' Her opening statement ('*It took*
me just three months') is thus clear enough evidence of her
intention; where her sister has been a butterfly she comes
running '*like a whistled dog*'. Prospect and retrospect, hopes
entertained and dashed, reproof and self-justification, startling
honesty and tenacious deception combine to delineate an
absorbing complex of embarrassment.

Evidently, Rosa now disgusts herself for having gone after the
man. She might, she says, have refused his '*ukase,* [his] *decree*'
when he proposed marriage to her, but how could she? He had
told her what she had secretly determined he should: that they
marry. He was, miraculously, playing the part that no-one but
herself knew had been prepared for him by her presently
'*surprised*' but always '*importunate traitorous flesh*' (p.165). She may
have hated him once but she is now prepared to believe in the

best in him and so conquer her aversion to him which, because it
is grounded in childhood, can be argued away as baseless. In the
brief, happy days of her engagement, he appears not as an ogre
but an anguished man ruined by war, '*villain true enough, but a
mortal fallible one less to invoke fear than pity*' while she herself
emerges, arrogantly as ever, as

> *that sun ... who did believe there was that magic ... which we call by
> the pallid name of love that would be, might be sun for him (though I the
> youngest, weakest) where Judith and Clytie both would cast no
> shadow....* (p.167)

She has surpassed herself as 'love's androgynous advocate' and
become the very principle of life itself, the centre of the universe
(Judith and Clytie, we notice, no longer sharing a community of
interest with her).

Alas, Rosa has forgotten that Sutpen is not the suitor she
imagines (or half-imagines) him to be but a man desperate to
rebuild his fortunes with a new family of sons, marriage or no
marriage. When he propositions her to this effect, the impact on
her is traumatic. Robbed of all hope, she breaks off the
engagement and begins to turn into the woman we know, one
who simply passes the time of day existing (and that off the
unadmitted charity of others) while ever more passionately
reliving the events of her youth. Yet she is not so innocent as to
believe that her salvation lies in memory. Formidable as that
faculty is, it is subject to the same limitations that govern all our
other senses.

> *That is the substance of remembering—sense, sight, smell: the muscles
> with which we see and hear and feel—not mind, not thought: there is no
> such thing as memory: the brain recalls just what the muscles grope for:
> no more, no less; and its resultant sum is usually incorrect and false and
> worthy only of the name of dream.* (p.143)

Every approach to the past is imaginary, as are all accounts of
experience, so that to the distortions of fantasy are added the
distortions of memory, which Rosa clearly, if sadly, recognises as
such, as when she admits of Sutpen, 'I had not lost him because
I never owned him' (p.171). People do exist beyond the scope of
our imaginations, after all. Strangely, it is the same lesson that

Mr Compson taught us in the previous chapter and one that Quentin can never learn.

III

Chapter 5 closes with Miss Rosa's cryptic announcement of the fact that someone lies hidden in Sutpen's house, a mystery which is to carry us through almost to the end of the story. Chapter 6 moves to Harvard in the winter of 1910. Until now, we have been in Jefferson on a hot summer's day in September 1909, the first chapter during the afternoon (until sundown), the next three after supper and for part of the night, and the fifth some time after that. Quentin hears something of what Miss Rosa has to say, returns home to listen to his father and then, having promised to accompany Rosa out to Sutpen's Hundred in the middle of the night, rejoins her, she being in a more baleful mood of revelation.[9]

At Harvard, Quentin is discovered reading a letter from his father which tells him that Rosa has just died. There follows a report of his conversation with Shreve, the latter doing almost all the talking. It is Quentin, however, who broaches Sutpen's death and then in an abbreviated form which leads us to suppose that he was murdered by Wash Jones in punishment for his violation of Wash's granddaughter, Millie. No mention is made of the resulting child's sex nor does Quentin adduce any evidence to support this new material. Moreover, as if suffering Miss Rosa's contagion, the writing is noticeably more ornate than anything in the opening chapters (one reason why it is difficult to accept the view that Rosa's style in Chapter 5 is intended dramatically).

Then the style moderates: where before it was elaborate, of dark and deep breath, it is now more controlled and evocative. Two pieces of description by the narrator may be compared. In the first, he is not so much presenting a scene as trying, detail by detail, to get into its skin:

That evening, the twelve miles behind the fat mare in the moonless September dust, the trees along the road not rising soaring as trees should but squatting like huge fowl, their leaves ruffled and heavily separate like the feathers of panting fowls, heavy with sixty days of dust, the roadside undergrowth coated with heat-vulcanized dust and, seen through the dustcloud in which the horse and buggy moved, appeared like masses straining delicate and rigid and immobly upward at perpendicular's absolute in some old dead volcanic water refined to the oxygenless first principle of liquid, the dustcloud in which the buggy moved not blowing away because it had been raised by no wind and was supported by no air but evoked, materialized about them, instantaneous and eternal, cubic foot for cubic foot of dust to cubic foot for cubic foot of horse and buggy.... (p.175)

—which is a reminder that when complaints are made against Faulkner's style, they concern less the individual phrase than the total sentence, as if we had asked for a string of pearls, say (not a single gem—that would never do) and had been given instead a treasure chest full of trinkets, baubles, jewels and coins in haphazard profusion. And the more we receive, the less we have to be grateful for.

Not many pages on, however, we read this.

They went on up the slope. They could not see the two dogs at all, only the steady furrowing of the sedge where, invisible, the dogs quartered the slope until one of them flung up his head to look back. Mr. Compson gestured with his hand toward the trees, he and Quentin following. It was dark among the cedars, the light more dark than gray even, the quiet rain, the faint pearly globules, materializing on the gun barrels and the five headstones like drops of not-quite-congealed meltings from cold candles on the marble: the two flat heavy vaulted slabs, the other three headstones leaning a little awry, with here and there a carved letter or even an entire word momentary and legible in the faint light which the raindrops brought particle by particle into the gloom and released; now the two dogs came in, drifted in like smoke, their hair close-plastered with damp, and curled down in one indistinguishable and apparently inextricable ball for warmth. (pp.187–8)

The syntax here now moves with it subject and no longer feels it is pursuing a reality it cannot transcribe. It can therefore relax into its powers where before it was anxious lest it (or we) miss anything. And how confident those powers are! Just as the preceding passage played on the idea of scattering or separation (without activity, paradoxically enough), so everything here turns on the conceit of gathering: the dark gathering in the cedars, the rain gathered into pearly globules on the headstones like drops from a candle, the hair of the dogs close-plastered by the damp—in the midst of which tearful assembly of effects stand the tombstone inscriptions which, by exception, are isolated and dispersed into the light, though their movement brings no release from grief, only an intensification of regret for the past which the final act of gathering—the dogs curling round themselves for warmth—forlornly repeats.

Mr Compson's contribution now returns us to Jefferson in the preceding September. Whilst heavily dependent on his own father's reports, it is still remarkably speculative, especially when it comes to describe Charles Etienne Saint-Valery Bon, Bon's son. Oddly enough, the tenuousness of the narrative here is not as nagging as might be expected, mainly because of the impression made by Quentin who, for the first time, begins to emerge as a character in his own right, one whose life is being steadily overtaken by the material he describes. This is evident not only in his memories of his boyhood visits to the derelict Sutpen estate (scenes evoked with an especially grave beauty) but also in the intricate narrative pattern that arises at this point.

It seems that Quentin's dialogue with Mr Compson the year before is concurrent with his present dialogue with Shreve who, since he sounds like his father and is, in any case, only repeating what he has learnt from him via Quentin, naturally reminds him of the earlier occasion. The result is a palimpsest of great complexity: Grandfather Compson tells Mr Compson about Sutpen, who supplements this information with material gleaned from other sources as well as from his own imagination before passing it on to Quentin, who tells Shreve, who now repeats it to Quentin (presumably after a first hearing, as if in incredulous response to it: 'I could hardly believe my ears'), thereby confirming its more important details while adding some comments of his own. Quentin, in turn, hearing Shreve repeat the tale, intersperses it with a few further reflections before finally ridding himself of this 'doubleness' of effect.

The numerous voices that surround Quentin at this point are

not unexpected. When he first listened to Miss Rosa, he heard through her a number of 'garrulous baffled ghosts'—garrulous because what they tried to understand left them baffled and what they did understand left them outraged. As it was for the 'ghosts', so it is for him. As he listens to the various voices rehearsing their mixture of fact and legend, his 'memory' begins to stir. He is now no longer an auditor but an active consciousness; the 'empty hall' has given way to 'the recognizable *I*', and he starts to develop an attitude to the stories he has been hearing. He is not just listening to the past, then—he sees it, both literally, as when he recalls the Sutpen tombstones, and metaphorically. (Faulkner's revisions show how deliberately he worked to gain this effect, transferring whole passages from Shreve to Quentin, who is thereby forced into a dramatic relation with his friend and, through him, with the material they are discussing.)

At this moment, Quentin the man emerges as the 'being' or 'entity' he was not before—*and he does so as a novelist, the Southern narrator*. The stories he has heard have created him as much as the facts of the past have done. This prodigious development is signalled by the multiplied number of speakers he hears and it leads the third-person narrator, who until now has been *Absalom, Absalom!*'s sole controlling intelligence, to share his task with him. This inner drama exists wholly between the lines and accompanies the book to the end. It is an impressive feat and, added to all the others we have observed, helps make *Absalom, Absalom!* incomparably ambitious in technique.

Unfortunately, the same voices that herald Quentin's emergence also signify how trapped he is by his novelist's role. Like Bayard Sartoris, he has been driven to literature as a substitute for the active life only to discover how tainted his birthright is. What he has learnt of the South, of its ideality no less than its culpability, teaches him what is of value but also how impossibly difficult it is to attain. At one and the same time, he has been given the basis of his existence and denied its fulfilment. One hand gives, the other takes away.

Quentin is not the only person to suffer like this, for we also have to notice (and it cannot then be overestimated) the coincidence that relates his emergence in the book with Sutpen's appearance *in propria persona* as a narrator. He, too, has been trapped by literature unawares and, as before, the moment is recorded by a complicated layering of voices. In conversation with Shreve, Quentin recalls what Sutpen said of himself to General Compson, who told Mr Compson, who tells Quentin, though closer study suggests that he owes as much to the omniscient narrator as he does to anyone else. Perhaps it is just that he is embroidering on his father's account, which itself may have been an elaboration of what the General had told him. (And if this creative habit is a family trait, then the General himself may have expanded on Sutpen's *ur*-narrative.) However that may be, we have to notice that Sutpen is now contained by an assembly of speakers and this fact is as instructive as any other we learn of as we launch into the central section of the story: the contest between innocence and history as figured in the adolescent Sutpen's crisis of identity.

IV

Sutpen comes from the mountains of West Virginia,

> where he had never even heard of, never imagined, a place, a land divided neatly up and actually owned by men.... (p.221)

Back home,

> nobody had any more [objects] than you did because everybody had just what he was strong enough or energetic enough to take and keep,[10] and only that crazy man would go to the trouble to take or even want more.... (p.221)

Here is a magic realm of dissimilar men who express themselves robustly but with an effortless equality that coincides with perfect freedom. When Sutpen exchanges this for Tidewater, he becomes a 'crazy man'; the little boy (he is barely in his teens) loses himself in finding the world.

> They fell into it, the whole family ... tumbled head over heels back to Tidewater by sheer altitude, elevation, and gravity ... the whole passel of them ... slid back down out of the mountains... (pp.222–3)

What a mighty fall was there!

Having lost 'the woodsman's instinct' which might have guided him home, Sutpen finds himself stranded in a land that is awash with distinctions between people, the first he discovers being the one that divides black men from white men. That distinction, in turn, depends on two others (is, in fact, representative of them): 'He had never thought about his own hair or clothes or anybody else's hair or clothes until he saw that monkey nigger...' (p.232). The moment of self-consciousness coincides with the moment when the social paradise is lost for the discriminations of ownership and prosperity—and both are identified with the presence of the negro. That is why, here as elsewhere in Faulkner's work, the negro is taken to signify the land's fall from grace, being both the foreigner, the bringer of disaster, to be loathed and feared, and a reminder to the Southerner of his criminality, and thus a figure to be respected and atoned for. Both values are present in Sutpen's critical rejection from the front door of a plantation mansion by a negro butler. At that moment, the butler brings to consciousness a knowledge of the white man's guilt and, with it, an awareness of 'blackness', of wrongdoing, in the South (as ever imaged by the big house).

> ... he did not even imagine then that there was any such way to live or to want to live, or that there existed all the objects to be wanted which there were, or that the ones who owned the objects not only could look down on the ones that didn't, but could be supported in the down-looking not only by the others who owned objects too but by the very ones that were looked down on that didn't own objects and knew they never would.... So he didn't even know there was a country all divided and fixed and neat with a people living on it all divided and fixed and neat because of what colour their skins happened to be and what they happened to own.... (p.221)

Owning land is the original crime, owning people a consequence of it.

West Virginia was a world apart and rogues like Sutpen's father could live in it happily because they were innocuous. Since myth is not made up of contingencies, their acts lacked consequence. They themselves may have been flawed, but their organism remains perfect because it lacks any moral status; it is simply in the order of things. Only when that state is lost can their misdeeds rebound on themselves and their communal use of land be seen to be invested with meaning.

But Sutpen has further to fall.

> He had not only not lost the innocence yet, he had not yet discovered that he possessed it. (p.228)

That discovery over, his education is complete: the fallen world is *about* such distinctions and expresses itself exclusively through objects—which object is mine, which object is yours, what object you are. At this point, he stumbles on his life's ambition:

> All of a sudden he discovered, not what he wanted to do but what he just had to do, had to do it whether he wanted to or not, because if he did not do it he knew that he could never live with himself for the rest of his life, never live with what all the men and women that had died to make him had left inside of him for him to pass on, with all the dead ones waiting and watching to see if he was going to do it right, fix things right.... (p.220)

That is the real dynastic theme, even if it comes to be expressed in actions that are inimical to 'all the dead ones'. The naivete of the language here is as revealing as the imagery of the spot he retreats to in order to think his thoughts:

> He went into the woods ... a place where a game trail entered a canebrake and an oak tree had fallen across it and made a kind of cave ... he crawled back into the cave and sat with his back against the uptorn roots, and thought. (p.233)

To think, the very act of 'ratiocination', is a consequence of 'uptorn roots'. (The words 'and sat with his back against the uptorn roots' were added by Faulkner in revision as if to emphasise the point.) Yet, if one is forced to think, it is best one goes to the woods, the source of all value. Hence the infantile and primitivistic associations of 'crawling back into the cave'.

> He was just thinking, because he knew that something would

> have to be done about it; he would have to do something about it in order to live with himself for the rest of his life, and he could not decide what it was because of that innocence which he had just discovered he had, which (the innocence, not the man, the tradition) he would have to compete with. (p.234)

And again,

> It was like . . . an explosion—a bright glare that vanished and left nothing, no ashes nor refuse; just a limitless flat plain with the severe shape of his intact innocence rising from it like a monument; that innocence instructing him as calm as the others had ever spoken. '. . . So to combat them you have got to have what they have that made them do what the man did. You got to have land and niggers and a fine house to combat them with. You see?' (p.238)

Indeed we do, for these are admirably exact passages. Sutpen is determined to stay loyal to 'all the dead ones' but he also wishes to 'do something' about the insult they have received through him, so he decides to found a dynasty of his own based on the possession of land, people and house. He has chosen to fight the enemy with the enemy's weapons, though he will wield them in the spirit of his ancestors and in pursuit of immediate ends which remain repugnant to him since his aim is not to emulate the South but to punish it. Accordingly, while he is prepared to fight Tidewater, he is also prepared to combat the very innocence that proclaims him a man of the mountains.

It is difficult, therefore, to tell with Sutpen which is the sheep and which the wolf's clothing, but it is imperative to give full credence to *Absalom, Absalom!*'s central statement:

> Sutpen's trouble was innocence. (p.220)

His vices and virtues are alike attributable to that quality and modified by it for in him innocence imitates experience by embarking on an impossible quest: to become its opposite. In a sense, he never begins to realise his ambition. By confusing ends and means, he has ensured that he will never stop being innocent, either unself-consciously or with the shattered innocence of Tidewater. Once more, our sure dramatic guide is his voice, which does not so much tell us about his continuing innocence as enact it. Indeed, as we overhear him draw up his plans, the point of view (the narrator's? the Compsons'? Quentin's?—it is not Sutpen's) grows almost ironic. This, it is implied, is what a young boy, without help or friend, would conceive of in the given circumstances; it is a mark of his dangerous incompetence as it is of his touching allegiance to the past. It is *this*, his 'worldly' innocence, which leads him to believe that such a design as his is possible, and this which ultimately defeats him; but only the truly other-world innocence he never lost could have allowed him to enter such a competition against the world with such an object in mind.

Sutpen's campaign begins with a visit to the West Indies. As though by instinct, he has decided that, if he is to beat the world, he had better learn the worst about it, so he chooses to immerse himself in a 'theatre for violence' which will reproduce the corruption of Tidewater in intensified form, settling at a point midway between the black of Africa and the white of emergent America. That, after all, is the point of the idea of paradise, the tension between order and dissolution; the child who was ripped from home pitches himself into the marginal realm and there learns of man's destructive passions the better to build his dreams on them. (Compare Conrad's *Heart of Darkness*.)

> ... not knowing that what he rode upon was a volcano, hearing the air tremble and throb at night with the drums and the chanting and not knowing that it was the heart of the earth itself he heard, who believed ... that earth was kind and gentle and that darkness was merely something you saw, or could not see in; overseeing what he oversaw and not knowing that he was overseeing it... (pp.251–2)

Everything is in violent disintegration but Sutpen 'oversees it', believes that he can convert it to his image of earth, despite the evidence before him.[11]

Sutpen's belief is no doubt a consequence of his foolish innocence but it is also a tribute to his radical innocence. It is the former which is justly condemned—

> that innocence which believed that the ingredients of morality

> were like the ingredients of a pie or cake and once you had
> measured them and balanced them and mixed them and put
> them into the oven it was all finished and nothing but pie or
> cake could come out. (p.263)

—and it is the former which may even tempt him to regard his
design as an end in itself. The South itself made the identical
error and

> erected its economic edifice not on the rock of stern morality
> but on the shifting sands of opportunism and moral brig-
> andage. (p.260)

—exactly the charge to be levelled against its hero.

> You see, I had a design in my mind. Whether it was a good or
> a bad design is beside the point; (p.263)

There speaks a moral brigand, all right. Yet there is a baffled
simplicity even in that chilling statement to remind us of his
genuine innocence rather than the one which permits him to say
such things with this degree of unabashed sincerity.

For Sutpen, everything has become willed. When he speaks
about his design being something whose goodness or badness is
irrelevant, he speaks as an ignoramus; sacrificing means to an
arbitrary end is surely the ultimate delinquency. Yet it is also
true that his design—his founding a 'dynasty'—is not in itself his
central preoccupation; re-establishing West Virginian innocence
in Yoknapatawphan history is. For him, any historical means
would be acceptable so long as the mythical ideal could be
achieved. His methods are thus consistently at loggerheads with
his ends—and would remain so, however he had chosen to act.

For these reasons, we must conclude that Sutpen is a
legendary creature, one so hedged about by contradiction that
Absalom, Absalom! has no choice but to give up traditional
character drawing if it is to come to terms with him. There can
be no exploration of his inner life because he has none worth
talking about. Nor can there be a considered narrative portrait of
him since there is not enough material to make the attempt
worthwhile. Sutpen has little to concern himself with other than
the raising of a house and family and this he does with a famous

speed. There is nothing else for him to think about outside his monomania, nothing else for him to do.

Yet he is also a real man living a real life at a particular moment of time, and the conflict between the two never ceases to cause trouble. When, for example, he learns that his Haitian wife is not wholly white, he discards her along with their son, Bon. He thus protects his 'design' but also avoids any further complicity in the white man's injustice to the negro. Again, years later, when Bon turns up at his house, he decides to meet him by telling him, in effect, 'Do not ask me to re-admit you into the family now, for that would only compound the failure of the land. Let us adhere to the ideal instead. Let us try to stop history. Until then, wait'. The reply might be, 'Whatever your motives, you are committing a wrong. You are sacrificing your own son to your cause'. Myth and fact, vision and morality, hopelessly clash.

Sutpen's acts have moral consequences, then, but they are not those of a man whose means and ends cohere within the same framework. Just criticism of him would have to take that into account, but there is no-one who can attempt it. The people he lives with do not know what innocence is and can therefore see only one aspect of him, the lover, the fighter, the man he *appears* to be, has *elected* to be, not the legendary figure he also is. And the same is true of the narrators. Miss Rosa creates a demon because, in her mind, he has become a treacherous god of love, Wash Jones creates a god who, because he turns out to be human, becomes a demon to be slain. Both attitudes suggest how difficult it is to estimate a man who is beyond logic, a figure of high romance whom history and literature have variously transformed into something suprahuman. In Sutpen we see the creation of a mythical creature *as a result of* irresolvable tensions in the South. Others may try to make him fit some scale of values, but he continually resists the attempt. And, in truth, there can be no solution to the problem of one who is both god and man, innocent and corrupt, at one and the same time. To grant him his innocence is to understand, if not to pardon, him; to grant him his corruption is to condemn him unequivocally. But the two attitudes are irreconcilable, forever hanging in the balance. No wonder that the omniscient author should beg leave of absence from his work and that the reader should concur in it, for when you are confronted by a character as 'inordinate' as

Sutpen, you have to do what you can with him.

> [The] inordinate character [is] not necessarily a giant of saga-
> like hero, but someone who has exercised a right to extreme
> conduct of aberration. Such people fulfil a new country's need
> for legends. A human being is required to be a myth, his
> spiritual value lies in the inflating of his tale.[12]

The same point is touched on by Patricia Tobin, who finds
that the cause of Sutpen's misfortunes lies in his failure to
integrate myth and history. For her, Sutpen is an 'inscrutable'
figure in what, following Mircea Eliade, she calls a 'sacred,
exemplary, and significant' tale that re-enacts the origins of the
South and is for that reason disqualified from 'the moral
impulses—responsibility, shame, doubt, guilt—that fall between
the actions of linear time and create its significant succession. . . .
The stasis of Thomas Sutpen renders him unfit for the dynamic
development of either a realistic or a tragic hero'.[13] Tragedy and
morality accrue instead to his descendants, who possess the one
quality he lacks: self-knowledge.

Actually, Sutpen straddles the distinction between myth and
history for he is an image both of the South's ideals (nature,
West Virginia) and of its past (Sutpen's Hundred, the Civil
War). Much warmth goes into the former but the latter
nonetheless leads Faulkner for the first time in his career to
suspect that the South was rotten to the core from the start. How
he did so is well suggested by F. Garvin Davenport, Jr. For
Professor Davenport, Sutpen's flaw rests where Professor Tobin
(rightly, I think) says it cannot, 'in his inability to live in history
as represented by the acts and relationships for which he is
responsible but for which he takes no responsibility. His flaw is
pride in his self-sufficiency'.[14] Now, Professor Davenport is
concerned with only one aspect of Sutpen's innocence and is
therefore ready to believe that 'the central concept of the novel is
the necessity of moral responsibility in history'.[15] (This, I hasten
to add, is a deduction we may make from *Absalom, Absalom!*, but
the work itself is otherwise concerned.) Even so, he is sufficiently
aware of the myth's force to come to this challenging conclusion:

> *Absalom, Absalom!* suggests that the nature of history makes
> impossible the American dream of economic plenty and

simple harmony with a docile nature. It also poses the question: Does the American Dream make responsibility in history equally impossible?[16]

It is a good question to ask of men who seek perfection in history but also—and simultaneously—its defeat. From the work that followed, particularly *Go Down, Moses* and *Requiem for a Nun*, we can tell that such, precisely, was the question that Faulkner was beginning to ask himself.

As it happens, the result only served to strengthen his attachment to the Dream, not because he was satisfied it was blameless (no such satisfaction is to be had) but because, by airing his fears, he came to a more profound grasp of its nature: namely, that it is not to be identified with history-as-belief over history-as-fact, any more than it is to be identified with a simple idealism; rather, it contains the conflict between them. That is why Sutpen remains never less than an ambivalent character. Unscrupulous he may be, but he is also

> Quentin's Mississippi shade who in life had acted and reacted to the minimum of logic and morality, [a severe qualification of Quentin's statement about his logic and morality a few pages back] who dying had escaped it completely, who dead remained not only indifferent but impervious to it, somehow a thousand times more potent and alive. (p.280)

This tribute to the man, coming from the same narrator who condemns him for his chef-like behaviour, is remarkable and is immediately reinforced by Wash Jones's encomium:

> *A fine proud man. If God Himself was to come down and ride the natural earth, that's what He would aim to look like.* (p.282)

Since *Absalom, Absalom!* grew (in part) from the short story dealing with Wash's worship of Sutpen, we may say that this was the view that Faulkner began with. However immensely he elaborated on it, he never lost it.

In *Requeim for a Nun*, Faulkner complains that

> a tragedy had happened to Sutpen and his pride—a failure not of his pride nor of his own bones and flesh, but of the lesser

bones and flesh which he had believed capable of supporting the edifice of his dream—(p.209)

Sutpen's dream was noble, so the argument goes ('edifice' = the big house and a lesser, though still powerful, conception of the dream), therefore he was noble too—precisely Sutpen's line of reasoning. It is the Henrys and Quentins we are asked to find culpable for not having been as devoted to it as he was. Faulkner is here harking back to Mr Compson's opinion that the house Sutpen builds is a house with 'a sentience, and personality and character'. It is, he says, 'as though [Sutpen's] presence alone compelled that house to accept and retain human life', the house itself representing

> an incontrovertible affirmation for emptiness, desertion; an insurmountable resistance to occupancy save when sanctioned and protected by the ruthless and the strong. (p.85)

How dismiss Sutpen, then? Without his ruthlessness and strength, there would have been no South.[17]

Sutpen's energy and enterprise, his love of the land, his greatness, without question or reserve, are Wash Jones's objects of faith. Both men come from poor white stock and, despite their separation in society (Wash is prevented entry into Sutpen's house by his daughter, Clytie, in echo of the monkey butler), both entertain the same hopes and beliefs. Indeed, Wash might be thought of as Sutpen's alter-ego, one who stays at home while the other ventures, with his approval, into enemy territory. But when Sutpen comes unstuck and, in a last, desperate effort to justify his activities, abuses Wash's granddaughter, Millie, Wash turns against him, not because he is offended by her pregnancy, it seems, but because Sutpen speaks of her as an animal, an object—the same offence that outraged him as a boy.

Sutpen's betrayal robs Wash of hope, so, following 'that morality of his that was a good deal like Sutpen's, that told him he was right in the face of all fact and usage and everything else...' (p.287), he kills Sutpen and Millie and their child and, last of all, himself. If his dream has been stolen from him, he can at least protect it from any further corruption, 'beyond all human fouling'. He is indeed another Sutpen, one whose idolatory can encompass—actually issue in—the killing of his hero. As such, he stands as one of Faulkner's rare essays in ironic portraiture.

V

In the eighth chapter, Quentin and Shreve discuss Henry and Bon, with the occasional help of the narrator. In doing so, they effect a remarkable change. Up till now, there has always been some attempt to provide a plausible mediator for the dissemination of material from one generation to the next. Now, the narrator, in one of his most daring acts, has Quentin and Shreve *become* Bon and Henry, and this for the obvious reason that *Absalom, Absalom!* demands further exploration of their lives even though there is no more information to be had of them. The feat is made more credible by the establishment of the interchangeability of character earlier on and further eased by the setting: the cold and snow of Harvard are now related to a Southern winter night where before the atmosphere of summer predominated.

Shreve begins by concentrating on the interview between Henry and Sutpen, in which, for the first time, Sutpen is made to declare that Bon is his son. In the previous chapter, Quentin's account of the same moment of time only has it that 'nobody ever did know if Bon ever knew Sutpen was his father or not...' (p.269). At first, Shreve, too, doubts if Bon knows who his father is, but then gradually revises his opinion. We can sense him going on to toy with possibilities, making his tale out of a mouthful of air as he conjures up Sutpen's first wife and her lawyer and tries to guess how they would have behaved. The prose here, as in Chapter 5, is of the most opaque, a sign, perhaps, of baseless speculation. The libertine fancy has been given its head in order to satisfy Shreve's need to establish antecedents for Bon, in the belief that a man's character is best understood by examining his 'psychology'. In other words, he is trying to fit Bon into the novel, whose pronounced tendency towards making character explicable has made this way of understanding people a reflex, though there is nothing inevitable about it. Indeed, Faulkner often betrays a tension in his work between the romantic and novelistic approaches. Faced with what Mr Compson calls 'acts of simple passion and simple violence', the poet in him responds energetically to the demands

made by the essences concerned—essences of wickedness or
innocence or whatever—while the historian in him tries to give
them realistic shape by imposing a pattern of cause and effect on
them. Joe Christmas and Popeye are the most prominent victims
of the habit, though the most important things about them are—
must be—left unsaid.

In the event, much that Shreve has to offer is both tedious and
irrelevant. It is an unnecessary attempt to satisfy an equally
unnecessary need. He does not understand (and neither, significantly, does the narrator) that myth and 'reality' are here once
again in endless conflict. A symbolic pattern of events centred on
a dynamic node of tension collides with the contingent world.
Contingencies cannot then be adduced to explain the symbolic
pattern; they can only state the opposition that exists between
them. The former invites analysis, discrimination and judgement. The latter demands the response, at once critical and
committed, of the imagination. It is the response that *Absalom,
Absalom!*'s narrators try to make, each in his own way, but what
they feel and what they think are not always in balance.
Judgement is weakened by emotion, emotion confused by
conscience.

This becomes particularly apparent when the narrator remarks of Quentin and Shreve:

> the two of them creating between them, out of the rag-tag and
> bob-ends of old tales and talking, people who perhaps had
> never existed at all anywhere, who, shadows, were shadows
> not of flesh and blood which had lived and died but shadows
> in turn of what were (to one of them at least, to Shreve) shades
> too, quiet as the visible murmur of their vaporizing breath.
> (p.303).

Mr Compson, we remember, believed that the Sutpens were
'inexplicable' though still 'men and women who once lived and
breathed' (pp.100–1), yet the more that is spoken about them,
the less secure they become until they threaten to dissolve into
air, mere ghosts of ghosts. As he registers the fact, the narrator
fills with a certain weary impatience. Here he is, almost at the
end of his story, and he is no nearer to settling its meaning than
when he started. By remarkable contrast, his protégés believe
they are within sight of success, but few are likely to share their

excitement. They are rather struck by the increasingly queered atmosphere at this point, a feeling that the whole Sutpen saga is about to vanish through their fingers.

> To pile like Thunder to its close
> Then crumble grand away
> While Everything created hid
> This—would be Poetry—
>
> Or Love—the two coeval come—
> We both and neither prove—
> Experience either and consume—
> For None see God and live—

To proclaim relief at Quentin's discovery of Henry in Sutpen's house is to avoid noticing that he and his fellow-narrators have had an experience but missed the meaning. Or rather, in this most Eliotesque of all works, they have

> ... had the experience but missed the meaning
> And approach to the meaning restores the experience
> In a different form...

Whatever it was that happened to the Sutpens is now passed recovery. Descriptions of it can offer only an approximation, tantalising and extraordinary but still an approximation. That is why *Absalom, Absalom!* repeatedly forms itself into climactic passages which give the appearance of resolving into a connected narrative but which have none of its substance. Motive and cause-and-effect do not seem adequate to its greatest moments.

It is significant that the narrator's remark about Quentin and Shreve 'creating ... out of the rag-tag and bob-ends of old tales and talking' should occur in the middle of Shreve's account of the first Mrs Sutpen's menage, a passage which (so far as we can tell) has no authority in 'old tales and talking' and is thus very different from the ones we have been reading. It appears that the narrator is anxious to confess the defects of his work in this regard but, as he proceeds, he touches on deeper matters. His defence is that love is the great forgiver. Characters from the past can be understood only by the heart which is sympathetically identified with them. Quentin and Shreve are therefore in 'love' as narrators, looking at each other

> not at all as two young men might look at each other but
> almost as a youth and a very young girl might out of virginity
> itself—a sort of hushed and naked searching, each look
> burdened with youth's immemorial obsession not with time's
> dragging weight which the old live with but with its fluidity:
> the bright heels of all the lost moments of fifteen and sixteen.
> (p.299)

This encounter with time returns us to *Absalom, Absalom!*'s *raison
d'être*, its description of youthfulness, and leads shortly afterwards to another of the narrator's interruptions, one which rises
to a grave beauty of utterance:

> That was why it did not matter to either of them which one
> did the talking, since it was not the talking alone which did it,
> performed and accomplished the overpassing, but some
> happy marriage of speaking and hearing wherein each before
> the demand, the requirement, forgave condoned and forgot
> the faulting of the other—faultings both in the creating of this
> shade whom they discussed (rather, existed in) and in the
> hearing and sifting and discarding the false and conserving
> what seemed true, or fit the preconceived—in order to
> overpass to love, where there might be paradox and inconsis-
> tency but nothing fault nor false. (p.316)

With immense resourcefulness, *Absalom, Absalom!* pursues its
enquiry into the nature of creativity and, now as before, declares
it to be personative.

What the narrator has to say here is prompted by a particular
circumstance but it has a wider relevance since, if Quentin may
be thought to answer to one side of Faulkner, so Shreve may be
associated with that side of him which stood sufficiently apart
from the South for him to regard it with detachment. (That his
first break with the South should have occurred in 1918, when he
spent four months with the RAF in Toronto, would support the
notion, Shreve being Canadian.) Moreover, the questions he
asks of Quentin, '*Tell about the South. What's it like there. What do
they do there. Why do they live there? Why do they live at all . . .*' (p.174),
are precisely the questions we can imagine Faulkner asking

himself when he returned to the South to discover that he was no longer an innocent boy from Mississippi but a writer in the 'faraway country'.[18]

Of the tenses *'was-not: is: was'* (p.324), we seem to be in *'was-not'*, that dream-like state which embraces the *'is'* of Quentin and Shreve and the *'was'* of the past. With suspense and puzzlement, they now begin to experience the 'spirits' travail of the two young men during that time fifty years ago...' (p.345). As they proceed, they vanish:

> Because now neither of them were there. They were both in Carolina and the time was forty-six years ago, and it was not even four but compounded still further, since now both of them were Henry Sutpen and both of them were Bon, compounded each of both yet either neither.... (p.351)

After a while, they return, Shreve asking trenchantly,

> What was it? something you live and breathe in like air? a kind of vacuum filled with wraithe-like and indomitable anger and pride and glory at and in happenings that occurred and ceased fifty years ago? (p.361)

The 'it' he refers to here is the imagination, which has transported them thus in and out of time. Is it, Shreve asks, a *substitute* reality, not so much a novel way of seeing the world but a new world in itself? Is it an emotional release, a 'vacuum' into which we escape? Is it a weakening preoccupation with the past in which we surrender to our obsessions? Do we fester in our imaginations?

Quentin's answer is his report of the discovery of Henry, the literal and metaphorical declaration of continuity within the South and justification of his activity as a narrator since, whatever Henry told—could tell—him about the Sutpens did not—could not—declare the whole truth of the matter. The past has a physical existence, but it is equally the product of that which we reveal to ourselves. Here, Quentin picks up the narrator's cue and is in league with him. The past has not 'occurred and ceased fifty years ago'. The imagination is not an indulgence which saps us of intelligence and control. The Southerner's attitude to the past is not a mania, any more than historical enquiry can proceed solely on documents and analysis. It offers him a new dimension of time, a whole new way of feeling, in which he discovers fresh perspectives of himself. As Faulkner was to declare of *Absalom, Absalom!*:

> The action as portrayed by Quentin was transmitted to him through his father.... It was the—the basic failure Quentin inherited through his father, or beyond his father. It was a— something that happened somewhere between the first Compson and Quentin, The first Compson was a bold ruthless man who came into Mississippi as a free forester to grasp where and when he could, and establish what should have been a princely line, and that princely line decayed.[19]

It is Sutpen's story all over again, or the McCaslins' or the Sartorises' (or the Faulkners', for that matter)—rightly so, since what is proposed is a character of general significance, one possessed of the very boldest ambition to whom, somehow, somewhere, something happened. Sutpen is a cipher of meaning buried within that mystery.

We run into confusion, however, with Shreve's suggestion that Bon came to him because he wanted recognition from him as his son. First we are told that Bon 'maybe' thought

> *He need not even acknowledge me: ... just as he will let me know that quickly that I am his son....* (p.319)

and then on the same page (no qualifications here)

> Because he knew exactly what he wanted; it was just the saying it—the physical touch even though in secret, hidden— the living touch of that flesh.... (p.319)

A little later, we are told that the briefest of letters, a lock of Sutpen's hair 'or a paring from his fingernail' would suffice. Is it a public or private acknowledgement that Bon is supposed to want? If the latter, is it to be tacit or more direct? When Henry and Bon visit Sutpen's Hundred to discover that Sutpen has gone to New Orleans, there was, Shreve says,

> only he, Bon, to know where Sutpen had gone, saying to

himself *Of course; he wasn't sure; he had to go there to make sure....* (p.329)

Isn't this the secret sign that Bon is supposed to demand or is it too negative or oblique? A few pages on, Bon, having taken a walk with Judith (who some ten pages before was said never to have seen him again), thinks,

> *Maybe even yet he will send for me. At least say it to me* even though he knew better.... (p.333)

Is this not the kind of announcement he has already decided he can do without? Or does he naturally hope for the best, emboldened by being in Sutpen's house? Henry's leaving home with him after quarrelling with his father is presumably not to be accounted a sign since, though it tells him that Sutpen knows who he is (which he wanted), no 'word' is sent to him (which he also wants). The same is true of the occasion in 1865 when he meets Sutpen and, looking into his 'expressionless and rocklike face', sees 'recognition' in it. Fancy makes heavy weather of Bon.

Matters are further complicated by the narrator's account of Henry and Bon's stay in New Orleans, during which he refers to the first Mrs Sutpen's

> drawing room of baroque and fusty magnificence which Shreve had invented and which was probably true enough...

and goes on to describe the woman herself,

> whom Shreve and Quentin had likewise invented and which was likewise probably true enough.... (p.335)

The two 'inventions' are of a quite different order yet they are spoken of in the same breath, in the same language and with the same teasing air of qualification. This parodic omniscience reaches its peak when we are told that Shreve and Quentin do not share Mr Compson's interpretation of Henry's reaction to Bon's octoroon mistress, though Shreve has not been informed what that interpretation is and Quentin had not been listening to his father when they discussed it. The young men therefore disagree with an interpretation of which they remain ignorant. It is not clear why this should be nor why Shreve should revise Mr Compson's statement that Bon was wounded in the war. He thinks it was Henry, with nothing to support him save his conviction that he is right, and the narrator confirms his amendment afterwards. It is, at any rate, his major act of revision.[20]

These are examples of a subtly discordant note to be found as the book draws to a close. The narrator adds to it with his report of Sutpen and Bon's brief meeting during the war, which is as deliberately speculative as Shreve's preceding account. We also notice an increase in instances of mental telepathy, especially between Bon and Henry. (Is it because they have been infiltrated by their erstwhile narrators? At one point, Henry repeats in precis one of Bon's speeches to him when conversing with his father.) The narrator does his best to tie up the loose ends by proposing (via Bon) that Henry killed Bon because he objected to the possibility of miscegenation rather than incest in the affair between Judith and Bon and (again via Bon) by supporting the theory of acknowledgement, though it is Shreve who shows how Bon no less than Wash Jones repeats the original Sutpenian injury. It is the best justification of the theory we have.

> He should have told me, myself, himself.... But he didn't do it. If he had, I would have agreed and promised never to see her or you or him again. But he didn't tell me.... He just told you, sent me a message like you send a command by a nigger servant to a beggar or a tramp to clear out. (p.341)

For all the efforts made on their behalf, the Sutpen children never succeed in emerging from the shadows, perhaps because they lack the sheer commotion of their father. What we are left with is a clear image of Sutpen as a flawed creature who held to the highest ideals but who was yet capable of enormities. Nothing is resolved—nothing asks further to be resolved— except this certitude of ambivalence, and it is to this that the narrator returns us when, in a last coup, he eventually takes over the book. Up to this point, he has encouraged us to think of Rosa, Shreve and the Compsons as the authors of *Absalom, Absalom!* but, in the ninth and concluding chapter, he steps back far enough to reveal its Chinese-box effect. ('Quentin said' and

Quentin himself disappears for some twenty or thirty pages.) It is no accident that this chapter, which tells of Henry's discovery, is the most nearly contemporary of all; the chronological gap between what is spoken of and when it is spoken has all but disappeared. 'Life is a tale. . . .' and we are tellers of and in it.

Where, in the end, does the emphasis fall then, on the tale or the tellers? Is the central figure Sutpen (as Faulkner insisted) or Quentin or both? I think the structure itself proposes the answer. If *Absalom, Absalom!* is the story of the South and if the recounting of that story is as much its subject as the story itself, Sutpen's cannot be the dominant perspective. But neither is it Quentin's, and not only because he is as much without the book (the only man who listens to all the tales) as within it (the man who finds Henry Sutpen). It is because there *is* no dominant perspective. If we are tempted to regard the whole book as that which is contained by him as a 'commonwealth', then there is behind him the mysterious narrator, who may more properly be described as a containing—though not a governing—intelligence. Quentin is rather a representative young man who listens intently to a tale which is robbing him of hope. *That* is the dynamo that feeds the book its energy and it leads him to break cover at the end with the great, repeated cries about the South: '*I dont hate it . . . I dont, I dont! I dont hate it! I dont hate it!*' (p.378). Nor does he. Saddened as he is by the South's history, he knows that its Dream will prevent his grief from ever becoming excessive. It existed before history began and exists again at this moment. He lives for it as Sutpen did, suffers for it as he did, loves it as he did. Nothing, not even the land's guilty memories, matters as much.

Yet these remain, and because of them, Quentin finds himself caught in an impasse (or, rather, a series of interlocking impasses) between myth and morality, faith and despair, bewilderment and understanding. The memorable scope and intricacy of *Absalom, Absalom!*, its passionate thoughtfulness no less than its confusions, are thus finally directed to impressing on us the paralysis of the South, its inability either to pass judgement on itself or free itself into action. As the narrator's last, measured words wind to a halt, the smell of defeat hangs everywhere. Once more, the howls of an idiot fill the air (the introduction of Jim Bond at this point is one of Faulkner's most striking revisions). His is the voice of the negro, symbol of the crimes committed by the South, and with it Faulkner discovers what was not present to him when he wrote *The Sound and the Fury*—the historical dimension of his people's suffering.

Did Mr Compson know? An afterword

Professor Brooks (1963) maintains that Mr Compson does not know that Bon is Sutpen's son until he is told about it by Quentin following his night ride to Sutpen's Hundred with Miss Rosa. Professor Langford (1971) believes that Faulkner intended Mr Compson to know about it but changed his mind, then returned to his original intention and finally abandoned it, though he failed to alter several passages which show that the truth could have been surmised all along. In Professor Langford's opinion, Faulkner did mean Quentin to discover who Bon was and tell his father about it, but, either through carelessness or indecision, only muddied the issue.

I think the matter worth pursuing, not just because I disagree with these views but because they reflect on the character of Mr Compson's contribution to the story, which critics still tend to regard lightly. The book has barely begun before Miss Rosa refers to Henry Sutpen as 'a murderer and almost a fratricide' (p.15). I take the phrase 'almost a fratricide' to refer, with almost comic exactitude, to a man who has killed his half-brother (though the phrase could conceivably be taken to refer to Bon's near status as Henry's brother-in-law). If that is so, then Quentin either knows or can easily deduce the truth about Bon's parentage (though not necessarily his tinge of coloured blood) from the start.

In view of this, and mindful of *Absalom, Absalom!*'s circular treatment of material, it is reasonable to assume that Faulkner intended his narrators and readers to know who Bon was from the beginning but wished to reserve treatment of the fact for a later point, both on the grounds of tension and because he wanted it to contribute to the drama of Quentin's developing consciousness. In both respects, he succeeded admirably. Take the following passage describing Sutpen and Judith's appearance together in a carriage:

> ... which certainly would not have been the case if the quarrel had been between Bon and *the* father, and probably not the

case if the trouble had been between Henry and *his* father.... (p.79; my italics.)

In the manuscript, Bon is simply referred to as 'the fiancé'. By introducing the balancing phrases comparing Bon to Henry, Faulkner teases with hints while allowing himself freedom to advance interpretations of Bon that are not dependent on his parentage (notably Mr Compson's). Such aesthetic finesse is considerable.

Shortly after describing Henry as 'almost a fratricide', Miss Rosa declares:

> I saw Judith's marriage forbidden without rhyme or reason or shadow of excuse.... (p.18)11

Now, either she has let her hatred of Sutpen run away with her or she genuinely cares not a jot for the fact that Judith is Bon's half-sister. Quentin and Shreve, too, debate whether incest (or 'almost incest', as Miss Rosa might put it) could have been a reason for Henry's opposition to the marriage only to reject it. So does Mr Compson—and there is no question that *he* knows about Bon. Sutpen, he tells us,

> named Clytie as he named them all, the one before Clytie and Henry and Judith even, ... naming with his own mouth his own ironic fecundity of dragon's teeth. (p.62)

The phrase 'the one before' can only refer to Bon, as the manuscript confirms. There, the sentence I have cited concludes 'which, with the two exceptions, were girls' (Langford, p.88). Professor Brooks has countered this argument by asserting, 'If Mr Compson, as early as page 62, had known that Charles Bon was Sutpen's son, he surely would have said: "... named Clytie as he named them all, Charles Bon, Clytie, Henry and Judith..." (*The Georgia Review*, pp.392–3). He is thinking of Quentin's later declaration, 'Father said he probably named him himself. Charles Bon. Charles Good. He didn't tell Grandfather he did, but Grandfather believed he did, would have. That would have been part of the cleaning up...' (i.e. following his decision not to 'incorporate' his wife and son in his design). (p.265).

Again, when Henry deserts his father to ride to New Orleans

with Bon, Mr Compson says he thinks he was 'doomed and destined to kill' Bon in order to prevent him committing bigamy with Judith. Nevertheless, he remains aware that bigamy is not the only grounds for murder since he tells us that, after seeing Bon but once, Sutpen himself went to New Orleans

> to investigate him and either discover what he already and apparently by clairvoyance suspected, or at least something which served just as well as reason for forbidding the marriage. . . . (pp.99–100)

From the context, it is clear that Sutpen is using his objection to Bon's mistress and child as a cover for his real objection, the one which 'clairvoyance' has alerted him to: that Bon is his son. To be able to report this, Mr Compson would obviously have to be less ignorant than some have supposed.

Quentin, then, does not need to tell his father what he already knows, nor is it only Faulkner's carelessness in revision that makes him appear to do so. True, Mr Compson's references to Bon's parentage are elliptical, partly for the reasons we have noted and partly because he is interested in pursuing a very different interpretation from the one that Quentin and Shreve are to advance. We catch the drift of his thinking in the following passage about Bon (significantly, it is not to be found in the manuscript):

> . . . a personage who in the remote Mississippi of that time must have appeared almost phoenix-like, fullsprung from no childhood, born of no woman and impervious to time and, vanished, leaving no bones nor dust anywhere. . . . (p.74)

It does not matter who Bon's parents were but what he *is*, not his antecedents but his bewitching *presence*.

Accordingly, when Mr Compson remarks

> It's just incredible. It just does not explain. Or perhaps that's it: they don't explain and we are not supposed to know. (p.100)

he is not confessing to ignorance of Henry's motive for threatening Bon's life. He is explaining the difficulties that await anyone who tries to interpret the past. Thereafter, he is free to concentrate on Henry's attitude to women, his love for Bon and the subtle way in which each man lives up to the other's conception of him: Bon the decadent he believes Henry thinks he is and Henry the country boy he believes Bon thinks he is. Throughout, he very deliberately avoids seeing any connection between Bon-as-Sutpen and Bon-as-fiancé.

It is true that Quentin tells Shreve in Chapter 7 that it was he who told his father that Bon was Sutpen's son. It is also true that Shreve, who is distrustful of Mr Compson's explanation of the Judith–Henry–Bon imbroglio, says that he thinks General Compson and Mr Compson are less well informed in the matter than Quentin. These passages, which, again, are not to be found in the manuscript, suggest that Faulkner was either seriously confused (or uncertain) about how to deploy the fact of Bon's birth—which I am disinclined to believe, granted the care with which he went about constructing this, the most elaborate of all his works—or that he intended the remarks to reflect on Quentin and Shreve, whose own unconvincing assessment of Henry's motive for killing Bon follows shortly afterwards. Whatever the case, both men's remarks are demonstrably untrue and contribute to what I have called the subtly discordant atmosphere of the last part of the book.

We should also notice that Bon's mixed blood (and hence the question of miscegenation) matters only to Quentin and Shreve—as it does, of course, to Sutpen. It may be that this is their only true source of privileged information.

PART TWO

The Waiting Past

5 The Sartoris War

[Perhaps the most decisive force] in the creation of the aristocrat is *absence of private life*. To live always in the presence of family and family servants subtly changes the most average of beings. Formality becomes a condition of survival.... Moreover, to represent one's family first and oneself second in all social intercourse confers a special impersonal character on human manners and actions.... The impersonal social code which permits a formal expression of inward emotion makes it quite pointless for people to interpret one another constantly, as they do in most 'realistic' novels. There is thus in the Southern novel a vacuum where we might expect introspection.... The stress falls entirely on slight human gestures, external events which are obliquely slanted to flash light or shade on character.[1]

I

[Joby] and Granny were like that; they were like a man and a mare, a blooded mare, which takes just exactly so much from the man and the man knows the mare will take just so much and the man knows that when that point is reached, just what is going to happen. Then it does happen: the mare kicks him, not viciously but just enough.... That's how Joby and Granny were and Granny always beat him, not bad: just exactly enough, like now.... (p.51)[2]

This man–mare relation represents nothing less than proof of what the fallen South can still manage to achieve by way of an equitable society, despite slavery. It contains, with precision, just enough freedom and authority to sensitise and validate the tie between master and servant, which the narrator seeks to show regulated life tolerably because it had the sanction of instinct, because it was maintained without outside interference and because it resists the abstract thinking of a later age— indeed, resists any direct statement, to be approached through the language of imaginative analogy and with the articulation of

112

a child.

The description does not confine itself to Jobies and Grannies, however (if it did, we should regard it suspiciously, especially in a novel of the Civil War), since *The Unvanquished* (1938) is full of such relations: Yankee and Confederate, Confederate and Confederate, negro and white, citizen and renegade, man and woman, youth and age. Within each, the master holds the whiphand, the mare usually kicks 'just enough' and the balance of society is restored. It is an extraordinary way in which to depict the War for it shifts attention away from the political nature of the conflict on to the character of the South itself, more particularly on the manner in which it managed to survive an upheaval very much greater in intensity but by no means dissimilar in effect to the ones it had previously experienced as a community which depends for its existence on perpetual subversion and renewal.

We first learn of the South's history when we meet the twin bachelors Buck and Buddy McCaslin.

> They lived in a two-room log house with about a dozen dogs, and they kept their niggers in the manor house. It didn't have any windows now and a child with a hairpin could unlock any lock in it.... And folks said that Uncle Buck and Uncle Buddy knew this and that the niggers knew they knew it, only it was like a game with rules—neither one of Uncle Buck or Uncle Buddy to peep round the corner of the house while the other was locking the door, none of the niggers to escape in such a way as to be seen even by unavoidable accident, nor to escape at any other time. (p.54)

The seemingly revolutionary arrangements of the brothers thus fall into the pattern established by man and mare; the pattern, which is not to be disturbed fundamentally, in peace or war, is that of a 'game with rules', civilisation itself, a view further illustrated by the opening story of *Go Down, Moses*, 'Was', which makes it clear that one of the primary purposes of 'game' in Faulkner is to negotiate the facts of Southern life and reconcile them to its ideals.

> [Buck and Buddy] believed that land did not belong to people but that people belonged to land and that the earth would

permit them to live on and out of it and use it only so long as they behaved and that if they did not behave right, it would shake them off just like a dog getting rid of fleas. (pp.55–6)

Or like a blooded mare kicking a man, no doubt. This attitude of the twins attacks the principle of ownership quite radically, whether it applies to people or to things, so that slavery, far from being identified with the mare figure, becomes an especial part of its burden of redemption. Indeed, it is as the McCaslins regard the land that they are moved to treat their slaves and poor white neighbours, both of whom they regard as members of a family: they not only swap homes with the negroes but inaugurate 'a system of book-keeping' whereby they encourage them to earn their manumission and persuade the hill-men to join them in pooling their farms.

We begin, then, with a vision of the South as a society whose type is the man-mule figure and whose expression is the code of impersonal gentlemanly behaviour, upright, courteous, trusting, sportive, brave. We next observe how the war comes to challenge this way of life not because of the threat it poses to its existence but because of the contradictory reactions it elicits from Southerners themselves. Ringo and Bayard at their war games in 'Ambuscade' are a remarkable introduction to the complex. As the two boys play, one black, one white, we see a ludic miniature of the country as an harmonious order protected from the discriminations of a divisive adult consciousness. To that extent, the world the boys inhabit antedates the South's recourse to the 'game' of civilisation, though likely soon enough to be pushed into it.

From another point of view, however, all is not friendship: Loosh, the negro who is to betray the whereabouts of the family silver to the Yankees, destroys the boys' model of Vicksburg. Not surprisingly, they fail to grasp the significance of his act; having been drawn into the war prematurely, they do not understand what it is about. All they are interested in is the 'smell of powder and glory'. Bayard senses in his father, an heroic struggle such as they pursue in their games, yelling 'Kill the bastuds! Kill them! Kill them!' (p.6) as they fling the dust about. A little later, their play comes nearer fact when they shoot at (and miss) a Yankee and Bayard comes home shouting, 'We shot him, Granny!.... We shot the bastud!' (p.30). Granny shields them by lying about their presence, prays forgiveness for so doing and orders them to wash their mouths out for using 'obscene language'. The ritual cleansing that follows climaxes the first confrontation of opposing forces; Bayard and Ringo's first lesson in civilisation is over. This achievement, however, is overshadowed by Loosh because with him the rules of the game so recently introduced to the boys have been broken. If the other Sartoris negroes are prepared to stick by their masters, he is not.

Bayard gradually comes to register the fact and with it his first adult perception, that the Sartoris realm is not monolithic or immutable. He also begins to understand that, while he may satisfy his bloodthirstiness in mock battles, fighting against real men has necessary consequences, physical ones for those who are shot at no less than moral ones for himself since, while defending the South is an honourable endeavour, it is not a licence which will cover every activity. For him, Yankees are 'bastuds' and opposition to them is expressed in the attempt to kill them. In such ways, he no less than Loosh has breached the conventions of game and spurned the civilities of gentlemanly behaviour. The point is made plain when we contrast the ambush he and Ringo engineer with the purposeful levity of the Colonel's accidental capture of a Yankee troop a little later, which combines playfulness and chivalry in a way that proves him to be still uncorrupted.

The result of the boys' first venture is thus ambiguous. They are both, of course, patently sincere in wishing to protect their own; Bayard, in particular, has a moment of nightmarish apprehension in which he sees his home destroyed.

> ... then all of a sudden I wasn't looking at it; I was there—a sort of frightened drove of tiny little figures moving on it; they were Father and Granny and Joby and Louvinia and Loosh and Philadelphy and Ringo and me—(pp.27–8)

Not long before, in an important passage added to the original story, Colonel Sartoris was superintending the building of a stock pen. Momentarily, the old regime was recovered: 'Joby and Loosh and Ringo and me on the edge of the bottom and drawn up into a kind of order'.[3] Such a listing of names—it recurs with some frequency—is indicative of the bonds the narrator is emphasising, roll-calls of the ante-bellum South. This is what must be saved. But how? Certainly not as Bayard does immediately after by firing a musket and so drawing the enemy down upon the very house he wishes to protect. In his ignorance, he has mistaken belligerence for the will to defend (thus paving the way for Drusilla); he has mistaken his father as a model for the enterprise (thus preparing for his habituation to killing) and he has implicated Granny in his deed. His lapse is indeed momentous.

'Retreat', the following story, deals with Loosh's betrayal of the family silver.

> 'Yes,' Loosh said, 'I going. I done been freed; God's own angel proclamated me free.... I don't belong to John Sartoris now; I belongs to me and God.'
>
> 'But the silver belongs to John Sartoris,' Granny said. 'Who are you to give it away?'
>
> 'You ax me that?' Loosh said. 'Where John Sartoris? Whyn't he come and ax me that? Let God ax John Sartoris who the man name that gave me to him. Let the man that buried me in the black dark ax that of the man what dug me free.' (p.90)

The silver, emblem of the South, is given away by the man who symbolises the corruption that supported it, so that when Loosh compares his position with that of the treasure, he repeats, with magnificent righteousness, the point made by the McCaslin brothers in their reforms. But Granny is too excited to pay him attention. As the negroes join the exodus, she leads the boys in a chorus of 'The bastuds! The bastuds!'. Whatever excuses may be offered for them, her words disgrace the cause she supports.

The triangular relation of Yankee, Confederate and negro complicates the effect of her behaviour. Between the first two there exists an unstated code of gentlemanly courtesy. It is immediately struck by Granny and Colonel Dick with their charade of polite lies in 'Ambuscade', she protecting the boys and he overriding Sergeant Harrison, whose enmity, like theirs, is in deadly earnest. (The simple-hearted Ringo plays Sergeant Harrison's part in the later ambush while the Colonel repeats Colonel Dick's.) Once more, serious game is preferred to open hostility. When Granny embarks on mule trading with the Yankees, it is another such game she joins, though, precisely because it mediates between tensions but does not resolve them, it is a difficult one to play; once ignore the rules or violate their spirit, all is lost.

Between negro and Yankee there exists a more neutral attitude. The latter is barely moved by the ostensible cause of the war while the former depends on his liberator as he might a windfall of nature, with no particular sense of obligation, aware only that an opportunity has been created which for many has been long awaited. Strangely enough, the Sartorises, too, accept the Yankees' presence as an incidental *fait accompli* in no way related to a dispute about principle since the apparent principle—that slavery is a sin—has already been conceded, most forthrightly in Loosh's exchange with Granny. Accordingly, when the South takes up arms, it does so not to preserve the status quo or even to defend the country against the outlander but to fight the Sartoris war, waged by Sartoris against Sartoris in consequence of the offence he has committed against himself, against, that is, his better self. That is why Faulkner declines to see in the Yankee-Confederate conflict anything more than the latter's wish to preserve a quarrel about themselves to themselves.

That, too, is why he does not enter into any arguments about the negro revolt. For him, this represents no more than a desire for movement which could have erupted at any time,

> one of those impulses inexplicable yet invincible which appear among races of people at intervals and drive them to pick up and leave all security and familiarity of earth and home and start out, they don't know where, empty-handed, blind to everything but a hope and a doom. (p.97)

There is thus in his account of things as little ethical content granted the Civil War as may be. All the usual contentious issues have been reduced to chance manifestations of a deeper theme which, while it finds itself expressed in a received historical sequence, is tied to it by no links of cause-and-effect.

In all this, it is evident that Faulkner had little appreciation of the motives that drove the North to intervene in the South. (The fact that its economic system was based on the same enormity the McCaslins complain of renders its intervention doubly redundant to him.) He had even less appreciation of the rights of slaves which, not even in *Go Down, Moses*, did he respond to with any inwardness. His knowledge of negroes was fundamentally nostalgic, that of family retainers, Aunt Callies, childhood playmates. That they had suffered injustices was recognised but it was always balanced by their formidable strength (the moral advantage they had won by the quality of their suffering) and then mitigated by the masters' conscience (the ameliorative efforts of such as the McCaslins). Besides which, no sooner was consideration paid to the iniquity of their bondage than it was promptly subsumed under the greater argument about the private ownership of land. Consequently, when Faulkner came to consider the war between the States, the only conclusion he was prepared to draw from it was that it represented the inordinately violent adjustments being made by an organism that needed to establish a new equilibrium of its parts based on a juster attitude to nature.

That is why the opening story of *The Unvanquished* deals with different points of view within a family, pointing to aspects of the established order that are dying or changing and discriminating between far-from-obvious alliances and animosities. Only by defining these and going on to show them at different times and in different moods could Faulkner hope to describe the impact of the war on the Sartorises. It helps greatly that he did so from the dual perspective of a youthful protagonist, through whose developing consciousness the material unfolds, and of the grandfather he has become who, camouflaged by his younger self, narrates the story, briefly touching on particulars and allowing them to gather emphases of meaning, often in retrospect, as the novel proceeds. To complain of the storybook flavour of the work or to concentrate only on the exposure of the flaws of the family is to overlook such complexities and misread the slight gestures in which the commentary is carried and hence to undermine the whole carefully-developed scale of values of which they are a part. Bayard's youthfulness certainly allows for overmeasures of piety and patriotism but there is the contervailing, if quieter, presence of the narrator to subject these to scrutiny and to show how part of the South's experience of war was precisely the element of wish-fulfilment they contain.

As the narrator goes about his work, his mood humorously naive and reflective in turn, he gradually emerges to form a character, one not directly announced but as important as any other we read of. It is that of an aged man who is determined to record the most important events of his life as honestly as he can by imitating the point of view of his childhood self while imperceptibly distancing himself from them. This unhappy, broken man, sincere, loyal, reserved and distinguished by no brilliancies of talent, embarks on a narrative that will rehearse events too disturbing to be more than briefly retold and so perplexing as to have left him with only clues to their meaning. He writes better than he knows.

II

'Raid' takes for granted the ravages of the Yankee–Confederate war. The Sartorises now live in one of their negro's cabins (ironic shades of the McCaslins), Granny writes with pokeberry juice— and the silver is gone. The mood, despite the energy of Granny and the ever-enthusiastic Ringo, is serious and the view panoramic, taking in the negroes marching to Jordan and the Sartorises forced from theirs, 'blind', like their former slaves, 'to everything but a hope and a doom'. The parallel between the two is reinforced by the grave, laconic episode in which Granny meets a negro woman and her child separated from the main body of marchers. They meet in equality of independence and the certainty of their faiths, though Granny can act contrarily, trying to bribe the woman to stay while disinterestedly abetting her escape.

As Drusilla's embittered speech on the collapse of the South indicates, all is now in a flux, magnificently captured by the marching negroes and the mêlée at the bridge which the Yankees proceed to blow up. Both the negroes and Granny's party are embroiled in the ensuing confusion and the effect is of a single doom embracing them all, negro hopes for freedom and white hopes of rescuing the old order caught up in the same cataclysm. It is against such a background that Granny Millard is to be judged, for the longer she continues to cheat her way to animals and money, the more she endangers herself until, by the time of 'Riposte in Tertio', the habit of deception is seen to have done for her; her game, in more senses than one, is up and the turning point to destruction reached. Yet, as ever in this careful novel, a balance has to be struck. A vestigial conscience still nibbles at

her mind, even if she has Ringo's zeal and Ab Snopes's support
to quell it. More importantly, the proceeds from her mule-
trading (and sometimes the mules themselves) are used to keep
what remains of society on its feet. An account book is kept;
Granny calls out the names of members of the local congregation

> Each time Granny would make them tell what they intended
> to do with the money, and now she would make them tell her
> how they had spent it, and she would look at the book to see
> whether they had lied or not. (pp.169–70)

With those last words, the scales of the balance tilt against her
again, for that she who has made a career of lying should affect
to be scrupulous about the behaviour of others is a measure of
the deception that has overtaken her.

It is the old hierarchical community that Granny strives to
resurrect, in which, as so often in Faulkner, only the extremes of
aristocrat and peasant or slave have any imaginative substance,
'unsoftened', as Roark Bradford notes, 'by any appreciable
middle ground'. (It is this, Mr Bradford thinks, that gives
Faulkner 'his feeling for the tragic and for the grisly humor with
which he relieves' their impact on him.[4]) Once, Doctor Worsham's church was patronised with much ceremony, plantation
owners down in the pews, their negroes up in the slave gallery.
Now, under Brother Fortinbride, it is in a decrepit state. Some
hill-farmers and a few bemused negroes are gathered together by
one wilful old woman and struggle to survive defeat, poverty and
growing despair. They are the 'unvanquished' (the original title
of 'Riposte in Tertio'), those who hold on by the skin of their
teeth.

It is before such improbable worshippers that Granny insists
on declaring her sins, explaining in her prayer to God that she
'did not sin for revenge. I defy You or anyone to say I did. I
sinned first for justice' (p.181), for the profits which she could, in
echo of the McCaslins, distribute among the farmers or offer
John Sartoris for rebuilding the family fortunes after the war.
Her honesty of purpose is not in doubt but the latent charity of
her earlier response to the sight of negroes marching away and
poor whites huddling for shelter in a charred land is muddled in
her prayer, a compound of nobility and arrogance that exposes
the defenders of the South as sharply as possible. During the four

years of the war, Granny has become 'littler and littler and straighter and straighter and more indomitable' (p.76) and much the same may be said of her supporters, if we allow the words 'little' and 'straight' full play to suggest a verdict on their diminution through singlemindedness as well as admiration for their resolution in adversity. The latter is nowhere more easily evoked than in the pages devoted to Brother Fortinbride's parishioners. Forlorn as they are and dubiously funded though they may be, the alternative to them is the irregular company that scours the land under the banner of Grumby's Independents.

Unfortunately, Granny tries to play with both and in so doing is infected by a greed differently motivated but nonetheless similar in effect to Ab Snopes's (who is out to line his own pockets) and to the Independents (whose sole means of sustenance is the booty they plunder). She who believes that even Yankees do not harm old women believes she can meddle with scavengers like Grumby with impunity, but she has forgotten that he is simply a pirate feeding off the miseries of war. By compromising herself with him, she has become one of the subverters.

Bayard threatens to go the same way in 'Vendee', which is the most sombre of the tales. (The title comes from Balzac's *Les Chouans*, whose first part is called 'Ambuscade'.) The story looks backwards to Granny's career and forwards to Bayard's attempt—prompted by what he presently experiences—to counter the effects of violence in Yoknapatawpha. Granny is dead, murdered by Grumby. Bayard, accompanied by Ringo and, for a while, Buck McCaslin, determines to punish Ab for his complicity in the crime and then to kill Grumby. That Uncle Buck should play a part in his vendetta is consonant with his earlier appearance as a Sartoris supporter (to the point of adulation) but his role as a thoughtful landowner is not ignored since the posse he joins is a paradigm of Southern society scourging itself of its baser elements, in this instance, Grumby, who is 'big and squat, like a bear' (p.226) and who, like the bear in *Go Down, Moses*, personifies the rankness within. In the circumstances, it is most appropriate that the metaphor of game should once again be raised and that the subject of hunting should call forth some of Faulkner's finest prose: taut, clear, atmospheric writing creating the cold and wet of approaching winter where before the warmth of summer prevailed.

Granted Grumby's character, the pathos of Granny's death and his own youthfulness, Bayard acquits himself much as we should expect, though the moment he cuts off Grumby's hand, like a hunter claiming a trophy, he is forced to consider the consequences of his actions. From what follows, we can deduce that such, precisely, is what he has done, so that when Uncle Buck salutes him as 'John Sartoris' boy', narrative tone and strategy combine to make us wince. Knowing what we do of the Colonel and what we have seen happen to Bayard, we can see how the son has again outstripped his father in violence and again foreshadows the latter's corruption, thus rendering the tribute strikingly ironical. Bayard himself senses it as such, for when he is called upon to perform a second act of retribution, this time against his father's killer, not the least of the factors urging him to a pacific decision is his desire to repudiate the cruelty of his treatment of Grumby.

Grumby's murder is a watershed in the drama of Bayard's developing consciousness, the act which finally causes him to recoil from violence. He has been made uncomfortably aware of the faults of his child's view of war and determines to rid the South of its taint—from wherever it might come—in his own way. It is a wholly silent conversion and one which is simultaneous with his revising his estimate of himself as 'John Sartoris' boy'. Ringo's bare, moving epitaph for Granny gives him the clue:

It wasn't [Grumby] or Ab Snopes either that kilt her. It was them mules. That first batch of mules we got for nothing. (p.229)

Bayard has been pursuing the least important enemy and will have to look closer to home—as close, that is, as he can.

He starts to do so in 'Skirmish at Sartoris' which, in one of Faulkner's most brilliant coups, returns the novel to the humour of the opening. There, the comedy, so blithe in appearance yet so oddly sad in effect, was needed to establish the innocent narrator and the controlling metaphor of play, after which the exceptions to the rule and those who pervert its premises steadily darken the mood until, in 'Vendee', play itself seems to have been corrupted and Bayard's goodness forfeited. Now, the mood suddenly turns and comedy returns once more to feed off the threatened anarchy of war; catastrophe is averted and the ground laid for Bayard's supreme act of gamesmanship at the end of the novel. When tragedy deals with such subjects, there is a sense of finality about it, of life lived through and seen through. In comedy, finality is made to yield to change and is thereafter seen to work its way through people of mixed virtues. Defeat is recognised but so is resilience, and if there is a major line of development in Faulkner's work, it is from a sense of collapse of the first intensity to a belief in man's capacity to survive the most crushing of defeats, a view given its first prominence in *As I Lay Dying* and now receiving its first major statement.

By the time of 'Skirmish at Sartoris' (whose moderated colloquial manner should remind us how varied a thing is Faulkner's 'style'), the War is over. Drusilla and John Sartoris are engaged in routing the Burdens at the ballot-box, thus reasserting their command over the South. 'Aunt' Louisa, on the other hand, is more interested in getting them married, thus regulating their relations. For her, Drusilla's involvement in the war is no more than a case of 'a young woman ... running about the country with no guard or check of any sort' (p.252). She must be corrected; neither war nor peace matters where questions of personal conduct are concerned. For Drusilla, however, fighting is all. The campaign waged on the battlefield may be over but another now claims her energies, the one Ringo defines thus:

> I ain't a nigger any more. I done been abolished.... They ain't no more niggers in Jefferson nor nowhere else.... Naw, suh, ... This war ain't over. Hit just started good. (p.248)

Indeed it has. Accordingly, she insists on retaining the dress of a soldier. When that is denied her, she presses on with the campaign against Reconstruction. As before, though, this fresh battle is only incidentally between Sartoris and Burden-cum-negro. Fundamentally, it is a continuation of the war between Sartoris and Sartoris, in particular for the soul of John Sartoris.

The decisive moment comes when, instead of submitting himself as arranged to a quiet marriage, the Colonel kills the Burdens. In exultant mood, he proclaims his house a polling booth not a wedding hall and Drusilla a voting commissioner not a bride. The cheers of the crowd that greet his announcement are as of nothing compared to Aunt Louisa's shocked reaction:

> 'And who are these, pray? Your wedding train of forgetters Your groomsmen of murder and robbery?'
> 'They came to vote,' Drusilla said.
> 'To vote,' Aunt Louisa said. 'Ah. To vote. Since you have forced your mother and brother to live under a roof of license and adultery you think you can also force them to live in a polling booth refuge from violence and bloodshed, do you? . . .' (pp.259–60)

Suddenly, the comedy releases a stirring protest against such an abnegation of morality and the implied elevation of end above means. Private conduct has been sacrificed to public policy and the crowd incited to cheer 'violence and bloodshed', not the ceremonial of marriage as emblematic of the communal domain. That is now in tatters with Drusilla as she stands

> in her torn dress and the ruined veil and the twisted wreath hanging from her hair by a few pins. (p.260)

The busy surface has shifted to reveal unsuspected depths.

Despite flinging the ballot box away, Aunt Louisa has to admit defeat and bursts into tears.

> So [George Wyatt] made a pack of the ballots and wrote them against his saddle and fast as he would write them the men would take them and drop them into the box and Drusilla would call their names out. We could hear Aunt Louisa still crying inside the cabin. . . . (p.261)

The reader, too, can still hear her crying while the acclaim of the Jeffersonians rings on: '"Yaaaaay, Drusilla!" they hollered. "Yaaaaaay, John Sartoris! Yaaaaaaay!"' (p.262), and it is with the commingling of these shouts and the tears of an old woman that the episode ends.

Drusilla has won her skirmish with her mother but it is, of course, John Sartoris who is her real victim, for the implied reminder in his subsequent conduct of any family life, of the feelings that a marriage would have sanctioned and the judgement which could order his business, is a wounding one. Aunt Louisa may be a sentimental old fusspot—we are meant to feel her limitations—but there is in her a domestic conscience which will not be stilled. Bayard notices as much. We sense his reserve, his watchfulness, growing all the while into a composed reflection on 'Sartoris'. He has shortly before seen Granny go to her death in fending for the South. He himself has killed a man in vengeance. What he now sees finally disabuses him of the belief that what Granny and he did is justifiable and makes him realise that his father is being fatally caught up—as they were—in public activity, public rhetoric, to the exclusion of all else. More than that, it makes him realise that Granny's appearance as prime mover earlier on can now be seen to carry its own meaning.

> Her fate is tragic, having both the moral flaw and the force of circumstance.... As enveloping action she represents the matrix, the core of the doomed South. It was her part as symbol and person to be protected by the Colonel Sartorises. That she herself must enter the conflict describes the failure of manhood in general and the aristocracy in particular.[5]

An excellent point, and one which Bayard is to act upon when he confronts Drusilla in 'An Odour of Verbena'.

It is important to note that neither Granny Millard (the Colonel's mother-in-law) nor Cousin Drusilla (a relative of the Colonel's first wife) is the genuine article. Granny is a Sartoris by marriage who becomes the thing itself as no born Sartoris could, the foreigner become more native than the native. Jenny du Pre, a Sartoris herself, is much more patient. She can both criticise and tolerate her menfolk but does not involve herself in action. She behaves as Sartoris women are expected to behave— as 'ladies'. Sartoris is, in its self-possession, its vanity, its daring and folly, something fitful, iridescently masculine. It is the quality Drusilla Hawk, the foreigner come to assume the native's destiny, absorbs in her passion to keep alive what Granny more circuitously tried to preserve. In 'Skirmish at Sartoris' (originally called 'Drusilla'), we see her will turn to stone. Just as the Colonel was once involved in light-hearted scenes like the capture of a Yankee troop or the escape from a search party only to become an autocrat who denies negroes their rights, kills people and generally spurns humane considerations, so she suffers under the impact of war nothing less than a transformation, as her manliness of appearance and partly of her manner indicate. The woman has become male has become 'priestess of a succinct and formal violence' (p.273). Like Narcissa in *Sanctuary*, though with infinitely greater emotion, she then devotes herself to defeating all that does not accord with her image of the South, seeking life, the resurrected life of the old country, first in Sartoris' army, then in Sartoris himself and finally, with terrifying singlemindedness, in Sartoris' son. The comic bustle has thus brought to prominence three lives (Granny, Drusilla and the Colonel) decaying under pressure. It is their combined fate which guides Bayard in his attempt to alter not their goal so much as their method of securing it.

His task is made very much harder by the filial devotions he feels and the awesome attractiveness of Drusilla herself. In a strongly wrought passage, he sees her standing

> not tall, not slender as a woman is but as a youth, a boy, is motionless, in yellow, the face calm, almost bemused, the head simple and severe, the balancing sprig of verbena above each ear, the two arms bent at the elbows, the two hands shoulder high, the two identical duelling pistols lying upon, not clutched in, one to each.... (p.273)

It is a boy's picture of formalised aggression, characterised by a sexual ambivalence we have met before in Joe Christmas and the Bayard of *Sartoris* and which is related to the same crisis of identity they suffered. 'An Odour of Verbena' returns to the subject with its repeated references to Drusilla's 'boy-hard body' and the obviously sexual imagery of the duelling pistols she gives Bayard. All these form part of the significance of the verbena itself, the smell one can smell above horses, above simple physical activity: glamorous male assertion. The one who best epitomises that quality is undoubtedly John Sartoris, so that there is a sense in which Bayard now approaches his father indirectly through Drusilla after years in which he was more a legend than a living person to the boy. In Drusilla, too, he sees a mightily tempting version of what he might have been, a close companion to the Colonel and combatant in the war untroubled by scruples and loyal only to his own kind. By the same measure, he is reminded of the warmongering boy he was and must now stop being.

> ... and this no poste and riposte of sweat-reeking cavalry which all war-telling is full of, no galloping thunder of guns to wheel up and unlimber and crash and crash into the lurid grime-glare of their own demon-served inferno which even children would recognise, no ragged lines of gaunt and shrill-yelling infantry beneath a tattered flag which is a very part of that child's make-believe. (p.115)

Sartoris and Drusilla have been too busy in the immediate conflict to notice what has been happening to themselves and their country and, despite his adoration of them, Bayard begins to turn from them and the odour of verbena they have come to be identified with,

> that quality of outworn violence like a scent, an odor; that fanaticism ... of some kind of twofisted evangelism which had been one quarter violent conviction and three quarters physical hardihood. (*Light in August*, p.325, when Doc Hines, of all men, is introduced.)[6]

Post-bellum Jefferson is an awkward kind of reality. John Sartoris rebuilds his mansion on the site of the previous one and is master of all he surveys, but his formidably attractive qualities have been reduced to the 'violent and ruthless dictatorialness' his son first senses in 'Skirmish at Sartoris' and which soon becomes apparent in his railroad activities. 'I'm for my land,' Sutpen tells him when he refuses to join his nightriders' campaign against the carpetbagger. 'If every man of you would rehabilitate his own land, the country will take care of itself' (p.277). It is advice, sound as it is, he cannot follow. Here, we are aware of a masterly obliqueness which reminds us of a scene in 'Raid' (another important addition to the original material) in which the Colonel returns home

> afoot like tramps or on crowbait horses, in faded and patched (and at times obviously stolen) clothing, preceded by no flags nor drums and followed not even by two men to keep step with one another, in coats bearing no glitter of golden braid and

with scabbards in which no sword reposed, actually almost
sneaking home to spend two or three days performing actions
not only without glory (ploughing land, repairing fences,
killing meat for the smoke house) and in which they had no
skill ... actions in the very clumsy performance of which
Father's whole presence seemed ... to emanate a kind of
humility and apology, as if he were saying, 'Believe me, boys;
take my word for it: there's more to it than this, no matter
what it looks like. I can't prove it, so you'll just have to believe
me'. (pp.114–15)

We are a long way from the returning warrior of 'Ambuscade'
riding the impressive Jupiter and armed with a sabre. The
glamour of the past has disappeared as Bayard has grown up.

Paradoxically, the effect is to enhance, not to diminish, the
Colonel's stature. In becoming more human, he becomes an
even more dominant presence and glamour is restored to him in
a different way, though it is not he who has changed so much as
Bayard. Indeed, a small drama, wholly implicit, inheres in this
scene. Just as the sabre-rattler was less a true representation
than Bayard's creation at a time when his patriotic blood was
up, so the portrait of him in 'Raid' is closer to the real man as he
tries to warn his son that the cause for which they are fighting is
not to be found in ambuscades, ripostes, raids, skirmishes and
retreats in 'vendee'. One is truer to it by mending fences. Having
since then yielded to the temptations his father cautioned him
against, Bayard recoils in the nick of time and returns to his
advice at the end by copying him in another act of 'humility and
apology', one which derives from 'Ambuscade', when the
Colonel announces his intention to build a stock pen:

> There would be all of us there—Joby and Loosh and Ringo
> and me on the edge of the bottom and drawn up into a kind or
> order—an order partaking not of any lusting and sweating for
> assault or even victory, but rather of that passive yet dynamic
> affirmation which Napoleon's troops must have felt.... (p.12)

Here is the corporate Sartoris ideal, and we realise once again
how the early stories deal lightly with matters that are to be
revealed as momentous later on. The full meaning of the title of
the novel, therefore, includes not only a salute to the Confeder-

acy but also a reference to Bayard's equivocal attempt to deny
victory or defeat to his country and aim instead for 'passive yet
dynamic affirmation', as he does in his meeting with Redmond.

It is John Sartoris' tragedy that he strives throughout the war
to make such an affirmation but—the crucial moment is
discovered in 'Skirmish at Sartoris'—just when he approached
reacceptance of the custom and ceremony of the old order, he
yielded to his worst impulses. In acting as he then did, no matter
the rights and wrongs of the case, his beauty became terrible. It
would have been unthinkable for him to surrender without a
struggle, yet opposition such as he and Drusilla undertake is
eventually as damaging to their cause as inaction. Drusilla
confesses as much when she tries to defend him.

> 'A dream is not a very safe thing to be near, Bayard.... But if
> it's a good dream, it's worth it. There are not many dreams in
> the world, but there are a lot of human lives. And one human
> life or two dozen—'
> 'Are not worth anything?'
> 'No. Not anything— ...' (pp.278–9)

It is as if the admission were too deadly to come from Sartoris'
own lips and must come instead from his alter ego, whom
Bayard is thereafter free to oppose. Four years after that
exchange, he goes out to confront his father's killer with George
Wyatt's elegy in his mind ('I know what's wrong: he's had to kill
too many folks, and that's bad for a man' (p.282)) and acts in a
way that he hopes will resolve his dilemma by cutting the knot
Gavin Stevens refers to in *The Town* when he talks of 'that
desperate twilight of 1864–5 when more people than men named
Snopes had to choose not survival with honour but simply
between empty honour and almost as empty survival' (p.40).

Simon, Sartoris' negro body servant, grieves over his late
master's coffin. Contemplating the scene, Bayard realises the
meaning of endurance.

> ... this was it—the regret and grief, the despair out of which
> the tragic mute insensitive bones stand up that can bear
> anything, anything. (p.301)

Ironically, again, his realisation of what it means to 'bear anything' recalls the moment in 'Ambuscade' when he smelt his father's

> clothes and beard and flesh too which I believed was the smell
> of powder and glory, the elected victorious but know better
> now: know now to have been only the will to endure, a
> sardonic and even humorous declining of self-delusion.... (p.9)

The 'will to endure' is that solvent which alone can reconcile loyalty to the Sartoris dream with an acknowledgement of the enormities committed in its name. More than that, it allows John Sartoris tragic stature as a man who fought the Civil War magnificently but faltered badly thereafter, who eventually realised the truth about himself and, in the manner of his death—when he refused to defend himself—declined 'self-delusion' and did something about it.

This is not to deny that the most important judgement Bayard makes is that his father is the arch-enemy. But this collides with another: that the Colonel is a man to be respected not just because the ties of sentiment insist on it but because he embodies virtues such as Yoknapatawpha is unlikely to see again. Like Sutpen, there is something about the man that will not let go of greatness. Consequently, where before the boy saw 'powder and glory', the young man sees 'the will to endure', a more principled compulsion to activity which he is to adopt as his own, and realises that his father was indeed heroic in a way he could not have perceived earlier. By adjusting his understanding, Bayard has not so much corrected as deepened his youthful impression and in the novel's developing drama of character he emerges as the Colonel's better self as Drusilla is his worst.

It has not, we know, happened at all easily since his adolescence, coinciding as it does with the war, has led him to associate the gallant life with emulating his father, with sexual potency and the claims of an emergent independence. As a result, the temptations to violence he feels are naturally power-ful—when honour and vengeance are invoked, they become almost irresistible. He is therefore intimately involved in the lesson he learns: that if anything is to preserve the South, it is the recovery of true courage, such courage, that is, as is not continually pressed into the service of a series of contingencies, large and small. Granny first tried to teach him that by insisting that moral values—truthfulness, avoidance of foul language, responsibility, courtesy to foe no less than to friend—are *especially* to be sustained in war, though she is no more successful a teacher than the Colonel and both fall victim to the dangers they warn of. It is ironical that the chain of events set off by Bayard's first act of bloodthirstiness should end (via Grumby) with another, the death of his father, calculated to touch him more deeply than any other. It is a further irony that he could emerge as he does from the test only because his father had become corrupted, thereby releasing him from claims he would have found impossibly difficult to discharge. It is the ultimate irony that it should be the Colonel's account of himself in his final hours that finally emboldens him to act for the good.

In his essay, 'The Unvanquished—The Restoration of Tradition', William E. Walker notes that the Bayard–Redmond meeting coincides with a preternatural (one might add 'poetical') event, a delayed autumnal equinox.[7] By behaving as he does on that occasion, Bayard manages to free the season—but also allows the high summer of Sartoris to pass. Consequently, there is something forlorn about him even in his moment of triumph. He has ensured that the South will survive with honour but he has not reversed its decline so much as arrested it. Worse still, he has crippled himself, for while his treatment of Redmond carries him to manhood, it also ensures the ruin of the wider conditions necessary to his fulfilment. Bayard's achievement is thus no sooner completed than it is called into question. Imaginative diplomacy on the path of compromise assumes certain stabilities and continuities, but these are no longer assured, so that, while the boy's playacting has been transposed into the real world, the real world cannot receive it as it should. It is not for nothing that his adult years should pass in the completest obscurity and that when we next see him, it is as the deaf, disheartened grandfather of *Sartoris*.

At this point, Faulkner's involvement in Bayard, never far from the surface, emerges. As Bayard embraces Drusilla, he realises

the immitigable chasm between all life and all print—that those who can, do, those who cannot and suffer enough because they can't, write about it. (p.284)

The very fact that he has narrated *The Unvanquished* suggests how much he has suffered and how his compromise with Redmond has failed to release him into life. But it is also an astonishing announcement on Faulkner's own behalf, apologising to the shades of Colonel Falkner as Bayard apologises to his father for the failure of his life which has made him into a novelist. The confession is all the more touching when we reflect that part of Faulkner's purpose in writing *The Unvanquished* was to examine the critical years during which the conditions making for his failure were established and to reprove the men who could have prevented it from happening for not doing so.[8]

The fact that John Sartoris has, despite his blunders, managed to retain his stature is thus one more reason why Bayard's attitude towards him should be so ambiguous. It also explains why the Colonel should have left him a relatively colourless figure, although Bayard's passivity (like the indirection of the Colonel's own portrait) is essential to the novel's strategy, as Donald Davie suggests when he describes the kind of figure Sir Walter Scott produced in Edward Waverley.

> ... the enormous advantage of the Scott method in this particular is that it makes of the central character a sounding-board for historical reverberations, or else, to change the metaphor, a weathervane responding to every shift in the winds of history which blow around it. This device, and this alone, of a weak hero poised and vacillating between opposites allows the historian to hold the balance absolutely firm and impartial, giving credit everywhere it is due.... it is designed to permit judgement of the parties, the ideologies, the alternative societies which contend for his allegiance.[9]

Bayard, of course, is more than weak or vacillating yet, in having become a narrator who contains within himself several competing points of view, he owes allegiance to the Scott tradition. We are all the more inclined to make the connection when we notice that Professor Davie links the weak hero with the theme of the lost father.

We are now in a better position to appreciate the benefit of having *The Unvanquished*'s perspective approximate that of a boy while at the same time being removed from mere youthfulness. It is as if the narrator were the old Bayard casting his younger self as an independent character. (Faulkner employed the strategy to excellent effect again in *The Reivers*.) This double figure stands inside and outside the novel. Inside it, he mimes the stealthy growth of a conscience and dramatises its development; he structures the events and comments upon them. There is no 'author' to communicate his conclusions to the reader. Only this double strategy could have allowed the narrator of 'Ambuscade' to show as intimately as he does that Bayard is no stranger to the behaviour he is later to oppose, having succumbed to it, in fact, long before his relations did. He has such a clear understanding of Sartoris transgressors because he is one himself; he has seen but he is also part of that which is seen.

At the end, two incidents concerned with swearing remind us of those which opened the novel. First, Aunt Jenny tells Bayard of an Englishman she met once, one of the blockade runners at Charleston she idolised not 'because they were helping to prolong the Confederacy but heroes in the sense that David Crockett or John Sevier would have been to small boys or fool young women' (pp.305–6). Or as John Sartoris was to small Bayard and fool young Drusilla. The Englishman's vocabulary was limited to seven words: 'I'll have rum, thanks' and 'No bloody moon'. 'No bloody moon, Bayard' Aunt Jenny ends, repeating her warning to him to act stealthily for the South, as the blockade runners did under cover of darkness. Bayard then goes to meet Redmond unarmed and allows him to take two shots at him, which Redmond deliberately aims wide. On returning, Aunt Jenny greets him by bursting into tears. 'Oh, damn you Sartorises! Damn you! Damn you!' (p.318). It is a fine art that gives us this mixture of affection and exasperation, gathering all the competing attitudes of the novel into one critical yet compassionate attitude.

The same sure touch prepares for Jenny's outburst with a reference to the contrasting dreams of Sartoris and Sutpen and follows it with Bayard's silent contemplation of Drusilla's parting gift, a sprig of verbena laid on his bed. The flower makes a complicated impression on him. He knows it is designed to reproach him for acting as he has done—indeed, it virtually accuses him of cowardice—but the charge leaves him unrepentant. Nevertheless, he is deeply moved by it and not a little guilty that he should have made it redundant when all he wished to do was restrain it. At the same time, he sees in Drusilla's gift a reluctant (if not unintentional) tribute to himself from his by-now-deranged victim, a token of surrender which recognises him as the new 'Sartoris', one worthy of accolade in the Southern way.

It has taken some time for *The Unvanquished* to be regarded as a novel rather than a collection of related stories. It should now be acknowledged as the difficult masterpiece of implication it is, the nearest Faulkner came to writing a novel of sustained and subtle moral enquiry.

III

The Unvanquished will also repay attention as the first novel to establish the Snopeses.

> ... it was Father that told Ab to kind of look out for Granny while he was away; only he told me and Ringo to look out for Ab, too, that Ab was all right in his way, but he was like a mule: while you had him in the traces, you better watch him. (p.146)

That, in embryo, is the whole story and it is the mule analogy that once again serves as an introduction to it. Snopes is evidently no stranger to the Sartorises: Sartoris manages, Snopes serves. In the normal course of events, what with the destruction of the wilderness and the arrival of city and machine, the old mare-relation would have been affected, yet the necessary modifications would have been made until a new balance was achieved. (In 'Was', Faulkner implies as much; in his contributions to the civil-rights debate and in *Intruder in the Dust*, he says as much.)

But the normal course is not to be. Sartoris goes to war and asks Ab to look after his mother-in-law much as one might ask a servant to be sharp about it. The break-up begins. It is worth remarking that the mule trading Granny then takes up prefigures the kind of activity we are later to associate with Snopes—but then bargain and exchange is the way all Yoknapatawphans express themselves. In the present business, Granny and Ab set out as comrades-at-arms against Colonel

Dick, she as diplomatist and tactician, he as wily skivvy but, despite (or, more truthfully, because of) their efforts, the family weakens and with it the man–mare relation. Snopes is faced with a weakening of the whiphand, the balance of the South is disturbed—and he kicks over the traces.

The souring brought about by the war touches everyone—Ab with his growing cupidity, Drusilla, Sartoris, Granny. Those in authority sicken and decay, for they are of the past; those who once served sicken and prosper, for theirs is the future. They are not, except superficially, two different and antagonistic parties. They are twin aspects of the same process. This, in turn, means that the conflict between them should be of a necessarily difficult kind. Ratliff's comments in *The Hamlet* repeat the point. Indeed, in opposing Pat Stamper, he makes Ab out to represent the 'honour and pride' of the county. In the present novel, the Colonel himself admits that Ab is 'all right in his way' (p.146).

Something of this tangle is caught in that accomplished story 'Barn Burning' (written a few months after *The Unvanquished* was published), which marks the change from Sartoris to Snopes by having Ab's boy, 'Colonel Sartoris', the filtering consciousness and documenting the movement through the contrast between his devotion to Yoknapatawpha's way of life and his father's contest with the riches and authority of the De Spains. The story is a sustained evocation of a community as it begins to fall apart: baron and peasant at odds, a peasant family divided against itself, the attempted settlement of conflict through the question-and-answer routine of the law and, beyond all, the neglect of that which should claim the energies of man but does not, the land itself. It is the land which is insulted by those who lord over it and those who burn barns. At this point, we can see why the real Colonel Sartoris should have failed. He could not remain whole and unself-reflecting. In the person of Bayard, it is the theme of *The Unvanquished*.

Two forces operate to touch Faulkner's creation of Sartorises and Snopeses, a nostalgia for the past and a crude reaction against twentieth-century America which invests it with all the aura of evil but, in the end, comparatively little of its substance. As has been observed before, the closer Faulkner came to the Snopeses, the weaker his animus against them became. A growing understanding of their place in the history of the land led him to alter what was undoubtedly an intention to create hostile characters into what we now have in the novels, something more confused but, by the same token, more revealing. The preface to *The Mansion* is a late acknowledgement of the fact and it is interesting that, as in the case of Popeye (with whom Ab shares the pre-eminent quality of 'tin'), Faulkner's compassion is aroused when he comes to contemplate the circumstances which go to help the Snopeses behave as they do. In the continuing tragedy of the South, they can no longer be regarded as villains. More than that, their plight comes to reflect the general one.

6 The Lost Domain

I

Of all Faulkner's works, *The Hamlet* (1940) is the most impressively written and organised, drawing from its author the fruits of a profound and protean engagement with his material. Faulkner was ever one for the multivalent expression of truth, needing access to his subject matter from several related but discrete vantage points with room enough to explore each fully so that from their interaction could emerge an embracing but unrestrictive unity. This strategy was well suited to his material but it was no less necessary to his temperament, since it must be remembered that he came to literature with a surfeit of feeling which depended on everything most dear to those who brood over a narrow, well-defined way of life. The instress of a familiar turn of phrase or gesture, the aura which attaches to names and events, the reflexes which may be started up by the most mundane object—all formed an amalgam of sensation and thought which permeated his sensibility. The creation of Yoknapatawpha was thus exactly the response needed to define his native fidelity, to order and deepen his emotions by relating time and locality to the myth which so exercised his imagination. We are reminded of one of Ezra Pound's sayings about poetry (he could have been referring to creative work generally):

> ... poetry is not greatly concerned with what a man thinks; but with what is so imbedded in his nature that it never occurs to him to question it; it is not a matter of which idea he holds but of the depth at which he holds it.[1]

Truer words were never said.

At the same time, Faulkner had to contend with a predeliction for the language of excess—adjectival, hyperbolical and given to the niggling no less than to the expansive and resonant. Such language, chasing after inflamed, often morbid emotions, was perhaps to be expected of a writer whose early circumstances were as unhappy as his were but it was no less a consequence of his Southernness, another manifestation of his involvement in the destiny of his people. A way of life came to a point in him and as he wrote, so it received expression, though the process was not without danger to himself, as he understood very well, for the history of his development as a writer shows time and again how, with true daring, he confronted himself at those points where he was most vulnerable but from which he could hope to draw his finest art. Accordingly, he had to allow his nostalgia for Confederate heroes, virgin ladies and hardy communities to fill his work as it filled his mind, along with grief for the decay of the past and anger against its betrayal. These were gut reactions, no doubt, but they are our starting point as they were his own.

Sartoris, *The Sound and the Fury* and *Sanctuary* show how extraordinary was the work that flowed from them. Each is a romance of the first intensity and in each the melodramatic strains proclaim Faulkner's despairing attitude towards the failure of the South. When, therefore, Ratliff, the itinerant sewing-machine salesman, entertains his fantasy of Flem Snopes as the Prince of Darkness in *The Hamlet*, he is only repeating what his creator had done frequently before—and does again now, somewhat against the grain, for it should be remarked how uncharacteristic the passage is of so sanguine a folk commentator as Ratliff. It should also be remarked how violently it contradicts the comic afflatus of the Snopeses' portrayal, towards which Ratliff himself has contributed most handsomely. (Ab Snopes, the head of the clan, is introduced to us via Pat Stamper, while Flem is woven into Yoknapatawpha's well-established pattern of Stamper-like chicaneries.) Of course, Ratliff's reaction here registers his shock at the discovery of Flem's true nature, yet it does not express hatred for the usurper so much as terror for the dangers he sees gathering about the South—and from more men than Flem. As Irving Howe has remarked:

Perhaps the most important thing to be said about the Snopeses is that they are *what comes afterwards*....[2]

to a people who, until the Snopeses' emergence, existed without tomorrows. Indeed, Ratliff says as much in the very disproportion between his reaction to Flem and anything Flem says or does in the book through which he moves so cunningly, like the cloud's shadow on a summer's day, forecasting wind and rain for

> a little lost village, nameless, without grace, forsaken, yet which wombed once by chance and accident one blind seed of the spendthrift Olympian ejaculation and did not even know it.... (p.147)

How characteristic the style is—the rhetorical cadence, the surplus of epithets, the tautologies, the strange alliance of dictionary and dialogue! How characteristic the sense of the distance between observable reality and the emotion which grows from it! It is from this commitment to the discharge of emotion through the cumulative impact of words that Faulkner now works to evoke the glorious 'accident' that befalls Frenchman's Bend in the person of Eula Varner—and this at precisely the same moment that the Snopeses arrive there. His ambition is fully commensurate with his subject, for it is the coincidence of Eula and Flem, myth and modernity, that is the theme of *The Hamlet*, their marriage of opposites that gives the work a presiding unity. We feel we are at the heart of the matter and it is fitting that *The Hamlet* should draw from its author his most perfect art.

In Ratliff's tall tales (with which the book effectively opens), the atmosphere is struck at once, Eula's eruption prepared for and the key points of the South's history quietly enumerated: the impact of the Civil War, the decline of Sartoris, the souring of Snopes, the growth of property and possessions. The norm is still that of desultory play amongst a people driven this way and that by contrary forces. They are a wayward lot, reacting sometimes foolishly, sometimes admirably, sometimes not at all, to their destiny. Every page is suffused with their presence, their talk, their passions, the 'marvelous and almost supernatural quality of beings and happenings in a remote, entranced world'.[3] Not so remote, though, for Frenchman's Bend is, by virtue of the intensity of its portrayal, something very real, almost contemporary, to Faulkner, a community of unambitious (in a worldly sense) poor whites, 'Democrat and Protestant and prolific', living a bare, sometimes harsh, agrarian existence. Their land is homespun made to appear rich cloth, something unpretentious made by love and effort the more precious, and their way of life one which is, in its broadest contours, easily regulated, somnolent and sufficient.

While by no means innocent, therefore, the mood of *The Hamlet* is marked by a sense of release, as if the burdens that had weighed on Faulkner from the start of his career had finally been lifted. It helps that, in the immediately preceding years, he had steeled himself to face the challenge of the past in *Absalom, Absalom!* (1936) and *The Unvanquished* (1938) and had slain the dragon of sex in *The Wild Palms* (1939). Once tested and protected by these works, as it were, and forearmed as he was by his knowledge of the eventual ascendancy of the Snopeses, he could at last approach the description of Yoknapatawpha he had so long contemplated, and then with a love tempered by a new kind of understanding. The resulting portrait of Frenchman's Bend is memorable. At this turning point in its history, it is still governed by natural law and it expresses itself in unformulated codes which work because they are observed by all. It is a homogeneous, self-regulating world, with no belief that life can be ordered any the more or better, a community of individuals who happen to share more than they dispute, with no sense of the future and little enough of the past save those aspects of it which have, in the ordinary sequence of events, been insensibly absorbed. It is a community very nearly free from chronological time, living entirely in the moment. And that moment is Eula.

Eula is a magical 'mammalian female' who brings to her schoolroom

> dedicated to the harsh functioning of Protestant primary education a moist blast of spring's liquorish corruption, a pagan triumphal prostration before the supreme primal uterus. (pp.113–14)

Faulkner's nature versus Faulkner's civilisation, in fact. Dressed in the awkward, hem-lengthened clothes of her childhood, she is

> like a slumberer washed out of Paradise by a night flood and discovered by chance passers and covered hurriedly with the first garments to hand, still sleeping. (p.131)

This gift of the gods was once the foetus whose mother bared her belly to the moon as if in acknowledgement of divine inspiration, a symbol of the spirit which animated the interaction of man and wilderness. In all her prodigious sluggishness, she personifies Dr Peabody's land:

> That's the one trouble with this country: everything, weather, all, hangs on too long. Like our rivers, our land: opaque, slow, violent; shaping and creating the life of man in its implacable and brooding image. (*As I Lay Dying*, p.40)

Her lazy bulk is thus an image of the 'sultry reverie' so finely characterised by W. J. Cash when he speaks of the Southern landscape and climate as being 'a sort of cosmic conspiracy against reality in favour of romance'.[4] With these associations, it is inevitable that Faulkner should have turned to hyperbole in his portrait of her. Indeed, he could appreciate her almost as if he were a nineteenth-century man struck with wonder at nature's bounty, its greatness and lethargy, its contentment, its awefulness.

But Faulkner is not a nineteenth-century man. Nor is he blind to the fact that the real nineteenth-century man did more than simply gaze admiringly at nature. Attached to Eula's appearance, therefore, is the grief of knowledge. She is a freak of nature as of time, an unseasonable manifestation. The early settlement is now village or town and will soon be part of an urban landscape; the farmer and trader are on the verge of demoralisation; the flood of the twentieth century is about to be unleashed on even the most backwater community. It is at such a time that there emerge a pair of contrasting and highly exaggerated versions of its fate: Eula, and the paradisal world from which it has sprung, and Flem, in whose career it may see the future towards which it moves. Such exaggeration reflects Faulkner's love for Eula and his anxiety that her appearance should coincide with Flem's, so that it is an impossible longing for the dying world and remorse for its successor that taint the celebration of her presence. These feelings are displaced on to others—Flem, Ratliff and company—or reflected in the love affairs between men and women (nearly all of them painful) while the joy is lavished on her and her kind exclusively. With that strategy, a structuring of satellites about a centre, Faulkner is able to weave his stories together with an effortless sense of their relation, spreading himself unhurriedly in anecdote, yarn, tall story, gossip and escapade. He thus captures in his writing something of the myth brought with her by the goddess.

Meanwhile, Flem emerges from the wings every now and then to suggest the dangers posed to a community when one of its families is soured. We catch the design in the body of the text: at first, the Snopeses belong to the yarns which traditionally give expression to the Southern character. Then, in the intricate double-dealing between Flem and Ratliff concerning Ike Snopes, Flem breaks the spirit of the yarn by insulting the boy's humanity, while Mink's confrontation with Houston shortly afterwards expresses such emotion as can no longer be contained by game or sporting contest—and before long others in Yoknapatawpha prepare to follow the same path. Like any other community, Frenchman's Bend cannot withstand sustained assaults on itself from within, especially when they come in the guise of conventions whose perversion few understand and none convincingly opposes.

In preparing for these developments, Faulkner concentrates his attention in Book One on the relations between the Snopeses and Frenchman's Bend. (Those who prefer to concentrate, here or in *The Hamlet* generally, on the Snopeses distort matters badly.) But if it was enough for his purposes that the Snopeses should be only lightly sketched in, Frenchman's Bend demanded more considered treatment, particularly in respect of the Old Frenchman place. The latter appears at once as a symbol of the former in pages of beautifully measured prose. (It also recurs at strategic intervals throughout: the first book returns to it at the close to mark Flem's 'arrival', the third opens with Ratliff's thoughts about it and the last ends with his search for treasure there.) The ruins of the place are all that is left of a once-grand plantation. Rumours of hidden wealth in its grounds persist but little else has survived the passage of years and the altered circumstances.

> Then they were in the old lane ... —the old scar almost healed now, where nearly fifty years ago a courier ... had galloped with the news of Sumter, where perhaps the barouche had moved, the women swaying and pliant in

heaped crinoline beneath parasols, the men in broadcloth riding the good horses at the wheels ... where the Federal patrols had ridden the land peopled by women and Negro slaves about the time of the battle of Jefferson. (p.336)

The echoes of *Sartoris* and *The Unvanquished* here are timely reminders of all that is comprehended by such overromantic feeling. But then exaggeration is needed to counteract the doleful impression made by the ruin and thus obeys the same logic which gives Eula outsize life. At the same time, it stresses the pastness of the past, in imitation of the somewhat suspect quality of a painted photograph: only a moribund country, it is implied, could encourage this sort of emotion, one which had been beaten in war and had then entered a stasis which tempted men to sentimentalise the past while slurring over the greater reality of the land on which it depended and which that war—itself a symptom of the breach with the land—helped bury.

This movement reaches its end when Ratliff, Bookwright and Armstid take over the Old Frenchman place for motives that have little to do with the house itself:

They got the mattress and the quilts...and carried them into the house, the hall in whose gaping door-frames no doors any longer hung and from whose ceiling depended the skeleton of what had been once a crystal chandelier, with its sweep of stairs whose treads had long since been prized off and carried away to patch barns and chicken-houses and privies, whose spindles and walnut railings and newel-posts had long ago been chopped up and burned as firewood. The room they had chosen had a fourteen-foot ceiling. There were the remains of a once-gilt filigree of cornice above the gutted windows and the ribbed and serrated grin of lathing from which the plaster had fallen, and the skeleton of another prismed chandelier. They spread the mattress and the quilts upon the dust of plaster, and Ratliff and Bookwright returned to the buckboard and got the food they had brought, and the two sacks of coins. They hid the two sacks in the chimney, foul now with bird-droppings, behind the mantel in which there were still wedged a few shards of the original marble. (p.357)

That last is a memorable conjunction, though it is important to stress that its nostalgia is by no means uncritical. Faulkner is not just decrying the death of the ante-bellum South (shards of marble) or attacking the imminent future (sacks of coin covered with bird-droppings) but lamenting their incongruity. That great houses should decay and be raided by countryfolk for whatever is useful to them is not in question, though there is naturally some regret felt. Change occurs and is (not without difficulty) accepted. The argument rather concerns the un-wonted disparity between the house and the treasure-hunters, money-sacks and marble. That most of the marble should have gone and the chimney be full of bird-droppings is no more than one learns to expect. It is the sacks of coin which rankle.

The symbol of the house is thus neither inert nor merely an indulgence of questionable historical validity. What is more, it is protected by a pattern of ownership that runs throughout the book—ownership of horses and separators, of cows, of money, of land, of Eula—and the debate about the principle of possession which that pattern encourages. The key terms of the debate are spelt out by the keeper of the house, Will Varner:

> ... he would be seen by someone sitting in a home-made chair on the jungle-choked lawn of the Old Frenchman's homesite. His blacksmith had made the chair for him by sawing an empty flour barrel half through the middle and trimming out the sides and nailing a seat into it, and Varner would sit there chewing his tobacco or smoking his cob pipe, with a brusque word for passers cheerful enough but inviting no company, against his background of fallen baronial splendour.... 'I like to sit here. I'm trying to find out what it must have felt like to be the fool that would need all this'—he did not move, he did not so much as indicate with his head the rise of old brick and tangled walks topped by the columned ruin behind him—'just to eat and sleep in'. (p.6)

Such cheery negligence is admirable. Varner behaves as if he were an actor who is delighted to find himself playing the lead part on a set of the most imposing dimensions but who does not for a moment doubt that it is all make-believe. He is evidently unimpressed by the 'baronial' past and can afford to cock a snook at its pretensions to grandeur because he is king of the peasants, an overlord who combines political, judiciary and pecuniary authority in himself and exercises it irregularly but not unjustly. Seated on his makeshift throne, he steadfastly refuses to surrender to the charms of such ostentatious private ownership. Certainly, the Old Frenchman place is elsewhere regarded with great affection but the affection is not, as we have seen, uncomplicated. It was, after all, the plantation which brought the principle of possessions and the distinctions of race and caste into the South. Accordingly, Faulkner makes to strengthen his attitude to the land by stressing the vanity of all such magnificence and the worth of men like Varner with 'his own invincible conviction of the absolute unimportance of this or any other given moment or succession of them ...' (p.107). At other times, particularly when he wishes to contrast the nineteenth and twentieth centuries or the South and North, he may turn to the house or 'aristocratic' behaviour for his yardstick of values, but it is in nature and plain people that he finds securer images because they form part of a mode that is less mixed and therefore less liable to confusion. Varner proves as much when he disregards the house (a mythohistorical figure) in favour of life lived moment by moment in the free and frugal manner of the pioneer (a more purely mythical figure).

In the context, Varner's nonchalance is alarming. He presides over Frenchman's Bend without realising how vulnerable to disturbance it has become and cares so little for the Old Frenchman site that he eventually palms it off onto Flem as a reward for marrying Eula. It would have helped if he could see the world as other than a stage, if he could see points of connection between events, thus alerting himself to what is happening in the Bend. But then it is the context that is at fault, not he. It is sad that the age should be such that we even have to question his competence. For him to behave otherwise would be to ruin him. His comic seigneurial air is proof of his innocence (despite his wordly acumen) and to lose that is to lose everything that matters.

Where we might lament the past or seek to preserve the ruins or restore the house, Varner leaves well alone, happy because he has no sense of such things. Where we might brace ourselves to deal with Flem, his custom of hospitality (not merely his caution against the threat of blackmail) prompts him to accept Flem, in the same way that Ratliff protects Ike. Where we might fret over the problems of daily life, he accepts Eula's pregnancy or arbitrates in the Houston–Mink quarrel (with which compare the legal action following the sale of the spotted horses) with a practised calm that is of a piece with his sexual amorality, his rough and ready personality.

It is very difficult for us, with our view of 'tradition', the one encouraged in us by practical problems like population and conservation and by writers like Yeats, Lawrence, Eliot and Pound, to appreciate Varner's attitude, to understand that there are for him no Urbinos and gyres, no twentieth-century conflict between machine and blood knowledge, no dissociation of sensibility, no Confucian or Provencal or Enlightenment eras, because history (as crises, cycles of recurrence, apocalypse, vortices or whatever) is meaningless to him. It is not altogether meaningless to Faulkner but in Varner and Eula we see how he wishes it were—which is why the results are so different when he and Varner view the Old Frenchman place. Varner's attitude is, I think, the sane one, but Faulkner is right to suspect that his kind of sanity may not be enough nowadays. Nevertheless, it would not be of much avail even if he were made aware of what is happening in the Bend. For all his powers, he is not the man who will determine its fate. He would never have gained his position had he been able to do so. It is no more than sufficient that he maintains it, no more than sufficient that, at this moment, he should lord it so delightfully. The best and the worst in the man, as well as the strengths and weaknesses of his people, may thus be summed up in one word: thoughtlessness.

That, too, is the quality, less benevolently intended, that characterises Varner's son, Jody. In everything he does, whether he be flirting with the Snopesian menace or constraining Eula, he is feckless, incompetent, and grasping, the very antithesis of his father. Understandably so, since it is not he who is Varner's natural heir but Ratliff, whom Faulkner describes as being 'a good deal nearer [Will's] son in spirit and intellect and physical appearance too than any of his own get' (p.158). Nor is Jody to be the next ruler of Frenchman's Bend; we shall have to look instead to the man whose calm, unobtrusive ways ape Will and Eula's (as his dress apes Varner's) and whose rapacity is but a magnified version of Jody's: Flem Snopes. Once more, the twin focus of *The Hamlet* binds Frenchman's Bend and the Snopeses into a single argument and reveals the latter to be a disaffected part of the community who go on to spread their disaffection more widely.

Such, then, are the issues raised by the Old Frenchman place. In seeking to build his portrait of the Bend on them, however, Faulkner was faced with a number of difficulties. He could not remain content with generalities nor merely chronicle settlement life. Neither could he concentrate simply on individuals. That would be to tilt *The Hamlet* towards the exceptional when interest resides primarily with the 'peasant'. The solution—one of his most consummate—was to use Ratliff and the tall tale, thus establishing a relation between speaker and audience that is of the greatest significance in these matters as well as being an integral source of information and analysis; to balance exactly the representative and individual by embodying *The Hamlet*'s two principal forces in Eula and Flem and withdrawing them from direct involvement in action; to fragment the narrative into related but distinct sections, each obliquely furthering the central argument; to capture the several tales through contrasting viewpoints and at different times and levels of intensity, thus implying his mythic concerns and only quietly registering realistic surfaces while concentrating, as the reader's immediate response will confirm, on men's actions and emotions—and all within the fixative of comedy. With abundant invention, he went on to populate his pages with a galaxy of characters: the Armstids, the Snopeses, Mrs Littlejohn, the Tulls, Jack Houston, the Varners, Pat Stamper, Labove (to mention only the most important), none of whom can stand detached as fully-rounded creations and all taking their bearing from Eula or Flem in pursuit of *The Hamlet*'s major theme, which is thereby greatly enriched, wholly bodied forth. Faulkner brought the American tall tale to a magnificent pitch. Theme and technique discover themselves in each other.

And in detail, for throughout the book Faulkner pours forth the particulars of the life of his 'peasantry'. We learn what they eat and drink (water from a cedar, never a metal, bucket, by the way)[5], what they buy from the store, what they farm (mainly cotton and corn), what they wear, how their children are educated, how and when wages are paid (and how much someone like Mink's wife can earn working at the Savoy Hotel), how they save, systems of farming (share-cropping, tenancies), the contents and structure of their houses (Varner's is the only one with more than one storey), modes of transport, the flora, fauna and topography of their land—the list is virtually endless. It would have been much less so had not Faulkner been in the habit of watching his characters as if they were independent men and women, not his own creations but creatures of the world. They are, as it were, real inhabitants of a real world, with this difference: they are seen in their imaginative aspect. As such, they belong neither to life nor to art and Faulkner approaches them with genuine uncertainty, confident only in what they do, as a gifted spectator might be, and describing their actions with an emphasis that suggests that he is trying to deduce from them their otherwise unknowable motives. As narrator, he remains implicitly in the public domain, being privy to no secrets and speaking to one and all about matters any of them might equally have seen, though with confidence (and not a little pride) in the spur these provide to his speculative ingenuity and verbal prowess.

Interestingly enough, Faulkner's characters, too, are in the habit of watching themselves, particularly when they perform actions, as if they also felt deed and thought, activity and words, to be separate entities. And since many of their actions are compulsive, they have excellent reason to watch themselves for they seem to be driven by motives which lie outside themselves. No wonder that the narrator has a contribution to make to their story. No wonder that, in his hands, the tall tale becomes such an expressive medium, capable of immense reverberations and radiances.

Frenchman's Bend is a magical solution holding all its disparate elements in suspension in much the same way as a novel does, so that, as we read *The Hamlet*, we feel a specifically fictive sensibility infusing its every page, the one described by Richard Chase:

> The American novel tends to rest in contradictions and among extreme ranges of experience. When it attempts to resolve contradictions, it does so in oblique, morally equivocal ways. As a general rule it does so either in melodramatic actions or in pastoral idyls, though intermixed with both one may find the stirring instabilities of 'American humor'.[6]

Eula's divinity is *The Hamlet*'s most obvious contradiction, while the marriages of Jack Houston and Mink Snopes, Hoake

McCarron and Labove's brief affairs and Ike's passion for a cow all exhibit an 'extreme range of experience', all of them untouched by the vagaries and embarrassments of daily life. The nearer we come to people, the more obsessive we find them and the more comical their exaggerations of feeling (a reflection, no doubt, of their 'inherited southern-provincial-Protestant fanaticism'). Each man is his own indestructibly individual self, a quiescent essence or energy owing as little as possible to the community to which, at other times and in more relaxed moods, he belongs. When paths cross, some spark or explosion is sure to result. Therein lie the seeds of destruction, though that is why Yoknapatawphans have their sovereignty as free men. A host of minor characters—divers Snopeses, Whitfield, Buck Hipps, Eustace Grimm, Uncle Dick Bolivar and all—give flesh to this notion of society as both a fellowship (the 'fun in companionship' poor Mr Polly longed for) and the romantically anarchic. The good spirits, the impassioned serenity of much of *The Hamlet* rest on this contradiction and are maintained in it, though if part of our delight in the comic world is our pleasurable anticipation of the characters' ability to repeat themselves in ever-fresh situations, then we must judge the comedy of *The Hamlet* to be of an ambiguous kind. If a character slips on a banana skin here, he more likely than not gets hurt and stays hurt. With a drifting thread of menace, Frenchman's Bend is altering. We have little assurance that it can last and none that it can recur.

II

Although *The Hamlet* was designed and executed as a unified work, it was first given airing in short-story form, beginning with 'Spotted Horses' and the creation of Suratt (renamed Ratliff). That is, both as character and narrator, Ratliff alerted Faulkner to the life of Yoknapatawpha at a time when he was beginning to emerge from the acute disarray of his own. This coincidence is remarkable and requires explanation. Faulkner had been thrown into despair when, as a young man, he lost his sweetheart, Estelle Oldham, and with her his sense of community (though Oxford offered him a closer approximation to it than any other place could). He tried to escape from these disappointments by joining, the Royal Air Force in Canada in 1918 but returned home,

much like Bayard Sartoris, an unsatisfied man disenchanted by
his surroundings and increasingly enamoured of the past,
despite the fact that it was stifling his feelings and disabling him
from purposeful activity. Internally, he was a regular Donald
Mahon, barely alive; externally, he prepared several faces to
meet the faces that he met, amongst them the bizarre Count
Faulkner, Leslie Fiedler's 'ultimate seedy Dandy'.[7] He drifted
from odd job to odd job, read and wrote a little and lasted a year
as a student at the University of Mississippi. As H. Edward
Richardson has argued, the poems that date from this period
(they were begun in 1919 and published in 1924 as *The Marble
Faun*) record the identity crisis of a man shut up with his
reveries.[8] More than that, they describe the nadir of Faulkner's
life, the death of part of himself. Thereafter, with the break to
New Orleans late in 1924, as if for freedom and self-discovery
once more (interestingly enough, an autobiographical sketch of
that year exists), he began to contend more seriously with
himself and his country in prose, not verse, and less in late
romantic terms—terms that made for poems which T. E. Hulme
regretted were always moaning about something or other—than
in the context of post-war Europe and America and, finally and
lastingly, of the South itself. He created another land from the
one he knew and created other people from those he knew of.
What he fashioned for the rest of his career was all of a piece,
part of a determined effort to reconstitute himself by finding in
literature a principled consolation for his failure as a man. He
wrote and rewrote, he struck out, he revised: the sole owner of
Yoknapatawpha ruled his land like a Sutpen of the imagination
with the sensibility of a Quentin Compson.

That the lives of the Falkner family from the time of the
novelist's great-grandfather came to be identified with the
South's history emphasised the pressure of personal commitment to the task. But the task itself went wider—and was
infinitely more ambitious—than this description of it might
imply, as becomes apparent when we recall that the germ of *The
Hamlet*, 'Father Abraham', was composed in 1926 alternately
with *Flags in the Dust*, the original of *Sartoris*.[9] That is to say, the
more personal complexion of Faulkner's suffering went hand in
hand with a concern for the character and destiny of the
plainfolk of the South. It was the former, 'the Benjy sickness', as
I have called it, that was explored in the works that immediately

followed. The other was, after all, much less known, less urgently felt. It was also beyond any powers of description he may have possessed at the time, for he had yet to prove himself a master of the form that defines it, the tall tale, and had yet to learn how to shape it to literature.

In that task, he was in every way a pioneer and he went about it with commensurate boldness. To call his novels 'experiments' would be misleading, since it would imply that there was a local literary tradition with which he was familiar and from which he departed with specific ends in mind. There was no such tradition. Even if there were, he would scarcely have been the man to possess it. What he *did* possess was an eye which created images of meaning and ears which picked up the rhythms and vocabulary of the spoken tale. Together with these went the ready tongue that led him to swap Sartoris and Snopes tales with his friend, Phil Stone, during their strolls through the Oxford countryside. And then there was the craft which could transmute such material into full-scale works of art. Caddy's drawers and Jason's monologue are early examples, Eula and the humorous anecdotes of *The Hamlet* later (and, I think, finer) ones of this kind of originality.

It is a consequence of the identification of oneself with one's country that there should be a blurring of the line between the 'private' and the 'representative', the two being fused without the intervention of overtly symbolical, still less allegorical, techniques. Another consequence (Walter Scott bears witness to it) is that past and present become coterminous—a description of the past will inevitably carry within itself a description of its consequences for a later point of time—while still retaining their separate identities. No 'historical' air hangs over the work. This feat is accomplished less by recreating than by transliterating an experience of time that is almost palpable to the senses and it has the effect of granting meaning to the present and future only in so far as they form part of an argument concerning the past. Whenever they escape from that argument, they are treated with little understanding because it is only in the past—properly regarded as being much more than and in important respects different from a chronological sphere—that one's difficulties can be sufficiently understood by being placed in a landscape that is both in and out of time—the 'apocryphal' world of Yoknapatawpha. A lost domain comes into being, one that can accommodate both nostalgia and the most disinterested sweep of inquiry. It is that lost domain that *The Hamlet* inhabits and expresses.

'Spotted Horses' (1931) harks back to it.

> Yes, sir. Flem Snopes has filled that whole country full of spotted horses. You can hear folks running them all day and night, whooping and hollering, and the horses running back and forth across them little wooden bridges ever now and then kind of like thunder. Here I was this morning pretty near half way to town, with the team ambling along and me setting in the buckboard about half asleep, when all of a sudden something come swurging up outen the bushes and jumped the road clean, without touching hoof to it. It flew right over my team, big as a billboard and flying through the air like a hawk. It taken me thirty minutes to stop my team and untangle the harness and the buckboard and hitch them up again.[10]

This—with its deft start *in media res*, its good-natured, unsurprised account of improbable events, its vernacular assurance— is perfectly judged. Who could doubt that, in the longer fiction that was to grow from it, the oral element was to play a part of the first importance? Yet 'Spotted Horses' remains no more than a fine tall tale. It has not the extravagant, burnished quality of its revision in *The Hamlet* and has yet to size up its characters (Mrs Armstid, in particular, has nothing like the severe power she is to be credited with later). Moreover, it lacks the Tull versus Snopes trial, its natural conclusion.[11] 'Spotted Horses' may have located a focus of interest but it lacks a spectrum for its diffusion, just as Suratt's voice, admirably suited though it is to its immediate task, needs amplifying. Accordingly, when Faulkner came to revise the story for its appearance in hard covers, he did more than merely stretch it. He prepared the ground for it by reserving its appearance for a point some two-thirds of the way through the book and then, in the forced grandeur of his language, acknowledged that Sut Lovingood is not twentieth-century man by robbing the story of its first-person narrator, of its spryness and artlessness. What was oral has become dramatic, part of a progression in time. 'Spotted Horses' is no longer a tale; it has combined with other tales to make up a narrative.

Faulkner's habit of building up his works from fragments is worth observing. *The Sound and the Fury*, as we know, emerged from Benjy's monologue and now comes to us in four inconclusive sections, while to the stories which make up *The Unvanquished* was added a final story but also important passages (such as that concerning the McCaslins) which help steer it to a convincing unity. 'Wild Palms', too, threw up the 'counterpoint' of 'Old Man' before emerging as *The Wild Palms*, while from the admiration of a poor white in 'Wash' and some early unpublished stories grew *Absalom, Absalom!*. The same casting and recasting of stories was to accompany *Go Down, Moses*. Even *Light in August* is unable to resist the claims of fragmentation, while the first two novels, *Soldiers' Pay* and *Mosquitoes*, are merely episodic, a congeries of parts. (*As I Lay Dying*, of course, is composed entirely of brief sections.) This tentative manner of writing, pursued with material like 'Spotted Horses' on and off over a long period of time—in an interview of 1939, Faulkner recalled having begun the book in New Orleans in 1924—gives *The Hamlet* the quality of something lived through, passed along the blood. The fact that its stories stayed in his mind for over fifteen years and that other parts of the human and physical geography of Yoknapatawpha were being explored all the while in his other work matter to the finished book as maturing does to wine or as memory to the mind of man.

Faulkner often writes in such a way as to bewilder his readers by depriving them of elucidatory matter, be it introductory paragraphs or contextual aids to understanding character and action. That he should do so is a reflection of the demand he makes on them to surrender themselves to his work as completely as he has done, a reflection of his ingrained familiarity with his material, meditated on for so long and so purposively as to have acquired the status of experience itself. As Malcolm Cowley has remarked, 'Faulkner's novels have the quality of being lived, absorbed, remembered, rather than merely observed'.[12] Of no work is this more true than *The Hamlet*. Consequently, readers are in the position of having to ease themselves into a narrative whose expression is not aimed directly at them; Faulkner is telling it to himself all over again.

If we are to get the measure of Faulkner's absorption in *The Hamlet*, however, we must go further back than 'Spotted Horses', back to the discarded *Father Abraham* or *Abraham's Children* (titles that no doubt ironically echo the idea of the Southern promised land). According to Joseph Blotner, the story opens with Flem, the local Abraham, looking through a window in the bank of which he is President. A flashback returns us to his early days in Frenchman's Bend, his work in Varner's store, his marriage to Eula, the sale of the spotted horses, Armstid's mishap, the various preparations for legal action and Suratt's reaction to these events. In other words, nearly the whole of what was later to become *The Hamlet* is contained in 25 pages and a little over 14,000 words written even before his first novel was published. It would therefore be no exaggeration to say that *The Hamlet* both inaugurates Faulkner's involvement in Yoknapatawpha and brings it to its summation.

It was also its mainstay, despite the attention paid to the line deriving from Bayard Sartoris, for, as the record shows, he prepared two versions of *Father Abraham* at some point during the late twenties, both concentrating on the spotted horses and both called 'As I Lay Dying' (a title picked up from a translation of *The Odyssey*).[13] Shortly afterwards, he started 'Omar's Eighteenth Quatrain', a forerunner of 'Lizards in Jamshyd's Courtyard' (the immediate source of *The Hamlet*'s concluding section) and kept working at it during the revision of *The Sound and the Fury* and the writing of *Sanctuary* and *As I Lay Dying* (which makes mention of the spotted horses). By August 1930, he had completed one more version of *Father Abraham* called 'The Peasants' and by November 'The Hound' (the basis of the Mink Snopes–Jack Houston material). The following year, 'The Peasants' reappeared as 'Aria Con Amore' before finally emerging as 'Spotted Horses' in 1931. In the July of that year, 'Centaur in Brass' was completed, while throughout the writing of *Light in August* (mid-1931 to early 1932) work continued on an unnamed book which Professor Blotner concludes was probably 'the Snopes novel', as he calls it. This carried on into 1933 and produced 'Mule in the Yard' in the following year. These last two tales do not appear in *The Hamlet* but they pursue the same subject and breathe the same atmosphere; moreover, they helped clarify Faulkner's mind about the course of his projected work. Not that any final decisions could be taken about it just yet, however, and this, combined perhaps with the fact that his purse could not afford the delay, led him to attend to more urgent matters in *Pylon*, *Absalom, Absalom!* and *The Unvanquished*.

Nevertheless, his first love was not forgotten; 'Fool About a Horse', that delightful tribute to Pat Stamper and finest of all Faulkner's comic tales, was published in 1936. (It may have been one of the yarns he liked telling his friends about in real, as opposed to literary, performance.)[14] By the time he got *The Wild Palms* out of the way, he could probably sense that his long labour was about to bear fruit. Only one task remained: an investigation into the root of the conflict adumbrated in the earlier stories. The result was 'Barn Burning'; page 1 of the MS is dated 7 November 1938, and its relation to *The Hamlet* made clear by the heading 'Book 1 Chapter 1 Barn Burning'.

As it happens, 'Barn Burning' turned out to be a separate short story (one of Faulkner's few good ones) and only a version of it appears in Ratliff's account of the origin of Snopes at the start of the book. No doubt this is to be attributed to the care which Faulkner took to subdue his effects for the sake of *The Hamlet*'s total impression for, had he included the story intact, Ab's passion would have upset the temper of the opening chapter and spoilt the effect of Flem's rise to power. In any case, his menace is of a different order and belongs to another time and immediate nexus of conflict. Likewise with the disappearance of Sarty, whose protest against what is happening to the South belongs to a specific situation within a family; within Frenchman's Bend, other voices, other presences register the same protest. 'Barn Burning' is too concerted a piece for the loose structure of *The Hamlet*. It is a prologue to the book, a key moment in the community's history as well as a foretaste of what is to come, and as such is reserved for publication in its own right.

The particular importance of the story in the present discussion is that it was the first of Faulkner's works to bring the Snopesian threat into clear focus. With its composition, the hints previously offered in *Sartoris* and *Sanctuary*, strengthened by the explorations of *The Unvanquished*, at last began to gather definition, with the assistance of the parallel process in the stories and novels wherein the character of Yoknapatawpha was established. (Faulkner's sketch of the county appeared in 1936, proof, perhaps, that he had only recently grasped it in its totality.) In fact, it is precisely because he had sensed what the human battlefield of Yoknapatawpha was like in stories like 'Spotted Horses' and 'The Hound' and had grasped the potential of

Ratliff as a positive source—his first appearance in 'Spotted Horses' is merely neutral, if not functionary—that he could contemplate expressing the necessary negative force of Snopes in 'Barn Burning'. And once Snopes became clear to him, two further consequences ensued: first, Ratliff himself, being too individual and realistic a character and too indispensable a narrative intelligence, could not be made to answer Snopes; someone else (in the end, Eula) would have to; and second, the earlier stories with the setting of Frenchman's Bend would have to be rewritten to accommodate the Snopeses if the conflict between the two were to be made definitive.

The way in which he went about doing so is best illustrated by 'Fool About a Horse' (1936). In its original form, the story offers a boy's account of the character of his parents (and, by implication, his country), two hard-working farmers. The father prides himself on having an 'eye for horse-flesh' and the ability to drive a good bargain but when he crosses Pat Stamper, he is quickly tricked out of the money entrusted to him by his wife for the purchase of a cream separator. On hearing of his loss, Vynie sets out to recover the money from Stamper but in doing so attempts no sleight of hand; rather, like Mrs Armstid after her, she simply requests the return of her savings and, unlike her, succeeds. In characteristic fashion, the men have had their fun, women apply the appropriate corrective pressure and order is restored. The contest has been essentially one between the mother and Stamper, between rootedness and vagrancy, the mundane and exceptional, labour and creative playfulness, simplicity of effort and brilliant feints. The agrarian paradise, it is clear, demands no choice between these sets of terms but their interaction, since the first term defines its ideals and the second everything that tests and reaffirms them.

When he came to revise the story for *The Hamlet*, Faulkner did his best to deepen this tension by introducing Ratliff as the narrator of the story and turning the father ('Pap') into Ab Snopes. Ab, that is, is being shown to us as he used to be, a typical Southern farmer, husband and father. Indeed, he *is* Yoknapatawpha but one whom 'Fate' (a word used with merely colloquial exaggeration in the short story) is in the process of converting into its enemy. By individualising Pap in this way, Faulkner converts the affair with Stamper into a point of departure where once it was part of the recurrent comedy of life.

The short story has become open-ended and now anticipates an unhappy sequence of events, especially since Ratliff and Ab appear in it as friends and neighbours whom we are later to see meeting in markedly altered circumstances.

In the midst of all this revision, one thing was left untouched: Pat Stamper's double-dealing. Rightly so, for it remains one of Faulkner's most inspired demonstrations of how competition between Yoknapatawphans once manifested itself and was resolved, though he is careful to note at which points such activity is vulnerable to disturbance. He has in mind the contest between Ab and De Spain in 'Barn Burning', where differences of talent are subsumed under the more dangerous differences of wealth, power and status. (There is a further contrast between De Spain and Will Varner, Varner being *primus inter pares* in Frenchman's Bend with none of De Spain's haughtiness.) He also has in mind the very different contests for possession later in *The Hamlet* between Mink and Houston and Flem and Armstid, while in Flem's defeat of Ratliff at the end he shows how the use of 'legerdemain' has degenerated into a contest that demeans the values of Yoknapatawpha. It is no longer part of a sporting rivalry (no doubt calculated to be profitable but not actually harmful) because men like Armstid now offer more than just a part of themselves as stake and men like Flem want to gain more than local, albeit real, advantages from them. Instead of the once-off event, there is now a pattern of aggrandisement to be followed. What was part of a man's expression of himself has become his business.

Once this analysis had formed itself in his mind, it is clear to see why Faulkner should have replaced the father and mother of 'Fool About a Horse' with Ab Snopes and his wife and why, in all that followed, he should have been careful to distinguish them from the Snopeses. People like Pap and Vynie are the subject of the stories but they are the object of the opposition between Eula and Flem. For this reason, they cannot enter too directly into the fray without distorting their character. It is Snopes, a related but distinct branch, who must do so and who must be shown to have appropriated their means of expression to his own ends. Like Eula, the plain folk must maintain a certain passivity. Theirs must be the confusion and irresolution which first nourishes and then capitulates to its own worst self.

It is with the aid of this scheme, now securely grasped, that

Faulkner was able to transform 'Lizards in Jamshyd's Court' (1932) from an untidy if inventive story to the fitting climax of an unfolding set of misadventures. The setting is no longer just a background but, thanks to the context provided by *The Hamlet*, a determinant of the scene's meaning, and the principals no mere treasure-seekers but characters engaged in a larger figurative argument which relates the decline of barter and swindle to Flem's rise in the community. The end result of this process is Henry Armstid, whose role in the 'Spotted Horses' episode prepares the way for his larger one here as representative—in outsize form, as is *The Hamlet*'s manner—of a demoralised 'peasantry'.[15]

'The Hound', published two months after 'Spotted Horses' in 1931, was probably the most thoroughly revised of *The Hamlet*'s stories. As potential material for a novel, it suffers from the fact that the argument between its leading characters, Cotton and Houston, is thinly sketched and the men themselves but ciphers, two bachelors without the histories and passion that are later to be invested in them. Nor has Houston's murder any wider meaning. It rests simply on a grudge—and that against a man of whom no more can be said than that he is overbearing. The narrative is well-paced but subdued in comparison with the magnetism and bravura, the sheer momentum of its counterpart in *The Hamlet*. Without before or after, how or why, it has only one interest in mind: the difficulty of getting rid of a dead body and, in particular, of overcoming a dog's loudly voiced grief for its dead master. It is the sort of idea which makes for a good 'yarn' but it is only the slenderest hint of what can be done to it when it is taken up by a work of art.

The dimensions of the transformation may be gauged from what follows. Suffice it to note here that, technically, the change involved playing down the laconic character of the magazine story and minimising its reliance on dialogue and plot. Instead, we have a closer interest in the psychology of human behaviour, a charged atmosphere and a much keener sense of place. These were all, no doubt, necessary if 'The Hound' were to be incorporated into the debate between Eula and Flem and if Mink and Houston were to be set free to express the growing desperation felt by their fellow men (so, incidentally, forewarning us of Henry Armstid), but they could just as truthfully be said to have been the issue of the process of revision itself, since the moment 'The Hound' was absorbed into *The Hamlet*, it lost the salient characteristic of the tall tale, namely its assumption that it is being addressed to men and women very like the speaker who can appreciate the characters and setting of his tale without having to be told too much about them. And that movement is itself suggestive of the larger theme.

Consequently, when the easy temper and anonymity of stories like 'The Hound' are dispensed with in revision, they are replaced by a feeling for history, human history, but also fictional history, since it is the presence of chronology rather than mere time in *The Hamlet*, the conversion of narratives of surprise or pleasurable anticipation into a prose which unfolds a circuitous but inexorable process, that gives rise, in turn, to our sense of the movement of a people from one stage of civilisation to another. Where, before, the type-figures were indistinguishable from the community, we could assume a restoration of equilibrium at the end of the short story. Now, however, the individual is no longer always restrained by his fellows and what he does becomes—perhaps paradoxically—more expressive of their wellbeing. When everyone belongs to an organism, no one person can upset its totality; now he can—and he is, ominously enough, surrounded by other, similarly errant individuals.

By way of exception, 'Barn Burning' reverses the general direction of the revisions and becomes more like a tall tale on its appearance in *The Hamlet*. The Snopeses, so it informs us, are fellow-countrymen whom the times have turned against and made unfriendly. The significance of this is measured by Ratliff as he warns his listeners about them in a friendly way (and in a mode familiar to them: no sermons, please), pointing out that what has happened to Ab could happen more seriously again. They had better look to themselves. A short story has been converted into a tale directed to a particular audience with a particular purpose in mind. It has become dramatic in quite another way.

The reworking of 'Spotted Horses' is particularly instructive in this connection. A great deal of it has been magnified seemingly out of all proportion to its subject matter. That which was once apt or amusing has become sharpened and hardened, while all the marks of a man addressing a group of sympathetic listeners—the relaxed air, idiomatic style and droll observation—have been diminished in favour of a gigantic imagination which so inflates the disparities that humour likes to feed on that it turns the story into something simultaneously comic and sinister, folksy and surreal. Much greater reliance is placed on polysyllables and rhetorical cadences and, though these sacrifice some of the story's pithy flavour, there is a contradictory emphasis, as of the muscular or statuesque, on detail. Most important of all, the collection of fine strokes within a loosely coherent whole which characterised 'Spotted Horses' gives way to the more cumulative novelistic procedures in which there exists a deferred but nonetheless apprehensible conclusion towards which the episode now moves. The conclusion, that is, will not be simply narrative; *The Hamlet* contains 'Spotted Horses' and their relation is an interanimating one in as much as they belong to two different stages of a community's life. Once more, technique enacts theme.

These remarks concerning the genesis of *The Hamlet*, speculative though they may be at times, inevitably lead one to remark the thoroughness of Faulkner's revisions, but this is only the first step to realising that, radical as these were, it is the alignment of the stories into a pattern that matters most of all. The process of revision, that is to say, was less verbal than contextual, as becomes clear when we notice that the characters who provide the context, Eula and Flem, are nowhere to be found in the stories; they make their first appearance in *The Hamlet*. (Flem, of course, appears elsewhere in Faulkner's fiction prior to *The Hamlet* but without the lineaments of his present character.) Once that fact is grasped, our appreciation of the book's specifically novelistic conception and execution is re-enforced. The stories by themselves, good as they are, might broach a major theme but they could never explore it. They are dispassionate, external narratives in which the personality and speech rhythms of the speaker command nearly as much attention as those of his characters. (Again, the exception of 'Barn Burning' proves the rule.) Thus, while it is proper to acknowledge their contribution to the finished work, it is impossible to grant them the status of 'previously published parts of work-in-progress'[16] or to discover in them a basis for proclaiming the unity of *The Hamlet*. That, such as it is, will have to be found in the book itself or not at all.

Faulkner once told a correspondent: 'I am quite sure that I have no feeling for short stories; that I shall never be able to write them, yet for some strange reason I continue to do so...'.[17] His 'strange reason' touches, perhaps, on the distinction between tall tale and literary short story but it raises a matter that has an even greater bearing on the discussion: his sense that some of his stories were sketches or cartoons, early rehearsals in a familiar and less taxing mode of some major work, not quite consciously executed as such but deliberately seized on whenever the occasion presented itself. The tales I have been discussing are of this kind, narrative samplers that allowed Faulkner to push his craft out against the day when he could put them to better use in the book he knew to be stirring within but whose composition he was prepared to delay until such time as he could claim to know what it was.

For all these reasons, *The Hamlet* may be said to have been the product less of revision than of recreation. It was a process that entailed the making of certain discoveries, stage by stage— discoveries about the folk element and Ratliff, about the way the various stories could be made to serve as spools for the book's winding threads, about the nature of Snopes. And once these had pressed the variety of his material into discernible shape, Faulkner could get to work and make his crowning contribution in the shape of Eula. A vital organising principle was born, one which could allow both broad expansion and concentration and which greatly expanded the resonance of individual episodes, even to the point of activating that feeble self-parody, 'Afternoon of a Cow', into the account we now have of Ike's afternoon.[18]

The Hamlet is a freewheeling work, then, but it does obey a pattern, just as some order, however ramshackle, obtains in Frenchman's Bend, though the closer we look for it, the harder it is to find—which, in the light of Flem's emergence, is central to the work's comprehension. Moreover, while it delights in miscellaneity, it acknowledges all that militates against its images of pleasure. As a combination of stories, it is vagrant, splendidly and variously rhythmical (I am reminded of what Denis Donoghue finds in the better poems of Robert Frost, a 'trust in numinous anecdote' which gives the reader a 'feeling for human axioms, in the press of rival commitments'[19]) but, as a fiction, it gradually, menacingly, finds its direction. Not to have had one, to have remained pointedly random, would, for its people as well as itself, have been best; to lose that randomness for direction is part of its tragedy.

The solution to the structural problems posed by his material is one of Faulkner's most original achievements, representing a major development of what C. S. Lewis called 'polyphonic narrative' and Gillian Beer after him calls

'entrelacement', interlacing stories so that nothing is ever finally abandoned or circumscribed.[20]

We are, in short, back with the romance, the literary form that stands in the closest relation to the vernacular and oral, with its

peculiarly precise register of the ideals and terrors of the age, particularly those which could find no other form. The romance is mimetic at a mythic level.[21]

That is memorably said, as is this:

... the infinitely supple tension, the prolific and apparently disorderly inclusiveness, the way in which events engender a whole range of disconnected happenings whose connections are yet felt though never pointed, the onward drift which dissolves the present into the past and remakes new presents which themselves dislimn. These narrative methods make the experience of reading the romances close to the experiencing of life.[22]

In the light of these quotations, it should no longer be necessary to insist that *The Hamlet* is a coherent whole. Nor should it be necessary to explain why, like most of Faulkner's work, it differs so radically from the traditional English novel. For one thing, there was not in Yoknapatawpha either a sizeable population with its tissue of habits and expectations nor the developed cultural matrix of a well-established community to support that sort of fiction. It is, rather, always crisis time in Yoknapatawpha, or something very like it. And the more crisis threatens, the more Faulkner responds in romances that seek to imitate his endangered myth. (When the Civil War erupts, *The Unvanquished* responds by collating itself into a series of would-be stories which are in fact episodes from a novel without its multifarious connecting matter.) His are thus no jumped-up stories or flawed would-be novels, but neither are they the products of a 'modernist' innovator. They owe their form (one which quite transcends the juxtaposition of related short stories) to the influence of an exceptionally strong tradition of rhetoric on a private sensibility in acute but fertile disarray.

III

The Hamlet is full of various kinds of trading. There is hardly a man who is averse to it because it is the great preoccupation whereby one Southerner declares himself to another, in the spirit of the delicate balance they have learnt from their exploitation of the land. Man-versus-man in the frontier settlement succeeds man-versus-nature on the frontier and is shaped by the same rhythms. Accordingly, when Pat Stamper and Ab Snopes pit themselves against each other, they do no more than rehearse the basic condition of the South's existence. The point is wittily elaborated on in the extraordinary deformations visited on the animals employed by Stamper or the scrub cattle 'transmogrified, translated complete and intact' into Herefords by the Snopeses a little later (like the Hait–Snopes mules in *The Town* and the Millard–Snopes ones in *The Unvanquished*). In both, we are presented with images of what frontier life was all about: the transformation of nature to man's design.

Man's relations with nature, founded as they are on the tension between his power over nature and his dependence on it, are potentially both difficult and rewarding. (Labove, Ike and Mink follow to remind us of that fact.) But his relations with other men are much more testing. What happens when these are affected by damaging animosities that upset the equilibrium between rivalry and co-operation concerns the rest of *The Hamlet*—and this at a time when, with the recent introduction of share-cropping and tenant-cropping and the simultaneous growth of towns in the South, the man–nature connection is itself being gradually eroded.

Faulkner's tall tales mimic this argument with marvellous spontaneity, beginning with the clash between Stamper and Snopes. Stamper is one of those lucky men who have made their work into an art, a trader whose 'legerdemain' frees him from whatever obstacles stand in the way to a happy life. His opponent is less lucky, one of those for whom the Stamper qualities have resulted in bitter misfortune, Ab himself contributing to the process. Yet his misfortune remains anything but personal since he is a victim less of character than circumstance, a point emphasised by the very existence of the Snopesless 'Fool About a Horse' and Ratliff's repeated assurance that Ab 'aint naturally mean. He's just soured' (p.27). It is fate that has brought poor whites like him into conflict with the Southern 'aristocracy' and fate that turns him out to work on one of Varner's farms and defend Yoknapatawpha's 'honour and pride' against Stamper—a combination of his wife's nagging, his own injured feelings and the fact that Stamper is a stranger who happens to be camped outside Jefferson on a particular day. It could have happened to anyone.

Jody Varner proves as much. That he works in his father's store (when he works at all) rather than on the land and that his attitude to nature in the person of his sister should be everything that nature is not suggests why he is the weakest link in the Varner chain—and why the Snopeses, far from being exceptional, are representative of an increasingly widespread process of alienation. When Jody invites Ab into Frenchman's Bend as an insignificant object whom he, the spoilt Stamper-type, can trick into swelling his profits, like calls to like. The victim selects his own executioner and method of execution.

The damage done to Ab himself is finely illustrated when, in an episode too little remarked, Ratliff drives out to visit him on his new patch of land. Their cold reunion, contrasted with the sympathetic humour of the Stamper episode and the friendliness of Ab and the eight-year-old Ratliff at that time, is painful to contemplate. Ab is now an embittered man, curt in speech and offhand in manner, though there is still some kindliness in him which Ratliff manages to tease out in his expert way. The old Sartoris and De Spain man (who crossed a negro butler with the same kind of shock Sutpen experienced) has become Varner's man. In that progress, we see adumbrated a whole drift of history. Gone is that loosely defined interdependence of men within the plantation hierarchy. In its place is to be found the impersonal economic relations of the present day which decree that Will and Ab are never to meet nor wish to do so. Whatever the reasons and wherever the blame rests, the results are woeful. All the self-reliance, thrift and energy of the one have been narrowed, all the authority and responsibility of the other weakened by the absence of the bonds which unite men. Our last sight of Ab is of a man savagely ploughing the infertile soil with no regard for it other than as the means for his survival. Every man is for himself now, and with a vengeance.

This scene between Ab and Ratliff is a good example of the brief, superbly judged modulations of tone essential to *The Hamlet*'s structure and tragi-comical temper. An equally good example is the ensuing description of Flem's impact on the store and cotton gin placed in his charge by Varner. Everything is promptly reorganised in favour of greater regularity. Customers no longer help themselves and settle for their goods. Will has to pay for his tobacco, no errors in conducting sales are henceforth made. Store and gin no longer run themselves and trust between people is neither assumed nor cultivated; business is business and 'muddling through' in the old fashion a thoroughly discredited practice. Not unnaturally, the townsfolk are somewhat disconcerted by all this but there is intermingled with their wariness a certain admiration for Flem. They show no understanding of the likely effect on them of his purposiveness, though it is only Faulkner's quiet handling of the matter that puts us on the alert. The narrative delicacy at this point extends to making Ratliff an authorial intelligence, one who, thanks to his absence from the stage for stretches at a time, provides infrequent reports that glance at rather than document Flem's rise.

In this way, the first book introduces us to a tension moving towards one kind of resolution. At the same time, it prepares us for themes that are to figure prominently later in the book— women who suffer from their husbands' actions (Ab's wife), men who are spoilt by adversity (Ab himself), overreaching duplicity by which one traps oneself in one's own designs (Jody). The narrative moves easily from the personal to the representative and from the past to the present, grouping its details rhythmically as much as chronologically and so accustoming us to the meaningful dislocations that are to follow. The second book, 'Eula', illustrates a strongly contradictory tendency. With it, we move from the silent menace of Flem to the fantastically gross sensuality of Eula Varner, she who represents everything in man that hungers for food, warmth, shelter, yet transcends all these, someone magnificently of the world yet released from it to enjoy a life richer than any the appetites could afford.

Like her father, Eula denies time. She is variously described as both eight and fourteen years old, simultaneously sixteen and thirty, a very pubertal foetus who 'possessed life but not sentience'.[23] She is the original American ('completely equipped ... to overcome anything the future could invent to meet her with'), that to which all free men rally, 'the queen, the matrix', an amalgam of nature and humanity at their most enchanting, something commensurate with man's capacity for wonder. Her presence is momentous, for it is she who gives *The Hamlet* its largeness and grotesqueness of life, its peculiarly forced intensity of feeling, and Faulkner responds to her with such extravagance that we may well talk of character being 'hyperbolized into pure quality':

> Ratliff [becomes] uncanny shrewdness; ... Mink Snopes, blind fury; Eula Varner, voluptuous sexuality; Flem Snopes, invulnerable cupidity. In becoming at one level, pure quality, the characters are suitable inhabitants of a mythical world.... To the extent that [they] approach pure quality they take on something of the archetypal....[24]

The Hamlet itself has it that Eula's

> entire appearance suggested some symbology out of the old Dionysic times.... She seemed to be not a living integer of her contemporary scene, but rather to exist in a teeming vacuum ...with a weary wisdom heired of all mammalian maturity.... (p.95)

This is no simple fleshy creature but a figure of myth, someone who defies exact description. There is a human Eula Varner, the plump girl who does nothing but exist, but within her lurks another, purer being, goddess of the 'teeming vacuum',

> one Eula Varner who supplied blood and nourishment to the buttocks and legs and breasts; [and another] Eula Varner who merely inhabited them, who went where they went because it was less trouble to do so, who was comfortable there but in their doings she intended to have no part.... (p.100)

To Jody, she appears

emanating that outrageous quality of being, existing, actually on the outside of the garments she wore and not only being unable to help it but not even caring. (p.101)

To Labove,

It was as if her muscles and flesh too were even impervious to fatigue and boredom ... , the drowsing maidenhead symbol's self.... (p.114)

She is the point, the centre,

swarmed over and importuned yet serene and intact and apparently even oblivious, tranquilly abrogating the whole long sum of human thinking and suffering which is called knowledge, education, wisdom, at once supremely unchaste and inviolable.... (p.115)

There is evidently a powerful impetus seeking release here and it drives Faulkner's language into a state of permanent purple. His imagination, having thrown up Eula, has in turn been provoked by her and now tries to seize her, to penetrate to her essence with the aid of that which, by definition, is alien to it—language. The words are expelled urgently, profusely, as if they were about to capture her bodily. The reader accustomed to classic English or American prose may resist for a while but is eventually battered into submission. And the more he senses that there is nothing merely fanciful about Eula, the more he senses a genuine struggle of language to express intensities which will wrest from him his wholehearted assent, not just his temporary sympathy, the more voluntary the submission becomes. As page after page is turned, the insistency works. Faulkner is never in doubt of his purpose and his confidence is measure enough for his vision.

For all the persuasion exercised on Eula's behalf, it is some shining quality about her that finally captivates the reader. In *The Mansion*, Charles Mallison excuses her adultery with Manfred De Spain on the grounds that she is a Venus who belongs to the whole community. For her to be 'a chaste wife or even a faithful mistress' would be an insult to the generosity of the gods. That is why Jefferson supports her;

only the preachers would hate her because they would be afraid of her since the god she represented without even trying to ... was a stronger one than the pale and desperate Galilean who was all they had to challenge with. (p.200)

We immediately recall Faulkner's comment on the phrase 'light in august', which he felt was

a pleasant evocative title because it reminded me of a luminosity older than our Christian civilisation.[25]

It is this quality Eula personifies, this saving element of barbarism and, with it, a sphere of living in which no shadows are cast. How should she not appear strange to us, who have long since lapsed into time and allowed knowledge to be channelled into various dogmas and abstractions? And how could the style associated with her not appear excessive to us, who trust to language as to the medium of our deepest perceptions?

Excessive to some degree that style remains, of course, however we look at it, though it should be remembered that its primary purpose is one of humorous celebration and that it draws for its licence on the same source that makes for Ratliff's tall tales, whose more temperate manner helps shade its passionate disturbance. Taken together, these two modes dominate *The Hamlet*. They give it its expressiveness, its extreme ranges of mood—from the vulgarest jest to the black comedy of Mink's disposal of Houston's body—its energy, its familiarity. Even so, it is Ratliff who claims the greater responsibility for these effects since the grand style is limited in duration; it is concentrated to make an impact, rising above the tall tales as Eula rises above her fellow-men. Thereafter, it virtually disappears from the book, remaining as a memory which is from time to time reinforced by those who share something of Eula's spirit, men like Ike and Mink Snopes. That is why there occurs with them a recrudescence of the 'Eula style' and why the writing, particularly in Ike's adventure, should occasionally overreach itself.

Eula's first dramatic engagement, with her schoolteacher, Labove, is an extraordinary one, related in a style that is both drugged and alert at the same time, with an atmosphere almost hallucinatory in intensity, like tropical air before a thunder-storm. No quotation can catch what Faulkner takes several pages to achieve, Jody as 'the jealous seething eunuch priest' (p.11) anxious to protect his sister, Labove, 'who did not want her as a wife, he just wanted her one time as a man with a gangrened hand or foot thirsts after the axe-stroke which will leave him comparatively whole again' (p.118) and Eula as the slumbrous centre of the 'priapic hullabaloo' (p.121). The pages fall away to transport us to the very scene.

Labove is a monk in his devotion to knowledge, with an 'invincible conviction in the power of words as a principle worth dying for if necessary' (p.105). Consumed by his mental passion, he wastes away until his 'gaunt body' is no longer 'shaped by the impact of its environment but [is] shrunken and leaned upon by what [is] within it, like a furnace' (p.106). Against such joyless effort, Eula unwittingly opposes another kind of wisdom.

> ... that face ..., even though but fourteen years old, pos-tulated a weary knowledge he would never attain, a surfeit, a glut of all perverse experience. He would be as a child before that knowledge.... He would grovel in the dust before it.... (p.119)

It is the kind of knowledge only she could possess,

> that ungirdled quality of the very goddesses in [Labove's] Homer and Thucydides: ... being at once corrupt and immaculate, at once virgins and the mothers of warriors and of grown men. (p.113)

Thus armed, she demolishes his 'faith in ... the white magic of Latin degrees' (p.117) and, after a feverish humiliation, arouses in him the ache of the body. He who had been 'above love' has been brought to life; effort, abstractions, seclusion have all been made to yield to impulse.

Eula's victory over Labove does more; it teaches him that she and all she represents are supremely good *and* never to be possessed. She is Venus to his Vulcan,

> who would not possess her but merely own her by the single

strength which power gave, the dead power of money, wealth, gewgaws, baubles, as he might own ... a field, say. He saw it: the fine land rich and fecund and foul and eternal and impervious to him who claimed title to it, oblivious, drawing to itself tenfold the quantity of living seed its owner's whole life could have secreted and compounded, producing a thousandfold the harvest he could ever hope to gather and save. (pp.118–19)

This passage—the text for the sermon of *Go Down, Moses*—offers *The Hamlet* its unifying theme. Set against the conflicts of possession that run through the book, it insists that the gargantuan Eula *is* the land, the paradise fair and 'foul' before such a fall as Thomas Sutpen experienced. She destroys the claims to ownership which money and knowledge make because she herself represents all wealth and knowledge, a wealth that every man instinctively responds to (*The Hamlet* uses the metaphor of sexual attraction) but which fewer and fewer know how to manage, save those who, like her former 'teacher', learn to do so: 'Show me what to do. Tell me. I will do anything you tell me, anything, to learn and know what you know' (p.119).

Having won her victory over Labove, Eula goes on to oppose the decay in Yoknapatawpha's forms of government, namely, the containment of rivalries within play-like affairs of trading and, when these fail, tribal arbitration of the sort provided by her father. This time, she works indirectly, largely through Mrs Armstid (with Mrs Littlejohn in support), and her enemy is no book-crazed schoolmaster but Flem Snopes himself, who is presently subverting the countryfolk to his own very different purposes with the sale of the spotted horses. Alas, she comes too late, for the merely pecuniary nature of the sale and the legalities that follow it prove that he has gained the ascendancy in Frenchman's Bend. The measure of his success can best be taken in the trial scene since, if it is true that a community at peace with itself is unaware of itself, the overt declaration that a struggle between its factions exists (such as the holding of a trial makes) signifies its deterioration. So, when Mrs Armstid, the heroically passive woman *par excellence*, departs the courtroom, the better side of Frenchman's Bend departs with her.

Old-fashioned regulation may still be attempted hereafterwards but it is no longer effective on the deepest level, as Varner discovers when Eula falls pregnant. Jody, stunned by the news, breathes fire, Mrs Varner sinks into bewilderment, the cook runs 'across the back yard toward her cabin, her apron over her head, as Negroes do when trouble starts among the white people' (p.142). Will, however, phlegmatically calls for calm.

> Hell and damnation, all this hullabaloo and uproar because one confounded running bitch finally foxed herself. What did you expect—that she would spend the rest of her life just running water through it? (pp.143–4)

Barefaced comic art reasserts itself. Varner remains unruffled because he believes that, while Eula's pregnancy is in one sense unexpected, in another it is not so at all; he shall have to cope with it as best he can, and this he does by bringing her and Flem together in an act of bargain and exchange. Just the sort of thing for a tall tale! Unfortunately, his plan misfires because Flem does not respect its premise: that it is a circumscribed act of self-correction designed to restore order by absorbing change. For him, marriage is a stepping-stone to success (he belongs to the novel) and he is confident that the villagers will not stop him from using it as such. To do so, they should have to become as corrupted as he is—which is why he has such an easy victory over them.

Ratliff alone shows any appreciation of the significance of the position. Though his grasp of Eula herself is somewhat confused, he knows that, for the first time, he has something to fear and from this grows his vision of the meeting between Flem and the Prince of Hell ('"What does (Flem) want? Paradise?".... "No." the old one says. "He wants hell."' (p.151).) He understands that Eula is, in essence, unconquerable but cannot help regarding her marriage to Flem as a catastrophe.

> What he felt was outrage at the waste, the useless squandering; at a situation intrinsically and inherently wrong by any economy ... : as though the gods themselves had funnelled all the concentrated bright wet-slanted unparadised June into a dungheap, breeding pismires. (pp.159–60)

There are still some reservoirs of right feeling to be found, though, and Mrs Littlejohn draws on them when she remarks on the stupidity of the men involved in the sale of the spotted horses. She is not the only one for, shortly afterwards, we find the smell of her ham cooking, the growth of the pear tree, the song of the mockingbird and the bathing presence of the moon gathered into a sensuous harmony which serves as background to the talk of the men as they discuss the events of the day. Even the horse-sale contributes to the prevailing mood, since there are elements in it which would not have been amiss had Pat Stamper had a hand in them—the bidders at the auction, Ratliff discomfited by a runaway horse, the overturning of the Tulls' wagon and Mrs Tull's outrage, culminating in a trial worthy of Dickens at his best, a series of mishaps impressive in its control, sweep and vigour.

It is Ike Snopes who is the truest of all Eula's devotees, perhaps. Certainly, his career bears a marked resemblance to hers: both are uncomplainingly used by Flem and both come into collision with monomaniacs, Eula with Labove, Ike with the farmer whose barn he raids for cow feed. When the farmer discovers his theft, he is filled with 'impotent wrath at the moral outrage, the crass violation of private property' (p.190) for, like Labove and Houston (whom Mink is shortly to cross with similar effect), he believes in

> the ancient biblical edict (on which he had established existence, integrity, all) that man must sweat or have not.... (p.191)

We contrast this 'embattled moral point' with the laziness of Eula and her father while at the same time distinguishing it from Flem's rapacity and Lump's exploitation of Ike, since it shows him to be engaged in what is potentially the most fruitful of activities, the contest with the land. As with Ab, though (and here we see why his plight touches on an experience which is widespread among the poorer farmers), the land has been so eroded and the farmer so dispirited by his labours that their interaction has been increasingly reduced to the utilitarian.

That is where Ike comes in. Like Benjy, he epitomises the failure of the South and, like him, complains against it more wisely than he or others can know, as is apparent from the Reverend Whitfield's suggestion that the cow he loves be given to him as cooked meat so that 'he won't want to chase nothing

but human women' (p.202). Whitfield does not understand—
nobody does—that Ike's cow is another Caddy and his love for
her one more version of the riches promised by the goddess. That
is why, as he struggles to reach his cow, Ike takes us back in time
to offer a record in miniature of primitive man's progress.
Thereafter, he retraces the various stages of the settlement of the
land—its seizure from Chickasaw Indians, its cultivation, its
denudation. The derelict sawmills he meets at one moment are a
memorial to that history and point the way Ab, the barn-owner
and Flem are to follow:

> [They] were not only their gravestones but the monuments of
> a people's heedless greed. Now it was a region of scrubby
> second-growth pine and oak among which dogwood bloomed
> until it too was cut to make cotton spindles, and old fields
> where not even a trace of furrow showed any more, gutted and
> gullied by forty years of rain and frost and heat into plateaus
> choked with rank sedge and briers loved of rabbits and quail
> coveys, and crumbling ravines striated red and white with
> alternate sand and clay. (pp.171–2)

How ambiguous the description is, torn between Faulkner's grief
that his ancestors should so have misused the land and a deeply
affectionate response to his home ground. The result is that, even
as we are reminded of the world Frenchman's Bend is in danger
of losing, we are afforded an explanation of why that danger
should have come to pass—indeed, should have been so richly
merited. And it is the same ambiguity that underlies Ike's
passion for the cow, a tribute to the feminine which, granted the
times, proves to be infertile and disruptive. For all the passionate
insistency of the prose, we are caught up in a transitional
movement from nature to civilisation and Ike is its embodiment,
looking backward to the confrontation between Labove and the
'bovine' Eula and forward to Mink's confrontation with
Houston.

Faulkner's description of Ike's adventures varies considerably
in quality. Take, for example, this fanciful description of dawn,
which develops the conceit 'that dawn, light, is not decanted
onto earth from sky, but instead is from the earth itself suspired':

Roofed by the woven canopy of blind annealing grass-roots

and the roots of the trees, dark in the blind dark of time's silt and rich refuse ... it wakes, upseeping, attritive in uncountable creeping channels: first, root; then frond by frond, from whose escaping tips like gas it rises and disseminates and stains the sleep-fast earth with drowsy insect-murmur; then, still upward-seeking, creeps the knitted bark of trunk and limb where, suddenly louder leaf by leaf and dispersive in diffusive sudden speed, melodious with the winged and jeweled throats, it upward bursts and fills night's globed negation with jonquil thunder. Far below, the gauzy hemisphere treads with herald-cock, and sty and pen and byre salute the day. (p.181)

This is an odd medley of effects. Rhetorical syntax, adjectival diction, synaesthetic imagery and rhapsodic tone all combine to suggest that Faulkner is not so much reporting as reliving the event he describes, himself the emergent dawn. His imagination has created such a credible world that he steps into it as if it were real and, once there, directly transcribes what he feels in the present tense. The reader may at first be affronted by the many breaches of decorum that result but he may in time be reconciled to them, even find a strange beauty in them, so authentic is Faulkner's belief in every particle of his description as necessary to a representation of a world in which appearances—and therefore approaches to reality—are turned upside down.

It is interesting to note that the language he uses here, 'lees of glory', 'ichor', 'coronal' and so on, is the language of his poetry, with this difference: it is being used on a much larger scale and with unaccustomed strength. The words no longer float in a mental landscape, mirroring their own progress as they move; they are part of an artist's range of effects, to be accepted or rejected according to need. Even so, it would be foolish to deny that Faulkner retained a weakness for the 'winged and jewelled'. Take the following description of raindrops: 'each brief lance already filled with the glittering promise of its imminent cessation like the brief bright saltless tears of a young girl over a lost flower;' (p.185). The first half has the poetic germ but not the appropriately 'poetic' language, which the second half goes on to provide. It constitutes a naive idea of what poetry is and its effects, as here, are often vapid but from it come such beautiful passages as this describing Ike collecting wild daisies for his cow:

At times his awkward and disobedient hand, instead of breaking the stem, merely shuts about the escaping stalk and strips the flower-head into a scatter of ravished petals. But before he reaches the windless noon-bound shade in which she stands, he has enough of them. He has more than enough: if he had only gathered two of them, there would have been too many: he lays the plucked grass before her, then out of the clumsy fumbling of the hands there emerges, already in dissolution, the abortive diadem. In the act of garlanding, it disintegrates, rains down the slant of brow and chewing head; fodder and flowers become one inexhaustible rumination. From the sidling rhythm of the jaws depends one final blossom. (p.184)

Southern tall tale has been crossed with late-romantic verse to produce a cadenced hybrid of its own. Since such moments of impassioned humour grow out of them, they necessitate our tolerance of raindrops weeping like young girls over lost flowers. We should otherwise lose the splendid language, no less than the conceit, of that 'abortive diadem' or, a little earlier, of Ike's withdrawal of the feeding basket 'from beneath the swinging muzzle which continues to chew out of the center of surprise . . .' (p.183).

With the Jack Houston–Mink Snopes conflict, we move (and the change matters) from assorted yarns, anecdotes and idylls to a concentrated narrative of great effect, beginning with the account of Houston's death ('He was still alive when he left the saddle . . .' (p.217) and ending with the brilliantly vivid descriptions of Mink's nights on the run. The obsessive character of these two men is pronounced. Both were—and to an extent remain—runaways from society, doomed solitaries of the type Faulkner used more than once to express the malaise of the modern. For both, time, events, life itself are all predestined qualities, something acknowledged by the precipitate nature of their actions and by the way in which the narrative is organised to allow for such coups as the placing of Houston's murder immediately after the passage relating the death of his wife or the introduction of a flashback concerning Mink's past into the aftermath of Houston's death.[26]

Houston begins life by fighting against conventionality. With nothing to learn about farming, he is sent to school to learn his abc. At the same time, he falls in love with Lucy Pate—or, rather, it would be more accurate to say that her kindness and consideration are forced on him and that his real feelings belong to the negro mistress he wins at the age of fourteen. When he realises that it is Lucy, not his mistress, book-knowledge ('Pate') not emotion, that he is expected to choose, he runs away. But his is no mere youthful rebelliousness.

> He is not wild, he was merely unbitted yet; not high-spirited so much as possessed of that strong lust, not for life, not even for movement, but for that fetterless immobility called freedom. He had nothing against learning; it was merely the confinement, the regimentation, which it entailed. (p.205)

Who else but Eula is 'that fetterless immobility called freedom'? And what else is Houston doing but trying, like Ike, to live by her standards rather than those of the new South?

Nevertheless, Houston is a divided man and his defiance of civilisation more ambiguous than might appear. After his futile attempt to prove that geography can provide escape, he comes back to the farm:

> There was still the mark of space and solitude in his face, but fading a little, rationalised and corrupted even into something consciously alert even if it was not fearful; the beast, prime solitary and sufficient out of the wild fields, drawn to the trap and knowing it to be a trap, not comprehending why it was doomed but knowing it was, and not afraid now—and not quite wild. (p.214)

The child of nature is also a child of civilisation and half-wills his own enslavement. It is his other self, the 'old mythical fanatic protestant' in him, that leads him to reject the prostitute he has lived with for seven years, come home and marry Lucy, she who represents education, family, security, everything that threatens Eula's 'fetterless immobility'. The moment he marries her, however, the 'beast' in him rebels and he buys her a stallion which soon afterwards tramples her to death. The stallion is, as it were, his poisoned gift to his wife, an unconscious willing to destruction of that willingly accepted, and with it he revenges his

loss of freedom. (The male–female conflict of *The Wild Palms*
hangs heavily over these pages.) After Lucy's death, his
misogyny is completed by the removal of almost all traces of the
feminine from the farm and he spends the rest of his life there a
spoilt man, neither captive nor free.

Mink Snopes, too, ran away from home in his youth, this time
in search of 'the sea' or, as an overblown passage has it,

> Perhaps he was seeking only the proffer of this illimitable
> space and irremediable forgetting along the edge of which the
> contemptible teeming of his own earth-kind timidly seethed
> and recoiled, not to accept the proffer but merely to bury
> himself in this myriad anonymity beside the impregnable
> haven of all the drowned intact golden galleons and the
> unattainable deathless seamaids. (p.236)

Prufrock was never like this. It is, in the circumstances, fitting
that Mink, who is more singlemindedly devoted to freedom than
Houston ever was and who married his whore, who had no
education and depended on nothing but his own and the land's
meagre resources for a living, should be Houston's murderer. It
is even more fitting that both men, like Ab Snopes, should have
been 'soured' by experience, the one a trapped animal who, in
fighting against his imprisonment, confirms it, and the other a
wild animal who discovers that his kind of existence is nowadays
another kind of imprisonment in which he is denied independence but instructed to be self-sufficient. Houston's lost 'freedom'
is Mink's 'oppression'.

After this, *The Hamlet* never quite recovers its buoyant spirits.
There is still a good deal of amusement to be had from the
mishaps of the 'peasants', while the humorous talk of Ratliff and
his friends still cuts like knowledge, but these come to us as the
last flares of a dying way of life. The truer note is struck by the
narrator. 'That,' he tells us between Mink's arrest and the
arrival of Buck Hipps and the spotted horses, 'was the fall before
the winter from which the people as they became older were to
establish time and date events' (p.258). It is a sombre moment;
history finally enters Yoknapatawpha and a new dispensation
begins.

Ratliff, as usual, is quick to take its measure when he explains
his entanglement with the Snopeses:

I wasn't protecting a Snopes from Snopeses; I wasn't even
protecting a people from a Snopes. I was protecting something
that wasn't even a people, that wasn't nothing but something
that dont want nothing but to walk and feel the sun and
wouldn't know how to hurt no man even if it would and
wouldn't want to even if it could, just like I wouldn't stand by
and see you steal a meat-bone from a dog. I never made them
Snopeses and I never made the folks that cant wait to bare
their backsides to them. I could do more, but I wont. I wont, I
tell you! (p.321)

When Ratliff falls into Flem's trap shortly afterwards, we
remember his little speech not with the satisfaction of irony but
with the disturbance of humour. Certainly, he is overanxious to
defend himself here but that only shows how insecure he has
become and how fearful for the continued existence of 'something that dont want nothing but to walk and feel the sun'. The
phrase immediately puts us in mind of Eula, who moves as
fitfully and mysteriously as Flem through the closing pages of the
book. She it is who is being lost and she whom Ratliff has been
trying to protect; she it is for whom nature and man once more
join in salute:

> Then the pear tree came in sight. It rose in mazed and silver
> immobility like exploding snow; the mockingbird still sang in
> it. 'Look at that tree,' Varner said. 'It ought to make this year,
> sho.'
>   'Corn'll make this year too,' one said.
>   'A moon like this is good for every growing thing outen
> earth,' Varner said. 'I mind when me and Mrs. Varner was
> expecting Eula.... I wanted some more gals.... So there was
> a old woman told my mammy once that if a woman showed
> her belly to the full moon after she had done caught, it would
> be a gal. So Mrs. Varner taken and laid every night with the
> moon on her nekid belly, until it fulled and after. I could lay
> my ear to her belly and hear Eula kicking and scrouging like
> all get-out, feeling the moon.' (p.307)

'A moon like this is good for every growing thing outen earth', 'I
could ... hear Eula kicking and scrouging like all get-out, feeling
the moon'—these are exact, energetic, caring words and the

voice that speaks them an enchanting blend of artifice and spontaneity. All things considered, it is the finest thing to emerge from *The Hamlet*—but, as Mrs Armstid suggests after her defeat by Flem, it is not to sound for long.

> She descended the steps, though as soon as she reached the level earth and began to retreat, the gray folds of the garment once more lost all inference and intimation of locomotion, so that she seemed to progress without motion like a figure on a retreating and diminishing float; a gray and blasted tree-trunk moving, somehow intact and upright, upon an unhurried flood. The clerk in the doorway cackled suddenly, explosively, chortling. He slapped his thigh.
> 'By God,' he said, 'you cant beat him.' (p.317)

Attention is divided between Mrs Armstid, noble in defeat, and the clerk, lost in admiration for Flem's 'legerdemain' to the exclusion of any concern for his victim, the former expressed in gravely beautiful Latinate fashion, the latter with candid simplicity, all unconscious of the dangers it applauds. The passage captures in microcosm what is happening to Frenchman's Bend—and it defies moral resolution. This becomes apparent when we notice that, like the pear tree in the preceding description, Mrs Armstid is captured in a Keatsian moment which reconciles the stasis of perfection with the motion of life. In that reconciliation, the realm of the absolute—where justice, order and love are attempted and escape us (the tragic mode)— merges with the world about us, a world indiscriminately composed of failure and recovery (the comic mode). That, in truth, is the hidden signature of Faulkner's mind and it allows him to describe Mrs Armstid and the clerk from two radically contrasting points of view without even trying to mediate between them.

The same rhythm recurs when Will Varner and Ratliff dispute the significance of the spotted horses. For Varner, the horses do no more than add to the variety of life. He is only sorry that he missed the fun and games. Ratliff politely demurs and distinguishes the menace his friend is blind to, doubting if 'there's any cure a-tall for that Texas disease Flem Snopes and that Dead-eye Dick brought here' (p.308). Varner–Yoknapatawpha is not impressed—not surprisingly, for Ratliff infects himself with the disease shortly afterwards. As he and his fellow treasure-hunters scrabble for their coins, 'four sets of blood ... lusting for trash' (p.346), old Uncle Bolivar, their guide, explains:

> God.... Just look at what even the money a man aint got yet will do to him. (p.343)

Greed and possession have begun their long day. The fact that the announcement is made by a member of Ratliff's own party could not be more helpful in insisting that the mania was, after all, a native trait which Flem has made the most (and the worst) of.

The book ends with the peasants congregating about Henry Armstid as they had earlier lined up to watch the spectacle of Ike making love to his cow or swarmed about Eula or rallied to the sale of the horses. In each case, they believe themselves to be spectators of life's immemorial comedy in a world that is always changing, always the same, and Faulkner does much to encourage this belief even as he shows them to be unconscious participants in events that are gathering to a very different end. Certainly, none of them understands that the tableau before them—Armstid digging for treasure with 'the regularity of a mechanical toy and with something monstrous in his unflagging effort', his wife bringing him pails of food and standing above him 'motionless, the gray garment falling in rigid carven folds to her stained tennis shoes' (p.365)—spells their doom. Nor do they care (or if, like Ratliff, they do, they are too compromised to do anything about it) that Eula is being taken from them, any more than Flem cares for the scene at the side of the road that meets him as he makes his way to Jefferson and the twentieth century.

Even so, *The Hamlet* refuses to take itself tragically. Yoknapatawpha's peasants may be unable to see what is before them, they may be unable to see that they are partly to blame for it inasmuch as it is they who have accepted the divisions consequent upon property, they who have yielded to 'law' and permitted individualism to become rampant. Yet, in their very ignorance is to be found an innocence that is very difficult to tell apart from blissful trust or culpable indifference. Either way, it signifies acceptance, endurance, an inability to conceive of, let alone make, meaningful choices. The integrity of Frenchman's

Bend remains intact even though its history is stained, and nothing could be more revealing in this regard than the contrast between Mr and Mrs Armstid—he the symbol of the folly of male activism, she of patient feminine wisdom—and the comparison between them both, as representatives of an albeit demoralised yeomanry, with the Snopeses. Eula abides. It is a lesson which comes to us with none of Faulkner's later exhortation but as something felt upon the pulse, a response to lively observation richly and evocatively recorded. So much so that *The Hamlet* is the work of his which, more than any other, remains imprinted in my mind—not only episodes and characters, atmosphere and setting but a grandness of feeling that embraces any number of contrasts: Eula and Flem, past and present, the humorous and the macabre, vernacular and ornate, almost hierophantic, modes of address, the individual and the body politic, an onward-moving plot and an eddying narrative. From these grew a romance which I hold to be Faulkner's greatest achievement, one that most fully stretched his fertile and penetrating imagination. There is no work more central to his art and, even above the book whose spirit it so resembles, *The Adventures of Huckleberry Finn*, none more central to the American temper.

IV

Our understanding of the tradition to which *The Hamlet* belongs is enhanced by Constance Rourke's *American Humor*,[27] which sets out to trace the interaction of 'the dark emotions and an earthy humor' in frontier life and the various descriptions of it which sprang up during the nineteenth century. In the course of her account, Miss Rourke places her emphasis on the

> strange new wonders on every side ... that produced the content of the stories—those natural elements that had brought terror and suffering to earlier pioneers ... but now were apprehended with an insurgent comic rebound and a consciousness of power. (p.49)

American 'humor' was born of the need to celebrate the frontiersman's victory over the wilderness and anticipated the civilisation that could be built on his achievement. In *The Hamlet*, however, it emerges in recoil from that civilisation and is directed towards the recreation of the young rural culture which made humorists like Ratliff possible. Timescale and purpose are thus neatly reversed as Faulkner develops his portrait of Frenchman's Bend through deadpan delivery no less than theatrical declamation, so mediating between the tremendous and the everyday and creating a rudimentary mythology in which the homeliest detail can rub along with the grandest of rhetoric.

An earlier, more relaxed example of the same sort of humour is to be found in *Mosquitoes*, where the novelist, Fairchild, tells of the sheep which old man Jackson took with him to the Louisiana swampland and which eventually turned aquatic. This is capped by the similar transformation of Claude Jackson, who ends his days as a lone shark terrorising women bathers along the Gulf Coast. The story, developed by Faulkner in an exchange of letters with Sherwood Anderson, is one of his most inventive and, in comparison with the unrewarding talk which constitutes the bulk of the novel, points all the more clearly to everything that was nearest his genius by recalling what Miss Rourke terms the

> ... exhilarated and possessive consciousness of a new earth and even of the wide universe [which] ran through this tall talk and the tall tales; ... Inflation appeared with an air of wonder, which became mock wonder at times but maintained the poetic mode.

The Hamlet's stories are nostalgic tributes in just such a mode and, like Miss Rourke's tales, become epical

> not merely because of the persistent effect of scale or because of their theme of wandering adventure, but because they [embody] something of those interwoven destinies of gods and men which have made the great epical substances.... Half-gods [have] taken shape and [walk] the earth.... (pp.64–5)

Yet the differences remain: Eula's appearance lacks the expectancy of folk tales while her status as a divinity is without answer from the people who surround her. Imposing as she is, she belongs to a context, and that context is dispiriting.

Similarly, while monologue, rhapsody and tall tale play an important part in *The Hamlet*, they are expanded into fantastically discordant shape. In part, this was because Faulkner wished to enrich the material on which his work was based and in part because he exaggerated the tall tale's already marked distinction between the bearing of the narrator and that of his characters. But it was also a reflection of the fact that, at the deepest level, he lacked the assurance of a public ready to listen to him. Whatever its other attractions, the post-bellum South could no longer supply him with that kind of audience. And it is this sense of separation that determines the style he employed in his work. More, it is the condition of his being as a novelist, as it was in the case of Thomas Hardy, who, late in life, remarked:

> The poet is like one who enters and mounts a platform to give an address as announced. He opens his page, looks around, and finds the hall—*empty*.[28]

Regarding Hardy's style, William Archer observed that he sometimes seemed

> to lose all sense of local and historical perspective in language, seeing all the words in the dictionary on one plane, so to speak, and regarding them all as equally available and appropriate for any and every literary purpose.[29]

Being displaced from home and yet set apart from the metropolis, both men employed an amalgam of language, derived from either and neither, as the means to their reality, be it Wessex or Yoknapatawpha, one that confirmed the attachment signified by a Max Gate or Rowan Oak but took it up into a far-reaching complex of attitudes which explored their sense of dislocation, of working—where it mattered—in isolation from others.

It is relevant to the point that the only memorable contribution made by Faulkner to a study of his art came in response to Malcolm Cowley, who had written to him to say that he thought Henry James's comments on Hawthorne working in solitude were equally applicable to him. Faulkner agreed, offering this definition of his

studbook style: 'by Southern Rhetoric out of Solitude' or
'Oratory out of Solitude'.... I think I have written a lot and
sent if off to print before I actually realised strangers might
read it.[30]

In an illuminating passage, he went on to explain why this
should be by giving Cowley an account of how literature
emerged in the South. According to him, the land was peopled
by peasants and aristocrats, neither of whom were interested in
creating a literature, let alone capable of doing so. After the Civil
War, however,

the strong among the remaining realised that to survive they
must stop trying to be pre 1861 barons and become a middle
class (;) they did so, and began to create a literature.[31]

Literature is the property of the modern South; in the 'pastoral
cityless land' of old, there was only oratory, 'the first art'. The
interesting thing about this view is that it comes from a writer
who was himself unconcerned with the 'middle class' (or middle
anything else, for that matter—Gavin Stevens is the nearest he
comes to it) and who cared very little to write about the period of
time when, as he saw it, a literature was born. For him, literature
is gained only when life falters; there is nothing to celebrate
about it.

By way of contrast, *The Hamlet* returns to the 'pastoral cityless
land' in its last flowering. In form and address, it is as far
removed from the novel of society as could be. But it is not
oratory either. It does not have the discrimination and stabilities
of the one nor the exuberant wonder of the other, so that, for all
the comfortable, unaffected air with which Ratliff launches into
his recital of the Pat Stamper story, we are aware of another,
more critical temper working behind the scenes to adapt its
material into highly developed narrative form. Ratliff is not the
author's mask nor the tale's sole creator as such narrators
usually are. He is himself a figure in a landscape and his story
one which can be appreciated only when it has been brought into
relation with the others that surround it.

Even so, *The Hamlet* continues to owe a good deal to the tall
tale, in this instance the 'turn toward entrenchment in local life'
that Constance Rourke observes occurred after the founding of

California and the end of westward migration.

> Retrospect, recovery, the ample possession, were to have their long day.... It was as if a people were trying to bury itself in its deeper resources. (p.288)

Miss Rourke links this mood to the emergence of short story as a distinctive American form, so bringing together two of the cardinal features of native prose, its fragmented or episodic nature and its dependence less on the life closest to hand than on the 'far view', 'the distant, the retrospective, the legendary'. Having made the connection, she can then rise to the announcement: 'It is not the novel which has developed but the romance, the cumulative tale, the saga, even the allegory' (pp.280–1).

Some three decades later, Richard Chase stressed the 'freer, more daring, more brilliant' character of American fiction, its

> picturesque and ... heroic [qualities], an assumed freedom from the ordinary novelistic requirements of verisimilitude, development and continuity; a tendency towards melodrama and idyl; a more or less formal abstractness and, on the other hand, a tendency to plunge into the underside of consciousness; a willingness to abandon moral questions or to ignore the spectacle of man in society, or to consider these things only indirectly or abstractly.[32]

It is not a uniquely American catalogue of features, of course, a point Graham Hough reminds us of when he discusses Cinthio's support of Ariosto's writing.

> Its structural principle is the 'interweaving' of diverse themes, and it can therefore admit a great variety of characters. It is tolerant of digressions and may comprise many actions and the actions of many men.
>
> Cinthio is feeling for the description of a fictional structure which can comprehend great diversity, but still is a structure not a muddle, still has its own kind of integrity and does not merely fall apart. In an extremely intelligent passage he tells us what the underlying principle is. The convention of the romance is that of oral narration.[33]

Professor Hough's historical perspective is amply documented by Northrop Frye, whose classification of fiction into four types—romance, novel, confession, anatomy—helps us to a clearer understanding of each, especially since it is one of his concerns to insist that criticism must first acknowledge the kind of work it is dealing with if it is to be pertinent.[34] As Hugh Kenner observes: 'Faulkner was neither an analytic nor a syntactic thinker, but a teaser into words ... —all necessary, all unwelcome—of what was, to start with, a simple unverbalizable pulsating impulse' and his expansion of such impulses leads to an 'unbounded interelatedness' within a 'vast interdependent oeuvre' whose convention is that of 'the tall tale spun on a timeless afternoon'.[35]

To grasp the romantic nature of Faulkner's fiction is to perceive that such verdicts as another novelist might make it his business to reach by careful description are nearly always assumed by him from the start—or ignored. Moreover, while his heroes often contend with life, they do so not because they are interested in mending manners but because they wish to dispense with morality itself in favour of the heart's knowledge. Should this coincide with morality, well and good (e.g. Horace Benbow in *Sanctuary*, Charles Mallison in *Intruder in the Dust*, and above all Bayard Sartoris in *The Unvanquished*); where it does not, the heart takes precedence (Quentin and Caddy, Ike McCaslin and Roth's women, Mink and Houston, *Sartoris*'s Bayard, Thomas Sutpen). Flem Snopes, we realise, is only the latest 'amoralist' to enter the scene and his line stretches back to the days before the entanglement which gave Jefferson its name.

That is why, when we look for the qualifying characteristics of Faulkner's work, we turn not to Lionel Trilling's 'hum and buzz of implication' but to Constance Rourke's 'humor' developed into Richard Chase's 'romance' which, while it does not preclude realistic observation, breathes a different air. Two features of the form Professor Frye draws attention to are worth emphasising: the subjective impulses of the romancer's creations and, second, his special relation to history, not only in the Jamesian sense of the lack of a developed culture but also in the belief that history itself can be mastered and banished. It is this article of myth that Faulkner absorbed through and through, the myth of America as seen by a Southerner. *That* was his 'ample possession'.

No precise time could be attached to it but it was not 'a pre-historical or a non-historical time, or a non-temporal existence, a point before and beyond time' nor was it something 'never mistaken for society' by those who believed in it.[36] It was located in the Compson and Benbow childhoods, the anonymous frontier community of *Requiem for a Nun*, Ike McCaslin's wilderness, Lucius Priest's Jefferson, Sutpen's West Virginia, Eula Varner's Frenchman's Bend, an active experience of reality at odds with the conditions we know to make for life yet nonetheless contained by it. No wonder that the romance was so apt a mode for Faulkner, for it is, as Professor Chase puts it, a 'clairvoyant' art in much the same way as humour is. To understand this is to understand his 'quickening sense of form'[37] and his concern for tragi-comic images of meaning. Since it is impossible to sustain such states effectively in narrative form or to maintain the 'clairvoyant' insights over any length, the fragmented approach with its bundle of interlocking perspectives is necessary, especially since the Faulknerian romance favours the broad canvas. If to this is added the habitual ranging from one temperamental extreme to another—the contradictory tensions which are the stuff of his art—then we can appreciate all the more the recourse to short story, anecdote, episode, in short, to a 'vagrancy of imagination'.[38]

Such art suits a young nation coming to consciousness, what with its youthful heroes and its tendency to find in them a representation of the larger problems of life. As Dawson Fairchild in *Mosquitoes* has it:

> Art reminds us of our youth, of that age when life don't have to have her face lifted every so often for you to consider her beautiful. That's about all the virtue there is in art: it's a kind of Battle Creek, Michigan, for the spirit. And when it reminds us of youth, we remember grief and forget time. That's something. (p.264)

The reference to Battle Creek, Michigan, is to the home of the Kellogg Cereal Company and its address for packet offers to the young. It is, by any reckoning, a startlingly belittling image of art—but then Faulkner could not care less about the higher claims of the imagination. All he cares for is its capacity to immerse us in childlike states of being, not in abrogation of our responsibilities but after a more inclusive sense of life.

Even so, childhood was never an uncomplicated quality for him. It was not merely instinctual; it could also be achieved. Nor was it regarded simply as a necessary condition for goodness. In *Absalom, Absalom!*, he comments on Sutpen's ability to utter

> calmly, with that frank innocence which we call 'of a child' except that a human child is the only living creature that is never either frank or innocent, the most simple and the most outrageous things. (p.246)

Again, in *The Reivers*, he comments:

> There is no crime which a boy of eleven had not envisaged long ago. His only innocence is, he may not be old enough to desire the fruits of it, which is not innocence but appetite; his ignorance is, he does not know how to commit it, which is not ignorance but size. (p.46)

'Innocence', then, seems to carry with it a more or less clear understanding of the contraries it contains. It is anticipatory but shielded from the knowledge it apprehends, embracing everything that is foreign to it while remaining free from its contamination. This is a difficult concept for us to grasp but it becomes more approachable when we notice its similarity to Keats's Grecian urn, an image especially prized by Faulkner for its ability to reconcile movement and stillness and thus defeat time.

When he came to resolve his attitude towards wilderness and civilisation in *Go Down, Moses*, Faulkner complicated the quality considerably by developing the distinction between innocent evil (figured in rank nature) and innocent good (figured in 'gentleman' hunters), the two locked together in a contest not for victory or defeat but as an expression of a duality wherein each depends on the other for its virtuous existence. It was not the wilderness, therefore, nor even the pioneering settlement (much less the plantation) that captured his imagination. It was the idea of their coexistence on the frontier, the settlement as an entity ramshackle enough to exist as an aggregate of free individuals but cohesive enough to be greater than the sum of its parts, the woods as the necessary point of external opposition. And it is in the woods that evil is located. In the community itself, there is only the rascality that is part of life, in intention and consequence no more serious than the mischief of boys, though as essential to growth and vitality. But no evil. The Southerner lives in goodness; he is born or reborn into it or falls away from it. When he falls, he falls into not-goodness and, despite the accusations levelled against him, the most one can say of Snopes is that he is not good.

The Adamic hero thus remains 'by some magic of art, morally *prior* to the world which nonetheless awaits [him]'.[39] Or, rather, he lives both within and without it, since the paradisal state is regarded by Faulkner as immanent; having been achieved on the frontier, it is always recoverable from it, in memory if not in fact. Yet that paradise was neither perfect nor static: the good life is good not because it is some flawless absolute but because it offers us a chance to hold in suspension what are otherwise logical, moral or historical impossibilities while actively encouraging us to seek their resolution. The greatness and sinfulness of the South are forever in the balance and forever available to its youthful questors at the moment of their awakening.

Here, we have a remarkable work of scholarly speculation to guide us, John Armstrong's *The Paradise Myth*.[40] Mr Armstrong's purpose is to enquire into the nature of paradise, which he does by examining the ancient figure of the snake-encircled tree, the tree representing order and the snake dissolution.

> ... the idea of the snake is one we feel to harbour something inimical to the permanence of all our designs upon nature: techniques, boundaries, moral systems, institutions, and even language itself. (p.36)

The snake's domain is the frontier, edge of the settled world, a realm of intuited knowledge and indeterminate being such as children possess, 'infinitely various', unrestrained, fertile of possibilities. Man himself is fascinated by such changefulness yet strains no less earnestly after stability—and this not merely in movement from one to the other but in recognition of a tension that answers to the deepest of his desires, the attainment of a state in which he shall be both secure and variable. In the emblem of tree and snake, he discovers just such a 'reconciliation of the inherited order with the marginal and the extra-systematic' (p.88).

Mr Armstrong traces this argument in various imaginative works, always to good effect but nowhere more memorably than in the plays of Shakespeare. (His discussion of *Antony and Cleopatra* is particularly fine.) In *The Tempest*, for example, he remarks the connection between the order which Prospero enjoys and its origin in 'the very elements making it unsustainable' (p.103). For him, Ariel and Caliban alike are creatures of the marginal world

> whose common principle of life is to liberate themselves from the tyranny they support, an apparent contradiction set forth with precision beyond the reach of abstract thought, by the ancient image of the snake-encircled tree. (p.110)

Paradise Lost, too, demonstrates the same principle, for Milton

> embodies in his construction at every level the imaginative principle which must subvert it. His splendid baroque paradise, . . . the epitome of the sure dispensation, would have been totally uncompelling without the satanic assault. The 'first grand Thief' not only breaks into the fold to destroy but at the same time energizes it and upholds it as an ideal form. (p.110)

Again,

> the ideal enclave . . . draws an essential part of its strength from the force which requires and effects its dissolution. . . . Milton gives new definition to the unitive principle of the tree-snake configuration . . . by setting forth the paradox of integrative power in dependence upon subversion at the heart of its own form-giving process. And it is this process . . . which brings together the divergent modes of fulfilment we seek: to stand rooted in a continuing order and to frequent that marginal region where every form is but for the instant. The greatest poetry and art . . . leave behind the pleasure-bound and passive conception of the earthly paradise, and are concerned to effect this all-important resolution. (p.121)

It is not difficult to see why the Yoknapatawphan paradise should obey the same rhythm for it, too, was established in the teeth of its enemies (be they history or nature) and is recoverable in the same way. Indeed, it may be said to exist nowhere other than in its opposition to them: man against nature, hunter against bear, Sutpen against Tidewater, Lucius Priest against Tennessee. The Southern myth does not so much deny reality, then; it is *about* its denial of reality. It is about a way of relating our better selves to our worst ones so that, whether the enemy is viewed with sympathy (as Ike McCaslin regards Ben) or hostility (as Sutpen regards the outside world) or a mixture of both (as Quentin regards Sutpen), his evil is a great good.

.., innocence is innocence not because it rejects but because it accepts; is innocent not because it is impervious and invulnerable to everything, but because it is capable of accepting anything and still remaining innocent; innocent because it foreknows all and therefore doesn't have to fear.... (*The Town*, p.178)

7 The Keatsian Moment

I

With *Go Down, Moses* (1942), we return to the debate between nature and civilisation in the South, this time seen through the eyes of Ike McCaslin. Like Sutpen, he is enamoured of innocence and baffled to understand why his countrymen's pursuit of the good should have produced such catastrophic results. If

> Once, man entirely free, alone and wild,
> Was blest as free—for he was Nature's child.
> He, all superior but his God disdained,
> Walked none restraining, and by none restrained:
> Confessed no law but what his reason taught,
> Did all he wished, and wished but what he ought.

how was it that he could have stooped to slavery and exchanged his freedoms for life lived (guiltily or not) under the moral law? And how was it that, for generations, he could have continued like this, despite all the encouragement he received? Yet continue he did, until the Civil War threw his Dream into eclipse. Since that time, the future has ground increasingly to a halt; in Quentin and Ike, it does just that. All that remains is the prospect of an over-populated, heterogeneous, mechanised civilisation covering earth like a blight, Armageddon in slow motion. Or, in an image derived from Faulkner's Nobel Address, an atomic holocaust. Or, in yet another formulation, an idiot negro burning down the Southern mansion or the corpse of another negro brought home to burial, both of them historical figures of guilt, symbols of the vision that miscarried.

However we put it, what was once a tension governing the relations between man and man and man and nature has degenerated into conflict and a hairline balance gone. Balance implies the organic, a life of seemingly endless perpetuation, but conflict argues a world in which time exists and victor and vanquished have meaning. As Auden noted:

> Nature is the dragon, against which St George proves his manhood. The trouble about that, of course, is that if you succeed in conquering the dragon, there is nothing you can do with the dragon, except enslave it, so that there is always the danger with a wild and difficult climate of alternating ... between respecting it as an enemy and expoiting it as a slave.[1]

Go Down, Moses is about just such respect and exploitation.

'Was', the opening story, is full of delicately balanced oppositions. It begins with a description of 'Uncle Ike',

> who in all his life had owned but one object more than he could wear and carry in his pockets and his hands ... ; who owned no property and never desired to since the earth was no man's but all men's, as light and air and weather were.... (p.7)

The one extra 'object' is a cot and mattress used for hunting, an activity expressive of his conviction that 'the earth was ... all men's'. The story which follows is designed to provide a framework for this belief, dealing with the activities of his father and uncle just before the Civil War. It is dominated by two episodes, the chase after Tomey's Turl, who has escaped from his quarters to woo his sweetheart, Tennie, and the gamble at cards between Hubert Beauchamp and Uncle Buck to determine whether Buck will have to marry Hubert's sister, Sophonsiba. In both, tension is rendered as game, in which the issue of ownership is debated primarily in the age-old terms of love and marriage and secondarily (but only secondarily) in terms of 'master–slave' relations. Slavery exists, yet the negroes are nominally manumitted and live in their masters' mansion while the masters live in their slaves' quarters. Racial discrimination exists, yet the negro Turl is his pursuers' half-brother. Moreover, while his wooing of Tennie broaches one of *Go Down, Moses*'s major themes, love and endurance (associated by Faulkner with negroes), his leading the McCaslins a chase makes him more of a white man caught up in that other leading theme of the book, the hunt. During the chase, being a nigger, Tomey's Turl should have jumped down and run for it afoot as soon as he saw them. But he didn't; maybe Tomey's Turl had been running off from Uncle Buck for so long that he had even got used to running away like a white man would do it. (p.11)

'Being a nigger', it seems, is a question of behaviour, not skin colour, so that when the dogs catch up with him,

it looked like they were trying to jump up and lick him in the face until even Tomey's Turl slowed down and he and the dogs all went into the woods together, walking, like they were going home from a rabbit hunt.... It wasn't any race at all. (p.15)

Nor was it, for the buoyant humour of the tale has served to disclose that, while tensions in the South exist, they are being continually dissolved or suspended. As happens whenever Faulkner turns to the past, memory and nostalgia (or wish-fulfilment) are in constant interaction, the former checking the freedom of the latter which in turn shades and deepens the otherwise bare facts of history.

Up to this point, the McCaslin brothers have managed to contain incipient conflict with playful skill. They are also determined, as we know from *The Unvanquished*, to do more than regulate the status quo since they are anxious to ensure a measure of justice for their slaves. They nearly succeed. (Hence the original title of the story, 'Almost'). At the end, Tennie is won, Uncle Buck is a free man, the war has not yet begun. We are witnessing the South's last moment of 'irresponsibility', when everything hangs in the balance.

But Buck and Sophonsiba do eventually marry.[2] She insists on moving into old Carothers' house, clears it of negroes and completes its building despite the opposition of Uncle Buddy. She chases Hubert's negro mistress from their old home, 'Warwick', bears a son (Ike) and establishes herself as the dispossessed member of the English aristocracy she imagines herself to be (and which, in a way, she is, for she has shown herself to be infected by the values of the Old World). The result is a little, light-fingered parable of how debilitating pretensions, sheer heedlessness and lack of spine allowed the South to throw away its chance.

It is against this legacy that Ike has developed his view about the principle of possession. He lives for a time when black and white were not so overwhelmed by guilt or oppression, when conscience and responsibility were alive within a system which at the same time harboured far worse qualities. It is as if the acts of the first McCaslin and those of his sons lay side by side and in separate compartments, as it were, the one free from the contamination of the other and pointing in a different direction, the former to destructive contention, the latter to tensions susceptible of amelioration and expressing mutual regard. *That* is the double burden of the McCaslin heritage and Ike has pledged himself to act against the one in emulation of the other.

Lucas Beauchamp, the oldest McCaslin still living on the land, cannot understand the motives which then lead him to surrender his ownership of the land.[3] He cannot see that ownership—that which the McCaslin brothers undermine with their housing arrangements and their communalisation of farming during the war—is the basic sin, though few know better than he the consequences of its extension into human relations. In his childhood, he and Zack Edmonds lived happily together but it could not last. As Faulkner was later to remark,

> ... there's no problem among the children, they play together and sleep together and eat together. It's only when they get old and inherit that Southern economy which depends on a system of peonage do they accept a distinction between the black man and the white man....[4]

And so it proves. When Zack grows up, he no longer regards men as men but as slaves and masters whom the latter can use as they like, as he himself does by 'borrowing' Lucas's wife for two years, Lucas's protest, bitter but dignified, notwithstanding.

The purpose of juxtaposing 'Was' and 'The Fire and the Hearth' is to compare two worlds almost a century apart by pointing to the difference between the racial attitudes they describe. Turl, the man being hunted in 'Was', is Lucas's father. Unlike him, Lucas is more a tenant farmer than a relation, his tie with Roth Edmonds (Zack's son) being part of the 'system of peonage' Faulkner takes care to demonstrate throughout the book: Sophonsiba's possessiveness spoils McCaslin and Turl, Zack's appropriation of Molly spoils his ties with Lucas, Ike's wife spoils her marriage by insisting on his retaining the McCaslin property, Roth exploits women in the manner of Old Carothers and the Indian chief, Doom. Only a love greater than any of these shows can generate the humanity with which, in the spirit of the 'old fathers', the ties of kinship are secured and, with them, a just social system. Accordingly, it is in the 'heart'—presently symbolised by Lucas's marriage and the fire on his hearth—that a central source of values is located, values inextricable from the stoicism and simplicity of the negro.

The McCaslins' attitude to women and to weaker, more dependent subjects presents no simple case of defective feeling, however, for showing deference to these subjects would not put an end to the matter; Sophonsiba and Ike's wife are no kinder than the men when they wield power, Fonsiba no less than Samuel Beauchamp defects from the South, Rider kills a man, the old bear pursues his ravages. It is rather a question of the quality of their relations, their ability to contain degrees of tension between unequal parts of a whole. This is what the McCaslins fail to do, usually aggressively but once by over-pliancy (Uncle Buck), and it is for these transformations of tension into hostility that they are to be punished. Tensions themselves cannot be abolished since they are both necessary and healthy, as the hunt demonstrates, a ritual which releases opposition but disciplines it to the exclusion of any excessive or inappropriate feeling. When Ike, who should have been another masterful McCaslin, chooses to be dependent, he does so because he feels the balance necessary to the South has been overweighted on the side of all that he renounces. It is the only way he feels that he, a white man, can emulate the negro, can *become* negro.

Lucas cannot understand this. He believes that the blame for the South's corruptive element attaches not to the founder (Carothers' line running, like Sutpen's, in negro descendants) but to the distaff side, a view supported by the harmful behaviour of Ike's mother at the time of her marriage and by white wives in general. It is as if the character of the South had been reduced to two branches of a family contending for domination, the one male, for the most part active, ruthless colonisers of the land, and the other female, what women in the Faulknerian ideal might be said to be. (The negro of whatever sex is aligned with the latter.)[5]

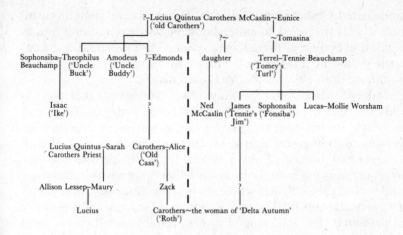

The answer to the South's problem is obviously not to be found in the white man, but neither is it to be found in the black man, rather in men of mixed blood—men like Lucas:

> Instead of being at once the battle-ground and victim of the two strains, he was a vessel, durable, ancestryless, non-conductive, in which the toxin and its anti stalemated one another.... (p.78)

His face is the face of 'ten thousand undefeated Confederate soldiers almost indistinguishably caricatured',

> *heir and prototype simultaneously of all the geography and climate and biology which sired old Carothers and all the rest of us and our kind ... who fathered himself, intact and complete, contemptuous ... of all blood black white yellow or red, including his own.* (p.88)

Here is an excellent example of how Faulkner neutralises opposition by suspending it, making it inherent rather than real. Lucas, we are told, is not a product of the clash between the races but its *denial*, a vessel that blends 'the toxin and its anti' into a stalemate. It is no accident that he should resemble Sam Fathers in the following story for, like Sam, he is instinct with 'the geography and climate and biology' of the South, all of which God guaranteed as good and which, despite a record of betrayal, still manage to survive (hence the 'ten thousand undefeated Confederate soldiers'). He is a proud anachronism, one who is prepared to suffer bondage while remaining free to remind everyone of the ancient virtues. And he could not have done so had he not been a confusion of the races, one capable of spanning both sides of the McCaslin divide.

Indeed, it is a signal fact (one often overlooked) that there is only one real negro amongst the principals, Rider in 'Pantaloon in Black'. More than that, Rider is endowed with superhuman powers of feeling and acting; his every quality is described with exaggerated intensity.[6] As a result, he is distinguished in the sharpest possible manner from his fellows, both within the story and within the book as a whole, so as to be more central to them. In particular, his fidelity to the memory of his wife (all the better appreciated for following Lucas's comic near-divorce from Molly) emphasises the value of 'the fire on the hearth' so powerfully that he emerges as the emotional justification for the appeal to the negro's way of life as the white man's salvation.

Yet if Faulkner sees in Rider a symbol for the kind of love that alone can redeem the white man's sins, he nevertheless does not wish the white man to go through the agony of becoming a negro only for the negro himself to become a white man, even if the white man is responsible for pushing him that way. Hence Samuel Worsham Beauchamp—and hence, a century before, Fonsiba's husband. He is first described entering the McCaslin commissary to claim her for his bride and the warning lights flash:

> ... wearing better clothes than McCaslin and most of the other white men the boy knew habitually wore, who entered the room like a white man and stood in it like a white man ... and who talked like a white man too, looking at him ... as a mature and contained white man ... might have looked. (p.195)

Once married, he and Fonsiba move to Arkansas, where Ike visits them in their ramshackle log cabin, the husband reading

> before that miserable fire for which there was not wood sufficient to last twenty-four hours.... (p.198)

We have before us a picture of whitened negroes betraying

themselves. Ike is desperate.

> Dont you see? ... Dont you see? This whole land, the whole
> South, is cursed? ... Granted that my people brought the
> curse on to the land: maybe for that reason their descendants
> alone can—not resist it, not combat it—maybe just endure
> and outlast it until the curse is lifted. Then your people's turn
> will come because we have forfeited ours. But not now. Not
> yet. Dont you see? (p.198)

Fonsiba's preacher-husband doesn't. His farm (a legacy from his
father, who fought with the Yankees in the War) may be barely
productive, but he is kept alive by the belief that he is seeing a
new era 'dedicated...to freedom, liberty, and equality for all'
(p.199). For Ike, this is sheer 'imbecility'. His plea to Fonsiba is
therefore urgent. What, he asks her, is the value of your freedom
if it merely allows you to join the white man's civilisation that is
the United States? Stay, rather, with the South, for only there will
freedom, if it ever comes, be worth achieving. Now, Fonsiba is a
McCaslin, Lucas's sister; unlike her husband, she is not black
but 'coffee-coloured'. Yet she, too, turns down his appeal: '"I'm
free", she said' (p.200). Ike echoes her a short while later when
he rejects his kinsman's pleas not to give up ownership of the
land. 'I am free,' he says, but his freedom is, in this context, a
true liberation in that it is designed to save his people from time,
not perpetuate their bondage to it, as Fonsiba's does.

It is impossible to understand Ike's reasoning here without
taking into account his interpretation of the Civil War which
follows, one of the most remarkable passages in Faulkner, I
think. The South is God's own land, yet the whites there have
betrayed Him so thoroughly that He has begun to doubt His
own purpose. Like the Northerners, they have reduced America
to 'the same worthless tideless rock cooling in the last crimson
evening' (p.203).[7] Before repudiating the South, however, God
decides: '*Apparently they can learn nothing save through suffering,
remember nothing save when underlined in blood*—' (p.204). The war
which followed was therefore his attempt to *save* the South, to
make the whites there suffer for their sins by undergoing the
tribulations of their slaves. Their vices are the 'vices aped from
white men or that white men and bondage have taught them'
but their virtues are their own:

Because they will endure. They are better than we are.
Stronger than we are ... And more: what they got not only
from white people but not even despite white people because
they had it already from the old free fathers a longer time free
than us because we have never been free— (p.210)

It is an astonishing conclusion: the white Southerner is the real
slave, the negro Man as created by God in His own image.

That is the divine plan but, like all such plans, it is liable to
human interference, particularly from 'New England mech-
anics', 'females of both sexes' descended from slavers, 'the
Boston-bred (even when not born in Boston)'. In a polemic of
uncontrolled bitterness, Ike (with Faulkner close behind him)
excoriates Northerners for believing the war was of their
ordering; for one thing, they did not know the negro, grew fat on
his slavery and were themselves corrupt Europeans at heart,
'spinster aunts and uncles whose hands knew no callus except
that of the indicting pen'. The men who led the armies of the
North were 'the farmers of the central and middle-west' who
were 'already looking toward the Pacific coast' (p.204). Southerners were no such rootless folk. Nor were they the racialists and
lynching mobs. These were, in fact, Yankees-in-disguise, descendants of carpetbaggers who had come South ostensibly to
save the black man but who in reality were part of the

nameless horde of speculators in human misery, manipulators
of money and politics and land, who follow catastrophe....
(p.207)

Fonsiba and her husband are the dupes of such people, two of
the countless negroes 'upon whom freedom and equality had
been dumped overnight' and who 'misused it as human beings
always misuse freedom' (p.206). They believe that the war, since
it gave them their 'freedom', was about their emancipation. It
was not. It was crucially God's act to prevent the white man's
freedom, it being no longer in accord with His will. True
freedom is true service.

It is, in the context, a bold conclusion and Lucas is intended to
demonstrate it. 'But Lucas remained. He didn't have to stay'
(p.79). After the end of the war, he stayed with the McCaslins,

unlike his brother, Jim, who vanished, and his sister, Fonsiba. In staying, Lucas acknowledges that the South's drama concerns the white man. Accordingly, in the quasi-religious drama that is to follow, the negro's role will be doubly passive for it is not the sin that acts and suffers but the sinner.

The importance of 'innocence', which Oscar Wilde characterised as America's 'oldest tradition', now emerges more fully than before. Only innocence, it seems, can mediate between love, courage and honour and the 'wrong and shame' of history, a point well illustrated by the story of Henry (Lucas's son) and Roth, which, like the Lucas–Zack one before it, tells of two boys growing up together happily before Roth eats the 'bitter fruit' of his heritage and becomes aware of the divisions that separate him from his playmate and foster-mother. 'Grief' and 'shame' spur him on to heal the breach, but too late. Not grief and shame but only *another kind of innocence* can hope to re-establish harmony. Only when the heart and mind have been cleansed of guilt can the Henrys and Roths, the Lucases and Zacks be reconciled. And it can happen, whatever the charity of our daily deeds, only when the Southerner has been freed from history by a miraculous act of perception which will allow him to carry the feelings of childhood into manhood, either through 'the fire on the hearth' or 'the big woods'. That is why it is important for Ike to stress, first, that the source of the South's values is natural rather than human and, second, that its sphere of existence is God-dominated. In such a regime, 'time' is as of nothing.

It is presumably to some such childlike quality that Lucas's hunt for treasure is meant to return to us, though I am so far persuaded by Marvin Klotz's views as to regard his behaviour as inconsistent with the significance granted him elsewhere. Professor Klotz has examined the revisions made by Faulkner to his published stories prior to their incorporation in *Go Down, Moses* and concludes that the additions (over a hundred pages of them) 'almost everywhere [blur] thematic forms, destroying established characterization'.[8] I do not think this is true, since it is often the added material that helps bind the stories together and deepen their meaning. Yet Professor Klotz is surely right to draw attention to the discrepancy between 'A Point of Law', the unpublished 'Absolution' and (to a much lesser extent) 'Gold is Not Always' and what Faulkner has made of them in 'The Fire and the Hearth'. 'A Point of Law' is a deft, amusing 'yarn' concerning a negro's attempt to eliminate a competitor in moonshining but it sorts uneasily with the introduction of a man like Lucas.

> Here is a Southwestern humor character, running a whiskey still, wily and inventive and funny, called away at the apex of his machinations, puffed into a heroic, a mythic figure in the Odyssey of the Old South, then returned to his natural habitat as a producer of excellent corn whiskey.[9]

It is Lucas as 'a heroic, a mythic figure' who dominates the interpolated and revised passages, but what he is and what he is called on to perform are not always commensurate with each other. When he tells Edmonds about George Wilkins's still, he becomes

> ... not Negro but nigger, not secret so much as impenetrable, not servile and not effacing, but enveloping himself in an aura of timeless and stupid impassivity almost like a smell. (p.46)

The Lucas who is essential to *Go Down, Moses*'s argument is precisely not 'Negro', much less 'nigger'.

In his revisions, Faulkner did his best to smooth things over by modifying Lucas's dialect (this is true of the negroes in general) and making Roth Edmonds less haughty and his attitude to Lucas more than merely one of master and slave. In 'A Point of Law', he may order him to finish ploughing his field and Lucas obey as a good 'hand' should, but in the book he attends to the field only because it was always his intention to do so; his wishes and those of Edmonds happily coincide.

The revisions also show that Lucas is changing his habits. For about the past eight years, he has stopped going into Jefferson. Now, he has decided to 'quit farming', a potentially momentous decision which might help explain his search for treasure. Yet it is by no means clear how this accords with his criticism of Ike for 'relinquishing the land', especially since the purpose of the revisions has been to make his ties with the land as emphatic as possible. Nor is it clear how his discovery of 'a simple coin' while digging on the face of an Indian mound fits in with his beliefs. As he burrows away, an overhang collapses;

striking him a final blow ... not vicious so much as merely heavy-handed,[10] a sort of final admonitory pat from the spirit of darkness and solitude, the old earth, perhaps the old ancestors themselves. (p.30)

Since we are repeatedly told how close Lucas is to 'the old ancestors', we must presume that this is intended as a rebuke for his present activities, just as the coin is intended to remind him of the values he is in danger of betraying, yet the handling of the treasure hunt that follows is never more than anecdotal and, while this affords us some amusement, we never have the same sense of serious fun we had in 'Was'.

Only in his conflict with Zack (which, like the similar Roth–Henry material, was added to the original story) does Lucas behave in a manner which is compatible with his general significance, nowhere more so than when he lights 'the fire on the hearth', an image given much expanded treatment in the book.

It was hot, not scorching, searing, but possessing a slow, deep solidity of heat, a condensation of the two years during which the fire had burned constantly above it, a condensation not of fire but of time, as though not the fire's dying and not even water would cool it but only time would. (p.40)

It is this warmth, this sense of 'mutual embattlement' that Lucas and Molly felt during their enforced separation, that young boys could—and still can—feel, and with it we discover what is central to all the positive relations in the book, the spirit of love in adversity.

'Pantaloon in Black' draws attention to it by emphatic if tangential variation. First, a certain progression is insisted upon. Where once there existed the man–mule order ('Was'), certain paradoxical freedoms were enjoyed. Rider pays tribute to them by building another 'fire on the hearth' on his wedding night. Unfortunately, he is no longer part of the extended family and, however deep his love for Mannie, the loss is felt. The fact that he is not named a McCaslin (though Faulkner continued to think of him as such) only repeats the point: the negro now exists in a purely economic relation with his white overlord.

If the connection between Roth and Lucas is an uneasy one,

that between Rider and the deputy sheriff hardly exists. For the latter, 'niggers' aren't 'human': 'when it comes to the normal human feelings and sentiments of human beings, they might just as well be a damn herd of wild buffaloes' (p.113). The contrast between this view of Rider and what we know of his reaction to Mannie's death could not be more painful or obvious. The deputy's wife goes one worse, however: Rider makes no impact whatever on her as she feeds her husband and prepares for an evening's entertainment at the movies. The sheriff is at least moved to hostility; she, sunk in the trivia of daily life, is quite untouched. As 'Go Down, Moses' is later to insist, it is now only the negro who holds fast to true values because only he cares for

> the dead who either will not or cannot quit the earth yet although the flesh they once lived in has been returned to it.... (p.100)

This passage refers to Rider's love for Mannie but, in a more personal way, it characterises the broader themes stated by Lucas and Ike. Rider's 'dead' are their 'dead' ancestors.[11]

It will be apparent by now that, while there is no central narrative in *Go Down, Moses*, its stories may be said to pursue related aspects of a common subject from different points of view. Attention is concentrated on isolated periods, critical moments of backward and forward looking rather than on the continuities of history which are the South's enemy. In that context, 'Pantaloon in Black' may be regarded as a pendant to 'The Fire and the Hearth' and 'Was'. As such, it enriches our understanding of three topics—marriage, the power of the dead and black/white relations. Particular details also benefit from the process: the fire on the hearth, Rider's gambling (nicely contrasted with the sheriff's wife's genteel club game) and a negro's killing of a white man with a razor are all restatements of material we have met before, while items like the presence of a timber gang, a faithful mongrel and the death of a loved one as marking the approaching end of a way of life are all to be repeated in later episodes. Even so, we should not be too anxious to press this or any of the other stories into too unified a relation. It is, I take it, Faulkner's contribution to the art of fiction to have developed the technique of composing his material in flexible yet coherently interrelated parts which span different periods of time and ranges of temperament. It is a technique he worked at frequently and intelligently, realising that it was by developing it that he could best approach his subject.

II

With 'The Old People', we turn from one aspect of the theme, man's relations with man, to another, more embracing one, man's relations with the land. In the person of the Chickasaw chief Ikkemotubbe, alias Du Homme, alias Doom, that story has its beginning, for it was he who passed 'ownership' of the land to the white man and so helped introduce the concept to the South; the white man, in turn, made it coterminous with private property and, the geography and economics of the South being what they are, with slavery. Sam Fathers represents both aspects of the theme but in so far as he tilts the balance in favour of man's communal interest in nature, he is a more profound figure than Lucas. He is a royal being 'who had been a negro for two generations now but whose face and bearing were still those of the Chickasaw chief who had been his father' (p.118). Negro-hood, we notice again, is not a matter of skin colour but a condition of being which we may have forced on us or which we may elect for ourselves. In Sam, it signifies his bondage 'way down in Egypt's land', 'Like an old lion or a bear in a cage' (p.119) (as a passage added to the original story has it). Having been sold into slavery by his own people when they passed the wilderness to the white man, he bides the time until he can return people and land to their original condition.

> And as he talked about those old times and those dead and vanished men of another race from either that the boy knew, gradually to the boy those old times would cease to be old times and would become a part of the boy's present, not only as if they had happened yesterday but as if they were still happening, the men who walked through them actually walking in breath and air and casting an actual shadow on the earth they had not quitted. And more: as if some of them had not happened yet but would occur tomorrow, until at last it would seem to the boy that he himself had not come into existence yet, that none of his race nor the other subject race

... had come here yet; that although it had been his grandfather's ... and someday would be his own land which he and Sam hunted over, their hold upon it actually was as trivial and without reality as the now faded and archaic script in the chancery book in Jefferson ... and that it was he, the boy, who was the guest here and Sam Fathers's voice the mouthpiece of the host. (pp.122–3)

As Sam speaks, time and space are suspended and Ike returns to a state where no inalienable possessions or distinctions exist, an innocent realm which yet *contains* the highest knowledge. At that moment, he discovers that innocence, like negrohood, is a state of mind which a man may cultivate in reaffirmation of root values.

Perhaps the real Golden Age is not in nature or in history but in between them: in the instant when men establish their group with a pact which simultaneously unites them among themselves and unites the group with the natural world.[12]

Sam's part in the drama is better understood once he is related to 'Jobaker' and Boon Hogganbeck, the former wholly Chickasaw, a recluse living by his hunting and fishing, the latter almost white, despite his Chickasaw grandmother, the 'almost unratiocinative'[13] servant of the McCaslins and De Spains. Sam occupies an intermediate position, neither wholly withdrawn from nor wholly subservient to the white man's world. As such, he can act as mentor to Ike, and what he has to mediate is

an unforgettable sense of the big woods—not a quality dangerous or particularly inimical, but profound, sentient, gigantic and brooding, amid which [Ike] had been permitted to go to and fro at will, unscathed, why he knew not, but dwarfed and, until he had drawn honourably blood worthy of being drawn, alien. (p.126)

Killing his first deer and being bathed in its blood by Sam is the boy's first experience of this 'sense of the big woods'. At the same time, it commemorates his emergence as a man—or, rather, the moment when he loses his childhood innocence for another, more 'adult' state of innocence. Innocence is preserved while being extended, and the process is seen as a Keatsian moment which defeats time, forever still yet forever active within the unchanging stillness. The vision of a leaping buck which no-one but he and Sam see is its expression:

> and ... the wilderness watched them pass, less than inimical now and never to be inimical again since the buck still and for ever leaped, the shaking gun-barrels coming constantly and forever steady at last, crashing, and still out of his instant of immortality the buck sprang, forever immortal.... (pp.127–8)

In killing the deer, Ike reanimates man's sacramental tie with 'the big woods' but he also, as a significant passage added to the original 'Delta Autumn' has it, accepts the obligation laid on him to vindicate its death by opposing

> the tamed land, the old wrong and shame itself, in repudiation and denial at least of the land and the wrong and shame even if he couldn't cure the wrong and eradicate the shame.... (p.248)

Accordingly, he resolves to remain all his life what he becomes at the moment of the deer's death, a hunter, the human incarnation of the spirit of 'The Old People', just as the ghost-buck is its natural one. In this way, he enters the mysteries of man's dependence on nature, which Sam salutes in traditional manner with the raising of his right hand, palm outwards: 'Oleh, Chief, Grandfather'. It is a hallucinatory moment. What is here revealed is Sr. Paz's 'Golden Age' of a makeshift community in contest with the wilderness and drawing its ideals from it in the ritual of the hunt, which formalises the tension between man's conscientious exploitation of nature and nature's disinterested reception of his design. Lost in this vision of the woods, Ike feels himself gathered up into nature and, for a moment, breathing ceases:

> ... there was only his heart, his blood, and in the following silence the wilderness ceased to breathe also, leaning, stooping overhead with its breath held, tremendous and impartial and waiting. Then the shaking stopped too, as he had known it

would, and he drew back the two heavy hammers of the gun.
(p.131)

It is the moment before discharge (a rite, that is, of puberty), an
absorbing state of unity with the world which carries Ike into the
heart of things. This is what the 'heart already knows'.

> The 'Golden Age is in ourselves' and it is momentary: that
> infinitesimal instant in which ... we feel not like an isolated
> ego, nor like an 'us' lost in the labyrinth of the ages but like a
> part of the whole, a throbbing in the universal respiration—
> outside of time, outside of history....[14]

It is an experience that Ike is to discover with increasing
complexity in deer, bear and snake, creatures at once fleshly and
ghostly, natural and supranatural.

III

In the next story, we are introduced to the bear, old Ben. Like
the deer, Ben represents the 'big woods', this time not in relation
to Sam's man-centred universe but the wilderness as seen by the
earliest hunter of the 'old wild life' in the 'old dead time'. (This,
perhaps, is why he should remind us of primitive man in some
ways.) As such he manifests a destructive principle, the one
described in a passage about an Indian mound from 'A Bear
Hunt' (an unrelated story first published in 1934).

> ... it possessed inferences of secret and violent blood, of
> savage and sudden destruction.... [A] dark power still
> dwelled or lurked there, sinister, a little sardonic, like a dark
> and nameless beast lightly and lazily slumbering with bloody
> jaws....[15]

Faulkner himself clarified the bear's identity in two passages of
commentary. Nature, he said, is 'a blind force, that by its own
standard is neither good nor bad'.[16]

> 'The Bear', as a story, was a truth of the bears and animals,
> was a natural force which represented not a deliberate evil,

not a satanic evil, but the quality of evil in sample size and force which exists, which man has got to face and not be afraid of, that force itself has certain rights which must be respected.[17]

And also

The wilderness to me was the past, which could be the old evils, the old forces, which were by their own standards right and correct, ruthless.... To me, the wilderness was man's past, that man had emerged. The bear was a symbol of the old forces, not evil forces, but the old forces which in man's youth were not evil, but that were in man's blood, his inheritance, his (instinctive) impulses came from that old or ruthless malevolence, which was nature. His dreams, his nightmares....[18]

Between man and nature there exists a tension since man uses nature both positively and negatively, as Sam and Ike do, serving it as priest and acolyte at the same time as they ritually despoil it. The bear is a hostile version of that tension whereas the buck and Sam belong to a later, more accommodating regime when nature and man enter a 'game' of opposition between hunter and hunted: 'there was something running in Sam Fathers's veins which ran in the veins of the buck too' (p.248). That Sam, who already owns black, red and white 'blood', should own animal blood, too, only emphasises his status as spokesman for the interdependence of nature and a rude state of civilisation. The bear, however, returns us to a realm in which nature was sovereign, so that when Sam, son of Du Homme, The Man, salutes him as 'the man', he recognises an animal chieftain, a *rival* centre of power that much nearer the root of life.

We may thus distinguish between three separate, successive states: the world of the bear, out of which man struggled to escape; then the world of Sam Fathers, when men achieved equilibrium with nature; and finally the world of today, when man is master of all he surveys—a world which is, ironically, as terrifying to hunters like Ike as the bear's was to the first Americans. The wilderness is therefore not only a phenomenal reality. Nor is it only a source of permanent value (since it is morally neutral, it can be used as a gauge of conduct; since it is inhuman, it will as often oppose as collaborate with man; either way, he draws his 'dreams and nightmares' from it). It is a record of how generations of men have responded to its challenge. It is true history.

When Sam baptises Ike in the deer's blood, he initiates the boy into the second state (the man–nature balance) in repudiation of the third (the man-as-master state), and the initiation is all the more convincing for being founded on an unsentimental view of nature's 'ruthless malevolence'. But the bear goes further.

> an old bear, fierce and ruthless ... with the fierce pride of liberty and freedom, ... seeming deliberately to put it into jeopardy in order to savour it and keep his old strong bones and flesh supple and quick to defend and preserve it; (pp.210–11)

The South has fashioned Ben after the image of its own aspirations and made them conditional on the occupation which brought it into contact with him. That is why, far from being owners of the land, Sam and his 'old people' have remained shiftless, and why, when Ike becomes a man, he becomes a *hunter*, one who is physically mature but who, in his relation with 'the big woods', is a very child.

> It was in him too, ... an eagerness, passive; an abjectness, a sense of his own fragility and impotence against the timeless woods, yet without doubt or dread; a flavour like brass[19] in the sudden run of saliva in his mouth, a hard sharp constriction either in his brain or his stomach.... (p.141)

As his encounters with the bear proceed,

> It seemed to him that he could see them, the two of them, shadowy in the limbo from which time emerged and became time: the old bear absolved of mortality and himself who shared a little of it. (p.144)

Thanks to Ben, Ike has become a perpetual youth of the race, one of those primitives who once roamed the woods with 'club or stone axe or bone arrow' in their hands. Bear, woods and man are now as they were centuries ago, without chronology, language, or self-consciousness. It is the desired consummation of existence.

More and more, we begin to understand that, whatever Part IV of 'The Bear' has to say, the real enemy of the South is time or linear process. Process means more people and therefore settlements and therefore Jefferson and therefore the United States. Process means civilisation, not culture, to men who can never be content with the hunting life because it entails growing up in mind as well as in body. And this, in turn, entails identity—what is me—but also possession—what is mine. If only process could be mastered! By the end of the story, it is, heroically, almost done, and all because of the wilderness' revelations. The bear himself defeats process:

> an anachronism indomitable and invincible out of an old dead time, a phantom, epitome and apotheosis of the old wild life ..., solitary, indomitable, and alone; widowered childless and absolved of mortality.... (pp.136–7)

This is insistent language gripped by a powerful surge of feeling and it tells us of a second 'phantom' that is taking Ike deeper into the myth. It is no coincidence that the description could as truthfully be made of him as an old man. He has become his beloved bear.

Ike sees the bear as immortal for a further reason, however: he has to place him in the context of contemporary America and wishes to secure him from it. In an early encounter, he is petrified by the bear:

> He did not move, holding the useless gun which he knew *now he would never fire at it, now or ever*.... (p.143)

The words I have italicised were added in revision to the story. They emphasise that, while Ike is a hunter, he is also a modern consciousness. Listening to Sam talk in 'The Old People', he had imagined that the 'old times' were returned but he has to strive to ensure that what he imagined becomes a permanent reality. Metaphor must yield to fact.

Yet if his renunciation of the McCaslin land follows from his discovery of the meaning of hunting as a way of life, his decision to spare Ben derives from another revision he has been forced to make: namely, that the hunt can no longer be the pursuit of quarry. Circumstances have made it imperative that it be valued for its effect on the hunter's heart, not the animal's body. Fact has here yielded to metaphor and the hunt become a Keatsian chase of love, with no before or after.

That is not how others see it. Old Ben behaves in the only way he knows, killing a colt and so inviting his own death, which Sam is instrumental in providing since that is the only thing he can do. Lion, his protégé, fulfils his duties as singlemindedly. Both Sam and Ben are aged beings without progeny, unaware of their condition, but Ike knows that, by acting as they do, they are destroying the only world that could support them.

For all these reasons, therefore, he is committed to a more complicated imagining of man's tie with earth than Sam is capable of. When, on one of his sorties after Ben, he divests himself of compass, watch and stick, he becomes the truest hunter, being guided about the woods simply by his wits and the wilderness itself. Eventually, he is led back to his starting point by the bear's prints and there experiences a vision that carries him to a new compact with nature. With much trepidation, the boy senses the woods 'coalesce'; a ray of sunlight picks out compass and watch, and the bear appears before him tremendously. At that moment, all is still. No action is promised or threatened. Then, Ben turns to go but, before doing so, gives Ike a parting look. Ancient enemies enter into an ineffable understanding of the tragedy that has brought them to the verge of extinction. The last bear and the last 'man' meet and, in their failure to attack, acknowledge their need for each other.

Three years later, this compact is put to the test when Ike and Sam ambush the bear. As Ike's little fyce prepares to launch an assault, Ike suddenly flings his gun away and throws himself after the dog. Once more, he refuses to press home the attack; once more, the bear excuses him his forwardness and vanishes. Sam may complain of the missed opportunity but is careful not to take a shot himself. As at the moment of Ben's death a few years later, it seems something within him breaks, as if to warn him of the fate that is about to overtake the woods.

Having acceded to his superior condition, Ike is soon enough isolated in it. The deaths of Ben and Sam and Lion are all traditionally executed and with them dies any immediate hope of recovery for the South. Nevertheless, when he turns twenty-one, he relinquishes his ownership of the land, giving up not the principle of ownership itself but his share in it (*pace* Thomas Sutpen, whose land, interestingly enough, forms the setting for Ike's drama). He is supported by the facts he discovers in the McCaslin commissary books. As he pores over the entries, he finds the seeds of hope and disaster lying juxtaposed together, first, his grandfather's miscegenation with his slave, Eunice, and his incest with their daughter, Tomasina, as well as the ownership of land practised by Ikkemotubbe and his forbears, men equally culpable for making 'the land already accursed ... , already tainted before any white man owned it' (p.184).[20] But these crimes can be corrected, he believes, if only the 'heart' can be touched afresh. And there, in the commissary records, lies the proof, for they tell him of other men besides his grandfather— men like Buck and Buddy with their 'manumission in title at least of Carothers McCaslin's slaves' (and that 'during the two decades before the Civil War'). Such men are after his 'heart', as are the anonymous farmers and hunters he reads about,

> not alone of his own flesh and blood but of all his people, not only the whites but the black ones too, who were as much a part of his ancestry as his white progenitors, and of the land which they had all held and used in common and fed from and on and would continue to use in common without regard to colour or titular ownership.... (p.191)

It is *this* version of the past that he prefers to the one inaugurated by Doom and his grandfather. In doing so, he becomes a man of mixed blood himself—and all because of that moment in the wilderness when he met a bear and learnt, long before studying the records,

> *Courage and honour and pride, and pity and love of justice and of liberty. They all touch the heart, and what the heart holds to becomes truth, as far as we know truth.* (p.212)[21]

In the fourth section, Ike discusses his inheritance with Cass seriously (Carothers, Fonsiba) and comically (Hubert Beauchamp, Percival Brownlee). Unfortunately, their discussion is no more than a mixed achievement, mainly because of Faulkner's view of the negro. While he was sincerely conscious of the wrongs of slavery, he was not as deeply agitated by it as he was by the sin against the land (a point suggested by *Big Woods*, a later collection of stories composed largely of material from the present work which all but drops the slavery theme in favour of the wilderness theme). For him as for Ike, the first task is to restore the land to its original purpose; thereafter, the racial problem will solve itself. Perhaps, but that is to avoid any adequate register of what life had been like for the slave, and it makes his art much less sure when it comes to describing the more human aspects of his theme. History is not as amenable to the perceptions of the 'heart' as nature, even when it is God's history rather than man's that is being adumbrated.

Much of Ike's talk about God is embarrassing in its arguments, as Glauco Cambon suggests:

The romantic South's reaction to what is to him an ineluctable desecration of his world sways between spontaneous myth and debatable ideology, or better, it verges on the latter at certain points where the experience of primal wonder and awe which throbs at the originating center of his writing makes room for tentative political statements.[22]

Or not so tentative, as the case may be. Such statements make for impure art and weaken *Go Down, Moses* by avowing views which invite party debate. *The Unvanquished*, too, proposes a revision of our views on slavery and the war, but its means are consistently creative. Disbelief may thus, if necessary, be suspended. Faulkner's impulse here is true but it has been pushed too far and the magnificent romance achieved elsewhere can only suffer for it. Ike's politics of civilisation are incommensurate with the myth of the wilderness. His greatest moments—and the truest—are accomplished in silence.

The lapse I have been describing is worth dwelling on since it marks the point in Faulkner's career which opened the way for the inferior works that followed, with the exception of *The Reivers*. We note the appearance in the fourth section of prolonged syntactical structures and an oracular tone of the sort which were later to be used extensively. It is surprising how infrequent these are in the earlier books and how often they are taken to be

representative of Faulkner's style. The fact that serious criticism
of his work coincided with the later, inferior novels is no doubt at
the root of the misapprehension. Indeed, such inflation usually
alerts us to insecurity of insight, being a sort of verbal fancy-
dress designed to bolster unprepossessing material and smother
the reader with impressiveness. The significance of this change
in style is all the more noticeable when we recall that *Go Down,
Moses* brings to an end Faulkner's middle period, a burst of six
books in almost as many years, beginning with *Pylon* in 1935 and
including four of his greatest achievements, *Absalom, Absalom!*,
The Unvanquished, *The Hamlet* and *Go Down, Moses*. The closer
Faulkner came to the contemporary scene, the more uneasy the
relation between myth and quotidian reality grew as the distance
between them widened. The conquest of nature has gone too far,
the traditional hero is now too isolated for any satisfactory
account of their connection to be attempted. Moreover, Faulkner
is no longer committed to youthful perspectives and there
effectively matures begins in *Go Down, Moses* the concept of
endurance, a powerfully felt emotion answering the failure of the
young to confront the realities of life in the twentieth century.
What is sought for are

> virtues not of a historical and accidental but of an ideal and
> permanent kind; qualities not given but achieved, by conduct
> and by art, through discipline and submission. The new
> innocence is not other than conscience.[13]

In a sense, anything that Ike did after 'The Bear' would be
unsatisfactory. It was brave of Faulkner as it was honest to
venture further. In 'Delta Autumn', we meet an old man
(characteristically, he has no life worth recording between youth
and maturity) who is just as ever beset by his McCaslin blood.
Nor has his environment prospered. The countryside makes way
for neon-lights and automobiles, trains move where panthers
once ran,

> and all that remained of that old time were the Indian names
> on the little towns and usually pertaining to water—Aluschas-
> kuna, Tillatoba, Homochitto, Yazoo. (p.241)

The wilderness itself still exists, albeit at crisis point.

He had watched it, not being conquered, destroyed, so much as retreating since its purpose was served now and its time an outmoded time ... until what was left of it seemed now to be gathered and for the time arrested in one tremendous destiny of brooding and inscrutable impenetrability.... (p.242)

The imagery of arrested movement here is significant. It tells us that, even now, Ike is trying to reconcile man's capacity for destruction with a belief in his ability to master it. He himself has tried to set an example, only to lose his wife (who is absent from the magazine stories in all but name) as well as any son he might have had. In return, he and the land have become 'coevals',

running out together, not toward oblivion, nothingness, but into a dimension free of both time and space where once more the untreed land ... of rank cotton ... would find ample room for both.... (pp.250–1)

Wilderness and agricultural settlement *can* coexist, after all, as Sam Fathers insisted they could, but they do so in 'a dimension free of both time and space', the Golden Age of 'the old-world people'.

When Ike passed ownership of the McCaslin estate to Roth's grandfather, he shifted the burden on to other shoulders so that he might alleviate it but he has inadvertently left Roth a harsh, cynical man, one who actively dislikes him for his virtuous air and devotion to the past. Ike's sententiousness is indeed annoying, though Roth himself is even less likeable. He is guilty of killing does, thus striking at the very continuance of the hunt, and callously discards his mistress, thus repeating the offence of the first Carothers. Nature and human beings are exploited as objects of use—the old sin of masters. But Ike, too, is guilty of an arrogant virtue. For him, the choice between Roth's dismissal of his mistress and her attachment to him narrows to a single question: is the fateful pattern of the McCaslins' behaviour to be broken (the woman being a descendant of Tennie and Turl and thus—unbeknown to Roth—related to him) or are the claims of love in this particular instance to be respected? His answer is not in doubt: he sends her away, oblivious of the harm this causes her. We know that his choice has been forced on him by his convictions and that it is not, as in Roth's case, made heedlessly. Even so, it is ironical that it should coincide with Roth's will— more, that it should oblige him to act for Roth in sending the woman away with a cash payment, though he placates his conscience by offering her General Compson's horn, emblem of the hunt. It is an immensely magnanimous gift, but the circumstances could not be less auspicious for its grateful acceptance. Nor will all Ike's motives for the gift bear close examination. As in his own marriage, he has been forced to sacrifice love for the goal he has set himself, in the belief that love is not yet possible for the McCaslins. They will have to suffer a great deal more before it is. But since it was the spirit of love which was to guide the white man, such sacrifice is critical. Ike's means are destroying his ends.

When Roth sent Samuel Beauchamp away for an act of theft, he condemned him to the white man's culture—hair treated, clothes inspired by glossy advertisements and speech betraying 'anything under the sun but a southern voice or even a negro voice' (p.259). To stay in the South is to suffer injustice but moving away from it causes even more injustice. That, precisely, was what Ike tried to teach Fonsiba and her husband yet he persists in ordering Roth's woman to leave.

> Go back North. Marry: a man in your own race. That's the only salvation for you—for a while yet, maybe a long while yet. We will have to wait. Marry a black man. (p.257)

Black and white must now stay apart if the South is to survive, with the proviso that the white Southerner accept his guilt and act upon it. If he does not (as Roth does not), no hope exists. If he does (as Ike and Gavin do), some hope remains, though, as Ike's encounter with Roth's mistress shows, it can never be more than tenuous. Indeed, the fear is upon him that, whatever he says or does, his people will destroy themselves as surely as they are destroying the wilderness.[24]

Ike's nerves now breaks. He sees a land ruined for the benefit of commuting white capitalists and upstart city negroes in the North while the labouring poor, black and white, suffer for them.

usury and mortgage and bankruptcy and measureless wealth, Chinese

and African and Aryan and Jew, all breed and spawn together until no
man has time to say which one is which nor cares. . . . No wonder the
ruined woods I used to know dont cry for retribution!. . . The
people who have destroyed it will accomplish its revenge.
(p.258; second ellipsis in the text).

The future mocks the past: there is wealth, but not nature's
wealth, mixed blood but without cultural homogeneity, the
plunder of nature but without a complex relation to bind man to
the woods. A passionate anger lets rip and the result is as
unlovely as Ike's meditations on God's plan for the South or his
camping pronouncements.

Contrast this with Mollie Beauchamp's grief for Samuel
Beauchamp, so profound and dignified—and so much less
lonely. Molly has Gavin Stevens (who, with his editor friend,
represents white Jefferson's better self) to help with the funeral
arrangements and Miss Worsham to comfort her, Miss Worsham's childhood friendship, unlike its male equivalents, having
lasted well into age.[25] Once more, we are directed to 'the brick
hearth on which the ancient symbol of human coherence and
solidarity smouldered' (p.267). The light is alive, but fading and
angry. It is a steadying image, one which just manages to renew
hope after 'Delta Autumn''s rush of despair.

Nevertheless it is Ike's gnashing of teeth that we remember
before Molly's fire and, above both, the sound of Boon trying to
piece together his broken gun at the end of 'The Bear'. Boon's
incompetent marksmanship, once humorously regarded, now
carries with it suggestions of a wider sense of failure, a sense that
the hunting life has all but come to an end. As in 'Go Down,
Moses', however, there is a counterbalancing source of strength
to turn to. Sam, Lion and Ben are all buried in the earth but they
are also alive, 'of earth, . . . leaf and twig and particle, air and sun
and rain and dew and night, acorn oak and leaf and acorn again,
dark and dawn and dark and dawn again in their immutable
progression and, being myriad, one' (p.234). Cass Edmonds had
earlier reflected on the rhythm of nature:

And the earth is shallow; there is not a great deal of it before
you come to the rock. And the earth dont want to just keep
things, hoard them; it wants to use them again. Look at the
seed, the acorns, at what happens even to carrion when you

try to bury it: it refuses too, seethes and struggles too until it reaches light and air again, hunting the sun still. (p.133)

We recall 'the dead who either will not or cannot quit the earth' from 'Pantaloon in Black' and Sam Fathers's evocation of men from the past in 'The Old People'. It is the same rhythm Ike experiences when he revisits his old hunting grounds and meets a rattlesnake,

the old one, the ancient and accursed about the earth, fatal and solitary ... , evocative of all knowledge and an old weariness and of pariah-hood and of death. (p.235)

He greets it as Sam had greeted the phantom buck (and as Issetibbeha's negro had greeted a cottonmouth moccasin in 'Red Leaves'): '"Chief," he said: "Grandfather."' His greeting, though, goes beyond a salute to the woods Sam Fathers knew, beyond even those of Ben, for it hails the presence of something greater than either of them: the quintessence of nature which characterises the wilderness Sam and Ben have, in their separate ways, represented.

The snake is even more malevolent than the bear, 'the old one, the ancient and accursed about the earth, fatal and solitary...'. When Ike meets it, he discovers the rankness of life. At the same moment, he is presented with another proleptic image of himself in nature, one which anticipates the time when he himself will apear as 'fatal and solitary' as the snake to men like Roth. Ike, that is to say, is being drawn to 'pariah-hood' in response to the 'death' he smells in the air and is increasingly identifying himself with the very forces that threaten destruction to his ideal of the coexistence of man and nature. It is a profound choice. Once more, as John Armstrong has it, we build our ideals on the flux. Once more, as Leo Marx has it, we seek to reconcile primitivism and pastoralism, play Prospero to Sycorax and Caliban.[26] The bear was more solid, manlike. The snake is evanescent, the repulsive reptile-other but, like buck and bear, it remains phantom in essence. This 'entity walking on two feet and free of all laws of mass and balance' is a metaphorical extension of Ike's declared state, the man who has elected 'freedom' to pursue the oldest world, 'all knowledge'. When Ike greets the snake, he makes the final pledge.

At this time, the woods exist: so too does the planing mill which will help devour them. The concluding scene of 'The Bear', in delicate symbolic fashion, helps us understand how the contest between them will go. Having greeted the snake, Ike goes on to meet Boon in a clearing between forest and open land— marginal territory. Boon sits under 'the Gum Tree'.

> At first glance the tree seemed to be alive with frantic squirrels. There appeared to be forty or fifty of them leaping and darting from branch to branch until the whole tree had become one green maelstrom of mad leaves, while from time to time, singly or in twos and threes, squirrels would dart down the trunk then whirl without stopping and rush back up again as though sucked violently back by the vacuum of their fellows' frenzied vortex. (pp.235–6)

It is a brilliant moment. Here, in variation, is Mr Armstrong's snake-encircled tree, combining the nourishing and threatening, stability and movement. Having a short while before projected his life into the snake's nature, Ike is rewarded with a phenomenal image of the moment which combines pursuit, activity, alteration—the dangerous wild woods—with settlement, decorum, order—the clearing. It is an image of man's reciprocity with nature, its 'concordant generality'.

> for vilest things
> Become themselves in her. . . .

Secure in this knowledge, Ike is at last ready to perceive that seeming irreconcileables may indeed be resolved into tensions, that change and movement are indispensable, as the snake suggests, to our notions of paradise. Why else should the woods have accepted the human intruder if not to enter into an adversarial relation with him? What ownership planted grew in time to the machine, at first the locomotive (the Sartoris railroad being the chief instance) and now the planing mill and urban centre such as Memphis, where the bears are found caged in a zoo and fed on ice cream and lady fingers. The ancient hierarchy is all but vanished and with it secret modes of understanding. Yet, as Cass Edmonds remarks, continuities and reconciliations within the bounds of conscience remain and this leads Ike to understand that life consists not of the *single* Keatsian moment but of a *succession* of them, each a durable but temporary balancing of oppositions, secure and, within its boundaries, vital.

A hint in this direction comes with the train, which 'resembled a small dingy harmless snake vanishing into weeds . . . [running] between the twin walls of unaxed wilderness as of old' (p.227). The train may once have 'brought with it into the doomed wilderness even before the actual axe the shadow and portent of the new mill . . . ' (p.229) but it *has* been accommodated. In the same way, the snake typifies change, hurtful change, but also a degree of stability, as in its movements, when the head appears static, almost complete in itself.

The questions posed by the train-snake simile are these: may not machine-age man enter into a new concordat with what is left of the woods? May not the process which has led the South into peril be adjusted to the very different process of nature, whose rhythms provide a clue to the fundamental structural solution? Ike's 'new innocence', that is, his conscience, alerts him to the drift. The contradictions awaiting him are, as 'Delta Autumn' shows, terrible and Faulkner keeps them steadily before us, but just as the negro's suffering has some effect on Gavin Stevens's generation in 'Go Down, Moses', so nature's suffering is exercising its influence on Ike and guiding him to his conclusion in the great images gathered at the end of 'The Bear'. These tell first of the collapse of the past: the gum tree is squirrel-infested round its trunk and in its branches; Boon, the last of the 'old people' and himself its meagrest representative, sits underneath, his gun 'dismembered', hammering at it 'with the frantic abandon of a madman', resentful of any intrusion into his solitude. Yet, above the failed hunter, the tree of stability and the squirrels of impermanence remain. As in a vision, they announce the death of one era and the birth of another. It will be centred on the old core of things but it will also embrace change, embrace even—as the squirrels suggest: 'frantic', 'maelstrom', 'mad', 'sucked violently', 'frenzied vortex'—the calamitous times that are upon us. As they dart about the tree, it is difficult to tell whether the squirrels' frenzy (and Ike's attitude to them as he observes them) is one of joy or grief. 'The pastoral design, as always, circumscribes the pastoral ideal'.[27]

The locomotive, originally regarded as harmless, actually

heralded the axe and the planing mill but it remains a 'labouring miniature puffing into the immemorial woods-face ... carrying to no destination or purpose sticks which left nowhere any scar or stump as the child's toy loads and transports and unloads its dead sand and rushes back for more ... ' (p.228). This description of the train as a toy, a mere plaything, is only a verbal victory, of course, a triumph of the imagination which translates the pastoral ideal from history (where it will always fail) into the heart (where it is sure to flower). After all, the logs *do* have a destination and purpose; scars and stumps remain for all to see. Yet Faulkner cannot help emphasising the absence of permanent value in such activity, especially when he compares the locomotive's 'crawling' movement with that of the buck, which Ike remembers bolting

> as the earth-bound supposedly move but crossing as arrows travel, groundless, elongated, three times its actual length and even paler, different in colour, as if there were a point between immobility and absolute motion where even mass chemically altered, changing without pain or agony not only in bulk and shape but in colour too.... (p.229)

Here again is that magical moment in space and time 'between immobility and absolute motion' when transformations that apparently defy both are realised. That is why, endangered as the woods are, Faulkner can only marvel at the puniness of its enemies.

> [The trees] did not change, and, timeless, would not, anymore than would the green of summer and the fire and rain of fall and the iron cold and sometimes even snow.... (p.230)

Timelessness and the seasonal, immobility and motion (as in *The Marble Faun*) are gradually being worked into metaphors whose substance is affirmative. Man *will* outlast the havoc he has wreaked. The woods *will* survive any number of axes. Did not Lena Grove flourish in a land full of planing mills? With that assurance, Ike's belief in endurance is finally confirmed, not because the possibility of catastrophe has been avoided but because it is so frighteningly sensed.

It is not easy for a man like Ike, in whose lifetime the hunting grounds have moved to the edge of destruction, to manage the sudden clash between nature and the machine. But both snake and squirrel-infested tree promise him that history is not linear nor only a flux: it has a rhythm, recurrent rather than repetitive, which saves as well as spends life. Nor is paradise ever lost for, so long as the possibility of its loss remains, so long will it survive—indeed, without that possibility, it would never have existed. In that light, the figure of Boon, while it attests to the breakdown of one human line, provides the assurance that the folly of man may protect as well as threaten. The squirrels are safe from *him*.

By an interesting coincidence, Ike remembers Ash, the cook (another poor shot), while on his way to the clearing. On the very day that Sam baptised him in the buck's blood, he allowed his prey to escape. The conjunction is comforting, as is the context. Moving once again without compass and with complete confidence through the woods, he pauses to pay homage to Sam Fathers at his grave. Nearby, he notices the concrete markers pegged out by the lumber company to establish 'the plot which Major De Spain had reserved out of the sale'. That much, at least, is secure from the axe. But nature promises more. These markers are 'lifeless and shockingly alien' in a place where

> dissolution itself was a seething turmoil of ejaculation, tumescence, conception, and birth, and death did not even exist. (p.233)

The same meaning awaits him when he finally gains the clearing to find Boon. Indeed, at first he imagines that the noise of Boon's hammering the barrel of his gun with the breech comes *not from the clearing but the railway line*. It is a revealing confusion, for this 'queerly hysterical beating of metal on metal' carries its own message as it reaches him from the woods: the woods, that is, contain the machine, have *always* contained the machine, as the snake itself (associated both with the woods and the machine) implies. Once that is grasped, he can see that Boon's dismembered gun obeys the same law which the bodies of Sam, Lion and Ben have already succumbed to. This, in turn, discloses the truth that, just as the 'machinery' of guns has been accepted as integral to the hunt, so the 'machinery' of train, axe and planing mill can be disciplined to human purpose. In the winter of earth, with death and sadness filling the atmosphere and snakes covering the ground in profusion, the promise of the difficult supersession of life, snake to bear to buck, is reasserted: 'Chief, Grandfather.'

The fifth section of 'The Bear' constitutes one of the greatest reaches of the imagination I know, greater than any other in the modern novel. In its lyric beauty, its simplicity and grave nobility of utterance, it achieves 'a sombre majesty beyond anything else in American literature'.[28] It is a finely orchestrated piece of writing in which every symbol yields the amplest riches, best glossed by Richard Wilbur in his 'Looking into History, III':

> Now, old man of the sea,
> I start to understand:
> The will will find no stillnesses
> Back in a stilled land.
>
> The dead give no command
> And shall not find their voice
> Till they be mustered by
> Some present fatal choice.
>
> Let me now rejoice
> In all impostures, take
> The shape of lion or leopard,
> Boar, or watery snake,
>
> Or like the comber break,
> Yet in the end stand fast
> And by some fervent fraud
> Father the waiting past,
>
> Resembling at the last
> The self-established tree
> That draws all waters toward
> Its live formality.

By taking the shape of his own lion, bear and watery snake, Ike, too, has tried to 'Father the waiting past'. Having done what he can, he passes the quest on to Gavin and like-minded Jeffersonians, though we are left in no doubt that, whatever he may have achieved at the end of 'The Bear', daily life throws up problem after problem which has to be faced not in the inspiring solitude of the woods but in the historical community.

The real conclusion to the book, however, comes with the fifth part of 'The Bear'. (James Early suggests that Faulkner once contemplated placing 'Delta Autumn' before 'The Bear' and that the fifth section of 'The Bear' was, save for the revision of 'Delta Autumn', written last.) Faulkner is no longer tempted by the language of argument, still less of low, mimetic narrative. Instead, he shapes his fiction about images of value. This is what he had done with Caddy's muddied drawers in *The Sound and the Fury*. In the same way, he took as the visual 'clue' to *Sartoris* John Sartoris' flamboyant leap to death from his crippled aeroplane, while the Luxembourg Gardens served for *Sanctuary*. A negro church in *Soldiers' Pay*, *Mosquitoes'* jungle and Lena Grove are further early examples. Meaning belongs with these images and nowhere else. Addie Bundren in *As I Lay Dying* represents the idea externalised, brought nearer the surface. Thereafter, the images begin to be grasped more securely: first, the brave new water-cum-land, men-cum-machine worlds of *Pylon* and *The Wild Palms* and then, in an accession to an altogether different level of understanding, the images of Sutpen's innocence, Eula's bounty and the wilderness of *Go Down, Moses*.

Why should this question of images matter so vitally? The answer, I think, is suggested by Ike's response to the snake-tree configuration. We have seen how this helps him to relinquish his claim to the land. We have also seen how giving up the land fails to have the effect he had hoped for mainly because, in trying to cure the sin against people simultaneously with the sin against the land, Ike has taken on an impossible task. The former is a moral question, the latter primarily a mythical one—related but different questions. In the same way, he has tried to show how both sins were part of a drama not so much human as divine: again, related but different questions. In both cases, the difficulty arises because he is trapped in the conflict between history and the imagination. Few men regarded slavery as he and his father did—or if they did, the history of the South would have been different; few Ikes gave up their land—or if they did, nobody noticed. What is more, his opposition to the McCaslins is intended to be selective. Yet, in giving up the title to the land, he has not acted to destroy the principle of ownership itself. Nor has he done anything, except indirectly (and then with confusion) to correct the injustice done to the negro. He may have won a small victory for himself but only at the cost of assuring Roth's defeat and, with it, his own. Nor is it enough simply to live the hunter's life. He may no longer be a landlord but others continue to hunt and own land or sell out to lumber companies before retiring from what has apparently become no more than a recreational activity for them. It may be that, in the circumstances, he has done as much as he can, but it is clear that it is nowhere near enough, particularly in the business of the land, where the mythical imperative has not been obeyed. It is not only that he has compromised where he should have stood firm; he has made the wrong *kind* of compromise. His father and uncle went further in their treatment of their slaves and, by keeping control up to the marriage with Sophonsiba, were able to steer their fortunes in the right direction.

Ike behaves *as if* he were living in a land that had been miraculously restored to its original condition; he does as he believes. Perhaps it is now impossible to find action which will cover all sides of the argument. Perhaps it can be done (if it can be done at all) by one who understands but does not actually know what either myth or history is. Until Part IV of 'The Bear', this was true of him. That is why that part of the story, like 'Delta Autumn', is so importantly flawed. Yet the images—those images symbolising patterned tensions unconstrained by circumstance—those images remain. In them, the heart's knowledge remains intact and triumphs over the world.

> Only by the form, the pattern
> Can words or music reach
> The stillness, as a Chinese jar still
> Moves perpetually in its stillness.

> Or say that the end precedes the beginning,
> And the end and the beginning were always there
> Before the beginning and after the end
> And all is always now.

Notes

PREFACE
1. Malcolm Cowley, *The Portable Faulkner* (New York, 1946); revised and expanded edn, 1967.
2. In *On Native Grounds* (London, 1943), p. 462. See, too, Delmore Schwartz's 'The Fiction of William Faulkner', *The Southern Review*, VII (Summer 1941), pp.145–60.
3. Walter J. Slatoff, *The Quest for Failure*, (Ithaca, new York, 1960).

CHAPTER 1: WRITER IN THE FARAWAY COUNTRY
1. The accent falls on the first syllable. 'Bayard' is pronounced 'Baird'. *Sartoris* is a shortened version of the original *Flags in the Dust*, prepared not by Faulkner but by his agent, Ben Wasson. Now that *Flags in the Dust* has been published, we can say that Wasson did his work with exemplary skill. Every virtue of the original was retained at the expense of the repetitious and redundant. *Il miglior fabbro*, indeed.
2. *Faulkner in the University*, eds Frederick L. Gwynn and Joseph L. Blotner (Charlottesville, Va., 1959), p. 285.
3. *The American* (London, 1949), pp.15–17. (First published 1877; the preface dates from 1906–8.)
4. *Faulkner in the University*, p. 22.
5. J.P. Sartre, 'William Faulkner's "Sartoris"', *Yale French Studies*, No. 10 (1952), pp. 95–9; 96.
6. Ibid., p. 98.
7. *These Thirteen*, p. 213.
8. Ibid., p. 271. We notice that this yearning for height is answered by Bayard's interest in flying machines, which reflect his enclosed, self-polluting world better than anything else could.
9. In 1926, the year before *Sartoris* was written, Faulkner elaborated his view that 'you don't commit suicide when you are disappointed in love. You write a book'—a book in which your hero commits suicide. (*Faulkner, A Biography*, Joseph Blotner (London, 1974), p. 228.)
10. Louis D. Rubin, Jr., *The Faraway Country* (Seattle, Washington, 1963), p.70.
11. Blotner, op. cit., p. 811.
12. See, too, poem XVIII of *A Green Bough*.
13. Rubin, op. cit., p. 14.
14. I refer to Faulkner's childhood love and wife-to-be, Estelle Oldham, who married Cornell Franklin, a lawyer, in April 1918. It is noteworthy that October 1918, is the month Faulkner's military ambitions came to an end

and that he should have identified it in this way with his earlier disappointment.

15. This complex underlies the view of art developed by Julius Kauffmann, Fairchild and Gordon. Their argument concerns Fairchild/Anderson's closeness to rural America and art's relation to universal truths. The greatest artists express these truths (associated with passion and suffering) with the immediacy of sculpture. Being young is associated with such revelatory concreteness, with Keatsian illuminations in which truth is captured but retains its particularity and potential in time rather than as an artefact.

16. Fairchild's girl, golden curls above the ordure, suggests how dangerously fragile this state is.

17. Both quotations draw from Poem xxxv of *The Green Bough*, where winter follows the death of the 'courtesan' summer and the poet senses 'An old sorrow sharp as woodsmoke on the air'. In *Sartoris*, the novelist describes September as possessing 'an ancient sadness sharp as woodsmoke on the windless air ... ' (p.27).

18.   The Raven bleak and Philomel
         Amid the bleeding trees were fixed,
         His hoarse cry and hers were mixed
         And through the dark their droppings fell...

   This is Faulkner's own poem, no. xxvii in *The Green Bough*, though the reader might be forgiven for mistaking it for the genuine article.

19. Anton Ehrenzweig, *The Hidden Order of Art* (London, 1967).

20. André Bleikasten, *Faulkner's 'As I Lay Dying'* (Bloomington, Ind., 1973), p.91.

21. In his review of *The Town*, Andrew Lytle drew attention to the triad composed of virgin (Linda Snopes), wife (Eula Varner) and mother (Maggie Mallison), complemented by Flem Snopes (legal husband), Manfred De Spain (physical husband) and Gavin Stevens (moral husband). He interpreted this as signifying the 'fearful impairment of man's competency towards womankind'. ('*The Town*: Helen's Last Stand', *The Sewanee Review*, lxv (Summer 1957), p. 479.)

CHAPTER 2: THE COMPSON DEVILMENT

1. R.W.B. Lewis, *The American Adam* (Chicago, 1959), p. 133.

2. See Winthrop Tilley, 'The Idiot Boy in Mississippi; Faulkner's "The Sound and the Fury"', *American Journal of Mental Deficiency*, lix (January 1955), pp. 374–7.

3. *Lion in the Garden*, eds James B. Meriwether and Michael Millgate (New York, 1968), p. 245.

4. *Faulkner, A Biography*, Joseph Blotner (London, 1974), p. 571.

5. Luster, we notice, thinks of Benjy as deaf and dumb, which shows how far from realistic such a mute is. Further proof of Benjy's metaphorical status may be gleaned from the fact that, although Quentin, Jason and Caddy appear in 'That Evening Sun' and 'A Justice', stories which were probably first written before *The Sound and the Fury*, Benjy does not.

6. Benjy's name is changed in 1900, when he is five years old and his deficiency apparent. Damuddy dies in 1898 (in his notes for the book,

Faulkner dated it 1900). Hence their association.

7. Nor only her. Versh tells Benjy his name has been altered because the family are 'making a bluegum out of you', i.e. a bogy.

8. Irene Kaluža, *The Functioning of Sentence Structure in the Stream-of-Consciousness Technique of William Faulkner's 'The Sound and the Fury'* (Krakow, 1967).

9. In 'Each in Its Ordered Place: Structure and Narrative in "Benjy's Section" of "The Sound and the Fury"' (*American Literature*, XXIV (January 1958), pp. 440–56), George R. Stewart and Joseph M. Backus suggest that Mr Compson's death coincides with the second anniversary of Caddy's marriage and that his funeral takes place on Mississippi's Memorial Day. His death thus marks the tragedy of the Confederacy and makes him a more substantial figure of interest than is usually allowed for.

10. A Prufrockian echo. 'Philoprogenitive' (p.121) and 'dust and desire' (p.122) also owe something to Eliot. Ida Fasel's 'A "Conversation" between Faulkner and Eliot' (*The Mississippi Quarterly*, XX (Fall 1967), pp. 195–207) offers an indiscriminate list of supposed correspondences, though Benjy's description of Caddy (p.70) and the fishing of the three boys (possibly Jason's hearing the lock at the end of his section) are more convincing examples suggested by her.

11. Elliott Coleman, quoted in Robert D. Jacobs, 'Faulkner's Tragedy of Isolation', *Southern Renascence*, eds Louis D. Rubin and Robert D. Jacobs (Baltimore, 1953), p. 174.

12. Blotner, op. cit., p. 573.

13. In 'Mayday', an allegory presented to Helen Baird in 1926, Faulkner also has the soldier-questor Sir Galwyn of Arthgyl join Little Sister Death by drowning himself.

14. 'Caddy' is 'Candace', an unusual name although it has a literary precedent in Charlotte Brontë's *Villette* (just as Temple Drake in *Sanctuary* may borrow her name from one of Jane Eyre's teachers at Lowood). Paulina Home's doll is called Candace 'for, indeed, it's begrimed complexion gave it much of an Ethiopian aspect', Candace being queen of the Ethiopians (Acts, 8, 27). In this, Caddy also owes something to Helen Baird, a dark-skinned, candid, vivacious woman with whom Faulkner fell in love in 1925. She contributes to the portraits of Cecily Saunders in *Soldiers' Pay*, Patricia Robyns in *Mosquitoes* (the novel is dedicated to her) and Charlotte Rittenmeyer in *The Wild Palms*.

15. *Faulkner, A Collection of Critical Essays*, ed. Robert Penn Warren (Englewood Cliffs, N.J., 1966), p. 252.

16. Richard Chase, *The American Novel and Its Tradition* (New York, 1957) p. 232.

17. Blotner, op. cit., p. 568.

18. Cleanth Brooks, 'Primitivism in "The Sound and the Fury"', *English Institute Essays, 1952*, ed. Alan S. Downer (New York, 1954), p.25.

19. Blotner, op. cit., p. 571.

20. Blotner, op. cit., p. 811.

21. Ibid., p. 811.

22. *Lion in the Garden*, pp. 147, 222 and 245 respectively.

23. James B. Meriwether, *The Literary Career of William Faulkner* (Princeton, N.J., 1961), p. 16.

24. Anton Ehrenzweig, *The Hidden Order of Art (London, 1967).*

25. Carvel Collins, 'The Interior Monologues of "The Sound and the Fury"', *English Institute Essays, 1952*.

26. Leon Edel, *The Psychological Novel 1900-1950* (London, 1955), p. 102.

27. Blotner, op. cit., p. 811.

28. *Faulkner at West Point*, eds Joseph L. Fant III and Robert Ashley (New York, 1964), pp. 109–11.

29. Robert M. Adams, 'Poetry in the Novel: or Faulkner Esemplastic', *The Virginia Quarterly Review*, xxix (Spring 1953), pp. 430–1.

30. Richard Chase, 'The Stone and the Crucifixion: Faulkner's "Light in August"', in *William Faulkner: Two Decades of Criticism*, eds Frederick J. Hoffman and Olga W. Vickery (East Lansing, Mich., 1951), p. 216.

CHAPTER 3: THAT TIME AND THAT WILDERNESS

1. *Essays, Speeches and Public Letters by William Faulkner*, ed. James B. Meriwether (London, 1967), pp. 62–4.

2. Gerald Langford, *Faulkner's Revision of 'Sanctuary'* (Austin, Texas, 1972), pp. 82–3.

3. More Eliot was lost in galley-revision: 'man's life ravels out in half-measures' (Prufrock); man is 'a shadow with an armful of feathers in a gale, on a black plain....' ('The Hollow Men').

4. Pertinently enough, he did so by capitalising on the method of retrospective biography first used to describe the Memphis gangster.

5. It is from such observations that the imagery of the Nobel Prize address derives.

6. Malcolm Cowley, *The Portable Faulkner* (New York, 1946); revised and expanded edn, 1976, p. xxii.

7. See Thomas L. McHaney, '"Sanctuary" and Frazier's (sic) Slain Kings', *The Mississippi Quarterly*, xxiv (Summer 1971), pp. 223–45.

8. *Lion in the Garden*, eds J.B. Meriwether and M. Millgate (New York, 1968), pp. 77–9.

9. In this reading, Popeye's life-history is a superfluous because factitious addition, though we notice the coincidence of Horace's wife and Popeye's mother being twice-married, a feature often repeated in the canon.

10. Langford, op. cit., p. 74.

11. Ibid., p. 76.

12. Ruel E. Foster, 'Dream as Symbolic Act in Faulkner', *Perspective*, ii (Summer 1949), p. 194.

13. Horace is not the first person to retch on learning that a girl has been physically intimate with a man. See pp. 120–1, where the imagery is, appropriately enough, paradisal.

14. Langford, op. cit., pp. 83–4.

15. Langford, op. cit., p. 117.

16. *Faulkner, A Biography*, Joseph Blotner (London, 1974), p. 613.

17. While in Paris in 1925, Faulkner composed what appears to have been a prose-poem concerning the Luxembourg Gardens, death and a young girl. It is unfortunate that this piece, which he admired inordinately, has been lost for it seems likely that it was the germ of *Sanctuary*.

CHAPTER 4: INNOCENCE AND HISTORY

1. John McCormick, *American Literature 1919-1932* (London, 1971), p. 102.

2. See Gerald Langford's *Faulkner's Revision of 'Absalom, Absalom!'* (Austin, Texas, 1971).

3. As I have implied, I think *Absalom, Absalom!* is an invaluable aid to the appreciation of Eliot's notion of tradition. I do not suppose that Faulkner shaped his work in any direct response to Eliot—the matter is too implicit for that—but the example of the older poet was never far from his mind, as is apparent from Charles Bon's description of life as 'breathing, pleasure, darkness', a paraphrase of Eliot's 'birth, copulation and death'. How deep the influence went may be measured by this passage from *Flags in the Dust*, which shows Faulkner to be not just Eliot's devoted reader but, by some uncanny trick, his medium:

> ... The fire had burned down again; its steady fading glow fell upon their musing faces and brought the tea things on the low table beside them, out of the obscurity in quiet rotund gleams—and they sat hand in hand in the fitful shadows and the silence, waiting for something. And at last it came: a thundering knock at the door, and they knew then what it was they waited for, and through the window they saw the carriage curtains gleaming in the dusk and the horses stamping and steaming on the drive, in the ceaseless rain. (p.340)

4. Patricia Tobin, 'The Time of Myth and History in "Absalom, Absalom!"', *American Literature*, XLV (May 1973), pp. 252–70, p. 257. See, too, Albert J. Guerard's *The Triumph of the Novel* (New York, 1976).

5. We note Henry's belief that virginity 'must incorporate in itself an inability to endure in order to be precious, to exist, and so must depend upon its loss, absence, to have existed at all' (p.96) together with Mr Compson's belief in masculine greatness and his preference for the martial to the amatory arts. Perhaps this accounts for the curiously subsidiary role he grants Judith, despite her supposed strength of character.

6. Cf. the image in Hemingway's *A Farewell to Arms* of a log full of ants placed on top of a fire and the effect of emptying a tin of water on to it.

7. A hasty correction lest we imagine she had been transfixed by him.

8. Meaning to say that she was forced to do so, but in fact confessing to an inner need.

9. In his 'Logical Sequence and Continuity: Some Observations on the Typographical and Structural Consistency of "Absalom, Absalom!"', *American Literature*, XLIII (March 1971), pp. 97–107, John A. Hodgson argues that the conversation between Mr Compson and Quentin in Chapter 3 takes place *after* Quentin returns from Sutpen's Hundred, that is, after the conversation described in Chapters 2 and 4. (He also believes that the italics of Chapter 5 represent not so much Quentin's memory of Miss Rosa's monologue as his mental re-enactment of it.) Cleanth Brooks regards Chapters 1 and 5 as continuous ('The Narrative Structure of "Absalom, Absalom!"', *The Georgia Review*, XXIX (Summer 1975), pp. 366–94).

10. Flem Snopes's 'taking and keeping' have a long ancestry, it seems.

11. 'Overseeing' contains a triple pun, I think: Sutpen plays the plantation overseer, he fails to understand what he sees and he sees better than he or anyone else can know the point of the 'volcano'.

12. V.S. Pritchett, *The New Statesman*, 9 February 1973, p. 200.

13. Tobin, op. cit., p. 258.

14. F. Garvin Davenport, Jr., *The Myth of Southern History* (Nashville, Tenn., 1970), p. 102.

15. Ibid., p. 102.

16. Ibid., p. 103.

17. Interestingly enough, *Go Down, Moses* presents the South's pioneers as evil (Lucius Quintus Carothers McCaslin) *and* good (the McCaslin twins, Buck and Buddy), thus projecting into different men the separate strands once found together in Sutpen. The effect is to make for a somewhat more optimistic reading of the South's history.

18. Interestingly enough, Faulkner once had the conversation between Quentin and Shreve conducted by two Quentins, thus making of it a more obviously inner debate.

19. *Faulkner in the University*, eds F.L. Gwynn and J.L. Blotner (Charlottesville, Va., 1959), p. 3.

20. Faulkner's hesitation may be responsible for the uncertainty here. He began with the idea that it was Henry who was to be wounded, changed it to Bon and finally reverted to Henry again.

CHAPTER 5: THE SARTORIS WAR

1. Herbert Marshal McLuhan, 'The Southern Quality', *The Sewanee Review*, LV (July–September 1947), pp. 357–83.

2. This passage is an addition to the *Saturday Evening Post* 'Retreat' (CCVII, 13 October 1934) and shows the importance that should be attached to Faulkner's revisions. In the context, it stands in sharp contrast to the break-up of the established order as the negroes march to their Jordan.

3. Appreciation of the closing phrase of *The Sound and the Fury* depends on our recognising its context, which is here provided.

4. Roark Bradford, 'The Private World of William Faulkner', *The Magazine of the Year*, II (May 1948), p. 91.

5. Andrew Lytle, '*The Town*: Helen's Last Stand', *The Sewanee Review*, LXV (Summer 1957), p. 479.

6. The title 'An Odour of Verbena' may derive from Hemingway's 'The Short Happy Life of Francis Macomber' as part of an attempt to present a somewhat loftier conception of courage in Bayard.

7. *Reality and Myth*, eds William E. Walker and Robert L. Welker (Nashville, Tenn., 1964).

8. I am reminded of Evelyn Waugh's involvement in Guy Crouchback's declaration of guilt at the end of *Unconditional Surrender*, a novel which bears comparison with *The Unvanquished* at several points.

9. Donald Davie, *The Heyday of Sir Walter Scott* (London, 1961), p. 41.

CHAPTER 6: THE LOST DOMAIN

1. Ezra Pound, *Profile, An Anthology in MCMXXI* (Milan, 1932), p. 130.

2. Irving Howe, *William Faulkner*, second edition (New York, 1962), p. 80.

3. Cleanth Brooks, *William Faulkner, The Yoknapatawpha Country* (New Haven and London, 1963), p. 170.

4. W. J. Cash, *The Mind of the South* (New York, 1941), p. 46.

5. See also: 'The sheriff had a shoe box of cold food and even a stone jug of buttermilk wrapped in wet gunnysacks' (p.255).

6. Richard Chase, *The American Novel and its Tradition* (New York, 1957), p. 1.
7. Leslie Fiedler, *Waiting for the End* (Harmondsworth, Middlesex, 1967 (first published 1964), p. 11.
8. H. Edward Richardson, *William Faulkner, The Journey to Self-Discovery* (Columbia, Missouri, 1969).
9. Stephen Neal Dennis quotes the fly-leaf of *Sartoris'* dust-jacket: 'These people will, as time moves by, be succeeded by the more worldly and pushing Snopes family'. (*The Making of 'Sartoris'*, Ann Arbor, Mich., 1969.)
10. *Scribner's Magazine*, LXXXIX (June 1931), p.585.
11. In 'Faulkner's Correspondence with *Scribner's Magazine*', *Proof*, Vol. 3, ed Joseph Katz (Columbia, S.C. 1973), James Meriwether points out that Faulkner shortened the material he had submitted to *Scribner*'s at the request of its editors, which may account for the omission.
12. Malcolm Cowley, *The Portable Faulkner* (New York, 1946); revised and expanded 1967, p. 445.
13. James Meriwether is of the opinion that *Father Abraham*'s version of the sale of the horses is itself a reworking of the second 'As I Lay Dying' (see his 'Faulkner's Correspondence with *Scribner's Magazine*'). Be that as it may, it is worth noticing how often Faulkner casts his stories in retrospective form, a practice suggestive of the influence on him of the tall tale and the wider Southern tendency to find the cause of a man's being in the past.
14. There was an earlier MS, done in 1935, related by an anonymous narrator who recalls what has been told him by V.K. Suratt, a sewing-machine agent. For details of this and Faulkner's subsequent revisions, see *Uncollected Stories of William Faulkner*, ed. Joseph Blotner (London, 1980), pp. 684–5.
15. In her M.A. thesis *Short Stories into Novels: A Textual and Critical Study of Some Aspects of Faulkner's Literary Method* (University of Leeds, 1962), Jane Millgate points out that the Suratt of 'Lizards in Jamshyd's Court' was often foolish and had already been worsted by Flem. In *The Hamlet*, he has been developed into a fit opponent for the Snopeses and his defeat reserved for the end, where it can be seen to be an altogether uncharacteristic lapse with ominous consequences for the South. For details of earlier versions of the story, see *Uncollected Stories of William Faulkner*, pp. 686–7.
16. Peter Lisca, '*The Hamlet*: Genesis and Revisions', *Faulkner Studies*, III (Spring, 1954), p. 8.
17. Blotner, *Faulkner, A Biography* (London, 1974), p. 600.
18. 'Afternoon of a Cow' was also a parody of the Hemingway persona. When it was first published, it appeared under the pseudonym 'Ernest V. Trueblood' (V for Very).
19. Denis Donoghue, *Connoisseurs of Chaos* (London, 1966), p. 167.
20. Gillian Beer, *The Romance* (London, 1970), p. 21.
21. Ibid., p. 58.
22. Ibid., p. 77.
23. Compare this with Hardy's description of Tess Durbeyfield, which works to the same purpose.
24. Florence Leaver, 'Faulkner: The Word as Principle and Power', in *William Faulkner: Three Decades of Criticism*, eds Frederick J. Hoffman and Olga W. Vickery (New York and Burlingame, 1963), pp. 203–4.
25. *Faulkner in the University*, eds F.L. Gwynn and J.L. Blotner (Charlottesville,

Va., 1959), p. 199.

26. In this regard, see Viola Hopkins's 'William Faulkner's "The Hamlet": A Study in Meaning and Form', *Accent*, xv, 2 (Spring, 1955), pp. 125–44.

27. Constance Rourke, *American Humor* (New York, 1931). See too, Cecil D. Eby's 'Faulkner and the Southwestern Humorists', Shenandoah, xi (Autumn, 1959), pp. 13–21, and Thomas W. Cooley, 'Faulkner draws the Long Bow', *Twentieth Century Literature*, xvi (October 1970), pp. 268–77.

28. Florence Emily Hardy, *The Life of Thomas Hardy, 1840-1928* (London, 1965), p. 386.

29. Quoted by Edmund Blunden, *Thomas Hardy* (London, 1954), p. 104.

30. Malcolm Cowley, *The Faulkner-Cowley File* (London, 1966), pp. 78–80.

31. Ibid., p. 79.

32. Chase, op. cit., p. ix.

33. Graham Hough, *An Essay on Criticism* (London, 1966), p. 21.

34. Northrop Frye, *Anatomy of Criticism* (Princeton, N.J., 1957).

35. Hugh Kenner, *A Homemade World* (New York, 1975), p. 198 and p. 207.

36. Frederick J. Hoffman, *William Faulkner* (New York, 1966), p. 24.

37. Richard Hughes, in *William Faulkner*, ed. John Bassett (London, 1975), p. 60.

38. Gillian Beer, op. cit., p. 4.

39. R.W.B. Lewis, *The American Adam* (Chicago, 1959), pp. 128–9.

40. John Armstrong, *The Paradise Myth* (London, 1969).

CHAPTER 7: THE KEATSIAN MOMENT

1. W. H. Auden, 'Huck and Oliver', *The Listener*, 1 October 1953, p. 540.

2. Such a reversal of expection is an important theme in the book, as Ike, Fonsiba, Samuel Beauchamp and Lucas are all to discover.

3. Hubert Beauchamp mock-comically points the way when he chides Buck for climbing into Sophonsiba's bed. The image of the bear he uses touches on the old animus against white women, especially in the marital connection. (Compare Turl's love for Tennie with Buck's reluctant involvement with Sophonsiba.)

4. *Faulkner at Nagano*, ed Robert A. Jelliffe (Tokyo, 1956), p. 167.

5. We notice that Ike's line, which should have been the main one, is in fact the shortest, having chosen to sacrifice itself in the attempt to reconcile the other two. The reconciliation occurs not here but in *The Reivers*, when Ned McCaslin (another negro descendant of old Carothers but of a line distinct from Lucas's) joins forces with Lucius Priest.

6. See Charles H. Nilon, 'Faulkner and the Negro' in *University of Colorado Studies*, 8 (September 1962), pp. 1–111, for an analysis of the portrait.

7. The Nobel Prize address returns to the same complex, as the quotation shows.

8. Marvin Klotz, 'Procrustean Revision in Faulkner's *Go Down, Moses*', *American Literature*, xxxvii (March 1965), pp.1–16.

9. Ibid., p. 12.

10. This is a good example of one of Faulkner's most characteristic tricks, the definition which appears to be precise but which is, in fact, otiose. No-one supposes a heavy-handed blow is necessarily vicious.

11. In 'Faulkner's Pantaloon: The Negro Anomaly at the Heart of *Go Down, Moses*' (*American Literature*, xliv (November 1972), pp. 430–44, Walter

Taylor expresses reservations. For him, Rider is Faulkner's only attempt to portray 'a genuine African hero' and he believes he could have succeeded only if he had been made to support Ike by displaying endurance. I take Professor Taylor's point but I find love, not endurance, to be the purpose of the story and suspect that Rider's inability to survive, coinciding as it does with 'Delta Autumn''s examination of the results of Ike's endurance, enacts a deeper point.

12. Octavio Paz, *Claude Levi-Strauss: An Introduction* (Ithaca and London, 1970), p. 106.

13. In the magazine version of the story, this reads 'almost unrational'. The alteration is not uncharacteristic of Faulkner.

14. Paz, op. cit., p. 139. Eliot's 'still centre' here receives its appropriate gloss, I think.

15. *Collected Stories*, vol. I, p. 47.

16. *Faulkner at Nagano*, p. 51.

17. Ibid., p. 59.

18. Ibid., pp. 50–1.

19. Perhaps Faulkner's version of 'the taste of pennies' experienced by the dying hero of Hemingway's 'Snows of Kilimanjaro', another, lesser tale of the hunting life.

20. The view that the South was 'primed for fatality' is, of course, Miss Rosa's and it is striking that Faulkner should echo her at this point. We also notice that it is now incest and not miscegenation that excites revulsion, as happens whenever the emphasis falls on the South's ideals rather than its history.

21. The words are spoken by Cass, Ike's cousin, after reading Keats's 'Ode on a Grecian Urn'.

22. 'Faulkner's "The Old People": The Numen-Engendering Style', *The Southern Review*, I (n.s.) (January 1965), p. 96.

23. R.W.B. Lewis, *The Picaresque Saint* (Philadelphia and New York, 1959), p. 207.

24. The situation here is replete with irony. Like Ike, Tennie's Jim (the unnamed woman's grandfather) came to a momentous decision on his 21st birthday and rejected his portion of the legacy settled on his family by the McCaslin twins, fleeing the South. Ike sought after him and tried to persuade him to accept, in vain.

25. Cf. Miss Habersham in *Intruder in the Dust*.

26. Leo Marx, *The Machine in the Garden* (New York, 1964). The main theme of Professor Marx's study is the attempt of American pastoral to define the middle ground between nature and civilisation by reconciling the claims of machine and garden.

27. Ibid., p. 72.

28. James Early, *The Making of* Go Down, Moses (Dallas, Texas, 1972), pp. 64–5.

Select Bibliography of Works by William Faulkner

NOVELS

All references in the text are to the London editions unless otherwise stated.

Soldiers' Pay (New York, 1926; London, 1930).
Mosquitoes (New York, 1927; London, 1964).
Sartoris (New York, 1929; London, 1932).
The Sound and the Fury (New York, 1929; London, 1931).
As I Lay Dying (New York, 1930; London, 1935).
Sanctuary (New York, 1931; London, 1935). (The Modern Library edition, New York, 1932, carried a preface by the author.)
Light in August (New York, 1932; London, 1933).
Pylon (New York, 1935; London, 1935).
Absalom, Absalom! (New York, 1936; London, 1937).
The Unvanquished (New York, 1938; London, 1938).
The Wild Palms (New York, 1939; London, 1939).
The Hamlet (New York, 1940; London, 1940).
Go Down, Moses and Other Stories—titled *Go Down, Moses* in all printings subsequent to the first—(New York, 1942; London, 1942).
Intruder in the Dust (New York, 1948; London, 1949).
Requiem for a Nun (New York, 1951; London, 1953).
A Fable (New York, 1954; London, 1955).
The Town (New York, 1957; London, 1958).
The Mansion (New York, 1959; London, 1961).
The Reivers - A Reminiscence (New York, 1962; London, 1962).
Flags in the Dust (New York, 1973).

STORIES

Collected

These Thirteen (New York, 1931; London, 1958—as Volume Two of the Collected Short Stories).

Dr Martino and Other Stories (New York, 1934; London, 1958—as Volume Three of the Collected Short Stories).

Collected Stories (New York, 1950; London, 1958—as Volume One of the Collected Short Stories under the title *Uncle Willy and Other Stories*).

Big Woods (New York, 1955).

Uncollected Stories of William Faulkner (London, 1980).

Hitherto Uncollected or Revised

'Spotted Horses', *Scribner's Magazine*, LXXXIX (June 1931), pp. 585–97.

'The Hound, a story', *Harper's Magazine*, CLXIII (August 1931), pp. 266–74.

'Lizards in Jamshyd's Court', *The Saturday Evening Post*, CCIV (27 February 1932), pp. 12–13, 52, 57.

'Wash', *Harper's Magazine*, CLXVIII (February 1934), pp. 258–66.

'Ambuscade', *The Saturday Evening Post*, CCVII (29 September 1934), pp. 12–13, 80–1.

'Retreat', *The Saturday Evening Post*, CCVII (13 October 1934), pp. 16–17, 82, 84–5, 87, 89.

'Raid', *The Saturday Evening Post*, CCVII (3 November 1934), pp. 18–19, 72–3, 75, 77–8.

'Skirmish at Sartoris', *Scribner's Magazine*, XCVII (April 1935), pp. 193–200.

'Lion, a story', *Harper's Magazine*, CLXXII (December 1935), pp. 67–77.

'Fool About a Horse, a story', *Scribner's Magazine*, C (August 1936), pp. 80–6.

'The Unvanquished', *The Saturday Evening Post*, CCIX (14 November 1936), pp. 12–13, 121–2, 124, 126, 128, 130.

'Vendee', *The Saturday Evening Post*, CCIX (5 December 1936), pp. 16–17, 86–7, 90, 92–4.

'Barn Burning', *Harper's Magazine*, CLXXIX (June 1939), pp. 86–9.

'A Point of Law', *Collier's Magazine*, cv (22 June 1940), pp. 20–1, 30, 32.

'The Old People, a story', *Harper's Magazine*, clxxxi (September 1940), pp.418–25.

'Pantaloon in Black', *Harper's Magazine*, clxxxi (October 1940), pp.503–13.

'Gold is Not Always', *The Atlantic Monthly*, clxvi (November 1940), pp. 563–70.

'Go Down, Moses', *Collier's Magazine*, cvii (25 January 1941), pp. 19–20, 45–6.

'The Bear', *The Saturday Evening Post*, ccxiv (9 May 1942), pp. 30–1, 74, 76–7.

'Delta Autumn', *Story*, xx (May–June 1942), pp.46–55.

'Afternoon of a Cow', *Furioso*, ii (Summer 1947), pp. 5–17.

POETRY

The Marble Faun (Boston, 1924).
A Green Bough (New York, 1933).

OTHERS

New Orleans Sketches, introduced by Carvel Collins (New Brunswick, N.J., 1958; London, 1959).

Faulkner in the University, Class Conferences at the University of Virginia 1957-1958, eds Frederick L. Gwynn and Joseph L. Blotner (Charlottesville, Va., 1959).

William Faulkner, Early Prose and Poetry, compiled and introduced by Carvel Collins (Boston, 1962; London, 1963).

Faulkner at West Point, eds Joseph L. Fant and Robert Ashley (New York, 1964).

Essays, Speeches and Public Letters by William Faulkner, ed. James B. Meriwether (New York, 1965; London, 1967).

Lion in the Garden, Interviews with William Faulkner 1926-1962, eds James B. Meriwether and Michael Millgate (New York, 1968). (Contains most of the interviews; two exceptions worth noting are Lavon Roscoe, *Western Review*, xv (Summer 1951), pp.300–4, and A.M. Dominicus, *Faulkner Studies*, iii (Summer–Autumn 1954), pp. 33–7.)

Selected Letters of William Faulkner, ed. Joseph L. Blotner (New York, 1977; London 1977).

Index

239